Friend

and

Foe

Friend

and

Foe

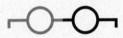

When to Cooperate,
When to Compete, and How
to Succeed at Both

ADAM GALINSKY *and* MAURICE SCHWEITZER

CROWN
BUSINESS
NEW YORK

Crown Business books are available at special discounts for bulk purchases
for sales promotions or corporate use. Special editions, including personalized
covers, excerpts of existing books, or books with corporate logos, can be created in
large quantities for special needs. For more information, contact Premium Sales
at (212) 572-2232 or e-mail specialmarkets@penguinrandomhouse.com.

Library of Congress Cataloging-in-Publication Data is available upon request.

ISBN 978-0-307-72021-4
eBook ISBN 978-0-307-72025-2

Printed in the United States of America

Book design by Christine Welch
Jacket design by Michael Nagin

10 9 8 7 6 5 4 3 2 1

First Edition

AG: To my parents, David and Maeda, for teaching me to be a more frequent cooperator, to be a more effective competitor, and to find the right balance between the two.

MS: To my perfect friend Michelle and the memory of my grandfather Arthur for teaching me that no matter what happens, we can always find our balance.

Contents

Introduction

At 8:20 p.m., one week before Christmas, 1996, an explosion ripped a hole in the garden wall of the heavily guarded Japanese embassy in Lima, Peru. With the smoke still rising, 14 armed guerrillas from the Tupac Amaru Revolutionary Movement (MRTA) stormed the ambassador's residence. Within minutes, everyone in the compound became a hostage.

The Japanese ambassador had been throwing a party for over 600 guests that evening; among the dignitaries were Peruvian congressmen, members of the Supreme Court, and chiefs of police.

This was a defining crisis for the Peruvian president, Alberto Fujimori, whose parents had emigrated from Japan. Although Fujimori had made significant gains against the MRTA when he came to power in 1990, by 1996 the Peruvian economy had slowed, prices were rising, and many Peruvians had become distrustful of his administration. On the eve of the embassy takeover, Fujimori's popularity had plummeted to 38 percent. Not only did the crisis put Fujimori's political future at stake, but worse, his own mother and brother were two of those taken hostage.

Initial reports revealed that the guerillas were "armed to the teeth" with machine guns and antitank weapons, and that they had wired rooms as well as the roof with explosives. They had chosen their target well—the ambassador's compound was encircled by a 12-foot wall, the windows had both bulletproof glass and bars, and the doors within the building had been designed to withstand grenades.

The guerrillas, who appeared to hold all the cards, began making demands: They wanted the Peruvian government to release 450 fellow MRTA members, enact market reforms, and improve living conditions in Peru's jails.

Negotiation appeared to offer the only solution. Not only did the prospects of a military resolution appear dim, but Fujimori faced both internal and substantial external pressure to reach a negotiated settlement. Japanese leaders, including Prime Minister Ryutaro Hashimoto, publicly called on Fujimori to negotiate with the hostage-takers to ensure the safe release of hostages.

Fujimori had a dilemma. He could cooperate with the hostage-takers and negotiate a solution. Or he could compete with them and launch an attack on the compound. Though there were serious drawbacks with both options, the debate focused on the dichotomy between these two approaches: compete or cooperate—act as a friend or behave like a foe.

The tension between competition and cooperation defines many of our interactions at home and at work, and to succeed across these realms requires knowing when and how to do both. In our most important relationships, from the negotiating table in the boardroom to the breakfast table with our kids, we routinely face challenges that appear to offer two opposing solutions. Yet the question—should we cooperate or should we compete—is often the wrong one. Our most important relationships are neither cooperative nor competitive. Instead, they are both.

Rather than choosing a single course of action, we need to understand that cooperation and competition often occur simultaneously and we must nimbly shift between the two, and that how we navigate the tension between these seemingly opposite behaviors gives us profound insight into human nature. In this book, we explore this tension and we offer advice to help you know when to compete, when to cooperate—and how to do both better to get more of what we want, at work and at home.

To understand this dilemma let's return to Fujimori. Instead of choosing whether to act as a friend or a foe, Fujimori did both.

Throughout the crisis, Fujimori publicly committed himself to a cooperative solution. In search of a negotiated agreement, he flew to Canada to meet with the Japanese prime minister, he flew to Cuba to meet with Fidel Castro, and he flew to London stating that his goal was to "find a country that would give asylum to the MRTA group." Even four months into the crisis, Fujimori proclaimed, "We are not contemplating the use of force [except] in an unmanageable emergency, which we don't expect to happen."

Fujimori not only made public statements about his cooperative intentions, but he also actively engaged in negotiations. He assembled a credible negotiation team that included the Canadian ambassador, an archbishop, and a Red Cross official. And the negotiations spanned a wide range of substantive issues including the release of prisoners and offers of asylum in Cuba and the Dominican Republic. They were also very successful: Through the course of negotiations, the guerrillas released hundreds of hostages and even allowed reporters into the compound.

This cooperative approach, however, reflects only the very public side of Fujimori's plan. As it turns out, Fujimori had also developed a second, secret plan soon after the crisis began. He had gathered the heads of the armed forces and the intelligence branches to formulate a military option. Over the four months of the crisis, the military smuggled equipment hidden in books and games to hostages, including miniature radios, microphones, and video cameras. The military also learned that although the guerrillas maintained tight security throughout most of the day and night, they routinely played an indoor soccer game in the early afternoon—a piece of intelligence that would prove critical to the competitive solution they later implemented.

Very early on in the crisis, the government played loud music throughout the day and performed deafening tank exercises near the compound. Although the noise might seem like an attempt to assault the senses of the hostage-takers or scare them with displays of might, in reality its purpose was to provide sound cover for a covert operation: to dig 170 meters of tunnels under the compound. At the same time, on a remote naval base, Fujimori built a replica of the ambassador's residence, and was training special units to practice storming the compound.

After more than four months, the negotiators had made real progress, so much so that the Canadian ambassador asserted that "both sides were close to settlement." At the same time, military preparations were also complete. And that was when Fujimori took action.

On April 23, 1997, during the hostage-takers' daily game of soccer, the Peruvian military detonated three charges, killing three of the hostage-takers. Commandos streamed into the compound through the holes created by the explosions, through the front door, and up ladders to the back of the building. When it was over, all 14 guerrillas, one hostage, and two soldiers had died.

Fujimori had deceived the MRTA guerrillas. While pretending to cooperate, Fujimori had bought time to engage in a high-stakes, competitive move that ultimately served his interest. Although he lost two soldiers, he had, without making a single concession to the guerrillas' demands, saved all but one of the 72 hostages who remained in the compound.

o

Humans are wired to cooperate *and* compete. Sometimes we cooperate enthusiastically with people and build enduring bonds with them. At other times, we engage in fierce competition with and have little regard for others. Even within a single interaction with the same person, we can oscillate between the two approaches. In the Middle East, if you negotiate the purchase of a carpet, you are competing over the issue of price, but the seller will invariably invite you to join him first in a cup of tea, an act of cooperation. Similarly, business deals in many parts of the world are preceded by an exchange of gifts, karaoke performances, and shared meals. A key insight of this book is that, both at work and at home, we are competing *and* cooperating all the time, often at the *same* time.

The question of whether people achieve the best outcomes in life by being fiercely competitive or by being fundamentally cooperative has fueled a fierce debate. We argue that this debate misses the mark. Focusing only on how humans cooperate overlooks our hardwired instinct to compete. Similarly, focusing only on how humans pursue their self-interest misses important insights into the social advantages of cooperation. Like the Peruvian hostage crisis, succeeding in most complex human interactions involves some measure of both competing *and* cooperating. This book will help you learn how to decide when to cooperate and when to compete—and how to be better at both. It is only by appreciating how humans find the right balance between the two that we can truly understand human nature and learn how to optimize our success at work, at home, and around the world.

Striking the Right Balance

The ongoing tension between competition and cooperation emerges from three fundamental forces. First, resources are scarce. Second, humans are social beings. And third, our social world is inherently unstable and dynamic (or what statisticians would call stochastic). Here is how we think about these forces.

Scarcity. We live in a world of scarce resources. Historically, the ability to acquire resources ensured our survival and the survival of our offspring. In modern times, these resources also secure our status and are central to our sense of well-being.

Scarcity triggers competitive reactions, often quickly and intensely. Consider this holiday example. The day after Thanksgiving in the United States is called Black Friday. (In finance, "in the black" means prosperity and profit.) Normally, the term Black Friday refers to the enormous volume of sales retailers enjoy on what has become the biggest shopping day of the year. But the fourth Friday in November of 2008 brought new meaning to the term. Throughout the night of Thanksgiving and into the early morning hours of Friday, a group of suburban shoppers gathered for a Walmart sale in Valley Stream, New York. Walmart, which would open at 5:00 a.m., had advertised a limited supply of bargain-priced items, some as much as 86 percent off their normal price.

The group of shoppers waiting outside, who only hours earlier had shared an American tradition that epitomizes cooperation—the Thanksgiving meal—transformed overnight into an unruly horde. By 3:30 a.m., the police had to be summoned to help control the chaos. As the opening time drew near, the crowd began to chant "Push the doors in," and one customer taped up a poster reading BLITZ LINE STARTS HERE. The employees, hoping to contain the crowd, formed a human chain. They never had a chance.

The 2,000 customers literally took the doors off their hinges and stampeded into the store, knocking employees out of the way and climbing over them. The lucky employees managed to climb on top of vending machines. Jdimytai Damour, who had just celebrated Thanksgiving with his half sister a few hours before, was not one of the lucky ones. He was trampled to death. But his tragedy was not an aberration. Black Friday turns dark every Thanksgiving, spawning headlines like this one from the *Huffington Post* on November 29, 2013: "Holiday Spirit: Shootings, Stabbings, Brawls."

These Black Friday stampedes highlight how quickly cooperation can disappear when a resource appears to be in short supply. But while scarcity breeds competition, cooperation is often
the best avenue for attaining scarce resources and holding on
to them. To secure scarce resources, in other words, we need to
nimbly navigate the shifting sands of our social world, and we do
this both by competing *and* by cooperating.

Social. Humans are inherently social animals. As humans
evolved, their brains grew in size and intricacy to manage the
complexity of human social networks.

The link between social connection and cognitive function-
ing is so tight that we literally cannot remain sane without social relationships. Consider for a moment one of the greatest
forms of torture: solitary confinement. Prison wardens learned
long ago how social disconnection can be far more painful than
physical torture. The human capacity to endure physical pain
is quite high, but within three days of social isolation the mind
descends into hallucination, spasms of anger, and ultimately
malaise and apathy. The damage caused by even a short period
of social isolation can be so profound that when people emerge
from it they both constantly crave and are often unfit for social
interaction.

Social connections are so essential for our survival and well-
being that we not only cooperate with others to build relationships, we also compete with others for friends. And often we do
both at the same time. Take gossip. Through gossip, we bond
with our friends, sharing titillating details. But at the same time,
we are creating potential foes in the targets of our gossip. Or
consider dueling holiday parties where people compete to see
who will attend *their* party. We can even see this tension in social media as people compete for the most friends and followers
or the most likes and retweets. At the same time, competitive
exclusion can also breed cooperation. High school cliques, fraternities, and country clubs use this formula to great effect: It is

through selective inclusion *and exclusion* that they breed loyalty and create lasting social bonds.

Unstable and Dynamic. We live in an unstable, dynamic world. Within a matter of moments, resources can vanish and social relationships can crumble. Simple events, like learning new information about how much someone else earns at work, can swing people quickly and dramatically from a cooperative mindset into a competitive one.

The interplay of these three principles—scarcity, sociability, and dynamic instability—can be clearly seen in the Grevy's zebras in Kenya. Work done by Dan Rubenstein of Princeton shows that the scarcity of a critical resource, in this case water, dynamically alters basic social relationships in zebra society. When the Grevy's zebras inhabit arid and parched climates, their mating relationships tend to be temporary and unstable. However, when the Grevy's zebras suddenly have greater access to water so that individual zebras no longer need to compete for water, their social relationships shift dramatically into more stable collectives.

Siblings—both humans and animals—understand how the interplay of these three principles drives the dynamic tension between cooperation and competition. Our relationships with our siblings often form our most cooperative relationships. We even have a name for it: *brotherly love.* On the other hand, our relationships with our siblings can also be some of our most competitive. We have a name for this too: *sibling rivalry.* Siblings are our friends *and* our foes.

Many babies start competing with their siblings before their siblings are even born. How? By breast-feeding. Breast-feeding can suppress ovulation, so the longer babies can convince their mothers to breast-feed, the more attention they will receive before a prospective sibling arrives. And it's not just food and material rewards that siblings compete for; they also compete for another scarce resource, parental attention.

On the other hand, the genetic overlap and shared identity between siblings fosters intense cooperation. In fact, this sibling cooperation has been measured in studies of the ground squirrel. Ground squirrels are surprisingly altruistic: When they see a predator near a fellow squirrel, they screech to lure the predator away from their endangered compatriot. This act epitomizes the spirit of altruism: The squirrel endangers himself to help another. What is interesting is that the volume of the cry rises when two squirrels are closely related. Among siblings, squirrels screech loudest.

Given their shared upbringing, siblings come to know each other particularly well. With this intimate knowledge, siblings develop both the greatest capacity to empathize with each other . . . and the greatest capacity to torment each other.

Some of the most dramatic shifts between cooperation and competition occur on the political stage. Consider the changing nature of relationships between countries in World War II. The Soviet Union and Germany formed a cooperative alliance on the eve of war in 1939. Their pact promised neutrality if either was attacked, and even described how Germany and the Soviet Union would divide Northern and Eastern Europe into different spheres of influence. Yet this cooperative deal collapsed less than two years later . . . when the Germans invaded the Soviet Union in 1941.

Conversely, within a remarkably short period the United States and Japan became friends instead of foes. In 1945, as World War II drew to a close, the United States firebombed 67 Japanese cities and dropped nuclear bombs on Hiroshima and Nagasaki, causing unimaginable destruction. The ferocity of these attacks convinced the Japanese leadership to surrender, and just days later American General Douglas MacArthur led the Allied occupation of Japan. Immediately after taking charge, MacArthur led the American pivot to cooperation. He made it illegal for any of the occupying Americans in Japan to assault Japanese people or even to eat any of the scarce supplies of Japanese food. One of the guiding principles of the occupation was to develop Japan's economy. Another was to build institutions to support freedom and democracy. This pivot transformed a bitter enemy into a stalwart ally.

This book explores a new way of thinking about the tension between cooperation and competition. We reveal how these three forces—scarcity, sociability, and dynamic instability— profoundly influence how we shift between friend and foe. In doing so, we draw on research across the social sciences (psychology, economics, sociology, political science). We explore animal studies to demonstrate that this tension between cooperation and competition is primal. And we draw on recent findings in neuroscience to reveal how this tension is wired into the very architecture of the human brain.

Every relationship contains the possibility of both cooperation and competition. Instead of orienting ourselves to cooperate or compete, we need to prepare to do both. By understanding that we are simultaneously friends and foes, we not only gain deeper insight into human nature but also gain insights into how to be more successful in our relationships at work, in our communities, and at home.

By revealing the fundamental facets of the friend-foe tension, we answer a number of intriguing questions, such as: Why are our fiercest rivalries with those who are closest to us? Why is hierarchy essential for some tasks but potentially fatal for others? Why are some teams better off when they have *less* talent? Where do gender differences *really* come from? Why do we let complete strangers sleep in our houses when we go on vacation? Why can teaching our kids to lie make them *more* cooperative members of society?

We also explain how the same skill that helps us avoid being called a racist can help us figure out just the right time to start a new business; why it can feel better to be on the job market during a recession; why you want to be first on an election ballot but perform last on *American Idol*; and when you want to make the first offer at the negotiating table.

Along the way, we draw lessons from both research and illuminating examples from all over the world. These studies and real-world illustrations will challenge many of the assumptions you currently hold about your friends and your foes.

We conclude each chapter with a section called "Finding the Right Balance," which offers specific advice to help you navigate your personal and professional relationships more successfully. Through this book you will learn: How to "lean in" without getting pushed back, how to gain power . . . and hold on to it, and how to turn your weaknesses into strengths. You will discover how to improve your ability to detect deception, and how to gain the trust of others quickly. And when you fall short, as we all invariably will, we offer strategies for how to deliver an effective apology. We offer insight into how to move the odds in your favor when you interview for a job and gain compensation for your talents.

To successfully navigate our social world, we need to find the right balance between cooperation and competition. This book offers a set of tools to help you navigate the shifting sands of our social world. By keeping your balance, in every area of your life, you will learn how to be a better friend *and* a more formidable foe.

It's All Relative

For years, David Miliband was poised to become the next prime minister of the United Kingdom. And then suddenly everything changed. Once on the precipice of leading England, he could no longer stand to live in his home country.

In the early 2000s, David had risen steadily through the ranks of political power. He held a number of senior positions, including foreign secretary under Prime Minister Gordon Brown, the kind of post that is a pathway to the top rungs of leadership. When Brown resigned as leader of the Labour Party in 2010, David seemed assured to succeed him. Indeed, David announced his candidacy for the top leadership position the very next day, flanked by 15 supportive members of Parliament. He was the clear front-runner.

But two days later, something startling happened. David's younger brother, Ed Miliband, announced *his* candidacy for the very same position.

The process of picking a new leader requires an outright majority, and the Labour Party would go through four rounds of voting until a single candidate finally won a majority. In the first round of voting, David led with 37.78 percent of the votes to his brother Ed's 34.33 percent. In the second round, David led again, 38.89 percent to Ed's 37.47 percent. And again David led in the third round, 42.72 percent to 42.26 percent.

Across the first three rounds of voting, David had edged out his younger brother, but his lead had narrowed. In the fourth and final round, Ed emerged as the victor, earning 50.65 percent of the vote to David's 49.35 percent.

By the slimmest of margins, Ed Miliband became the new leader of the Labour Party. David remained in Parliament for the next two years, but in his own words, "the permanent invidious comparisons made professional life impossible." In April of 2013, David left his home country to live in New York City, far away from his brother.

It is always painful to lose a close contest. It understandably leaves us with regret and remorse, haunted by what might have been. But why is it *especially* painful to lose a close contest to someone like your younger brother?

We answer this question as we explore the power of *social comparisons*, the process of figuring out where we stand relative to those around us. We'll discuss how, as inherently social beings, we are programmed to compare ourselves to others—to our siblings, our neighbors, our friends, our officemates, our high school buddies, and our old college roommates.

Depending on the circumstances, social comparisons can motivate us to collaborate more effectively, compete more vigorously, or even, as David Miliband did, retreat from the game altogether. To understand these effects, we need to appreciate a few key ideas about social comparison:

First, *social comparisons are inevitable.*

Remember that our social world is unstable and dynamic: Social comparison information helps us make sense of where we fit in at any point. The way we come to understand how well we are doing is by looking at others. As a result, we have an insatiable appetite for social comparison information. This is why seven hundred million people check Facebook every day; not just to share information, but also to see where they stand relative to all of their friends—in everything from who got married first, to who is ahead in their career, to who took the best vacation.

The second insight about social comparisons is that *they come in two directions: up and down.*

We can look *up* at people who outperform us and we can look *down* at people to whom we feel superior. Whether we look up or peer down has critical implications for both our life satisfaction and our motivation. Looking up makes us feel worse, but can motivate us to strive harder. Looking down makes us feel good, but can lead to complacency. Thus, social comparisons have the potential to motivate us to perform better but feel worse. Or perform poorly and feel great. In order to thrive in life, we need to find the balance between feeling good about ourselves while feeling motivated to perform well.

The third key insight is that people can become *too* motivated by social comparisons. As a result, social comparisons can tempt people to cheat, to sabotage their rival, or to take crazy risks to come out on top.

Ironically, it is the people with whom we collaborate most closely who serve as our most intense points of comparisons. We most often compare ourselves with our friends, but these comparisons can turn our friends into our foes. Here, we offer insight into how to use social comparisons effectively to find the right balance of cooperation and competition.

Making Sense of Our World: Why Expecting Fathers Gain Weight

Do I earn enough money? Do I need to redo my kitchen? Are my kids doing well in school? Do I need to lose weight?

It is nearly impossible to reflect on these questions in a vacuum. Inevitably, we find ourselves looking to others for answers.

Other people provide a benchmark to help us figure out where we are in the world and how we fit in.

Consider your weight. Do you weigh too much or just the right amount? To answer this question, we often, consciously or not, think about our friends and their weight. When researchers at Harvard Medical School repeatedly measured the weight of 12,067 people over a period of 32 years, they found that when one's friends gained weight, it increased that person's own chances of becoming overweight by 57 percent! Why? Because our brains tell us it's okay to reach for that second doughnut as long as we don't weigh much more than Monica or Brad! Our own weight gain doesn't look so bad if our friends have put on a little themselves.

A particularly poignant example of the role that social comparisons play in weight gain involves pregnancy. Women's bodies undergo an amazing transformation during pregnancy. As a woman carries a child, she naturally gains weight. This is hardly a surprise; she is eating for two, after all. But what we find really interesting is what happens to *men's* bodies when their wives are pregnant.

There is no biological reason for an expecting father's body to change. His initial contribution to the process notwithstanding, there is absolutely no biological function that he needs to perform as the mother carries his baby during pregnancy.

In practice, however, research shows that expectant fathers gain considerable weight during their wives' pregnancies. In one study, a full 25 percent of expectant fathers claimed the need to buy a "paternity" wardrobe to accommodate their weight gain. We believe that social comparisons powerfully drive these effects. How? Bit by bit, as the expecting mother gains weight, the expecting father loses just a bit of motivation to maintain his own weight. And before he knows it, this lost motivation has led to quite a few packed-on pounds. In very extreme cases, men even develop pregnancy symptoms that match those of the expectant mother. This diagnosis is both common and real enough to have earned its own diagnosis: Couvade syndrome.

Whether it is our weight, our salary, or our kitchens, comparisons help us make sense of how we are doing. But it's not just a matter of how you compare, but *with whom* you compare, that can determine whether the comparison motivates you to work harder or simply feel worse.

Similarity Matters

"Two households, both alike in dignity." In this opening line of *Romeo and Juliet,* Shakespeare introduces the now iconic competition between the two noble families by describing how similar they were to each other.

Although we constantly compare ourselves to others, not all social comparisons are created equal. Some social comparisons matter more than others. In the weight-gain study, same-sex friends influenced each other's weight gain more than opposite-sex friends. The more similar the peer, the more our comparative instincts kick into high gear.

This is precisely why it was so painful for David Miliband to lose the election to his brother. And indeed, few people are as similar as siblings—people who share the same parents, the same DNA, and most often the same upbringing. For David and Ed Miliband, they also shared similar ambitions. David and Ed both went to Oxford. Both became members of Parliament. Both vied for leadership of the Labour Party. And both were serious contenders to be prime minister of England. It is the full weight of all these similarities—and coming up short—that made his defeat too much for David to endure.

In the Milibands' case, their similarity fueled an intense rivalry that ultimately derailed David's career. But other times, sibling rivalry can intensify motivation, propelling us to new heights. Let's consider another pair of siblings, the Williams sisters. Venus and Serena have dominated women's tennis for over a decade. At different times in their careers, each sister has been ranked No. 1 in the world. But early in their professional careers, it was the older sister Venus who was most lauded by critics and most feared on the court.

Reflecting on those early years, Serena recalled that she "always felt like the underdog." Yet instead of accepting her fate as number two, Serena drew inspiration from it: "Venus was the big star. When we were growing up, it was a lot about Venus—it needed to be about Venus, because she was an incredible player. And that actually, being the little sister, the one that wasn't as strong, wasn't as good yet, gave me encouragement and the fight I have in my game."

Today it is Serena who has since eclipsed her big sister to dominate women's tennis. In their 24 head-to-head finals meetings, Serena has won 14 to Venus's 10. Serena has won 18 Grand Slam titles. Venus has claimed seven. As of this writing, Serena is ranked No. 1 in the world, while Venus is ranked No. 18. Serena can no longer be considered the "underdog."

But as we've seen, competition and cooperation can be simultaneous. This is why the Williams sisters have shown such a remarkable ability to put aside any sibling rivalry and succeed as a team, racking up a gaudy 21–1 record in women's doubles finals, including three Olympic gold medal performances in the 2000, 2008, and 2012 Summer Games.

Time columnist Josh Sanburn explained, "The Williams Sisters' rivalry is highly unusual and utterly remarkable. They are two of the greatest tennis players of all time and from the same family playing in the same era. And with all of their fiery competitiveness on the court, they're still incredibly close off of it." Their relationship exemplifies how siblings can be our closest friends . . . *and* simultaneously our most intense rivals.

Yet the social comparison phenomenon goes beyond just

sibling rivalry. Any similarity can intensify competition. Take shared history, for example. Ever notice how colleagues who start working in the same industry at the same time often become ready rivals? This was the case for Larry Bird and Earvin "Magic" Johnson, who entered the NBA in the same year, 1979. From that point on, they would always compare themselves to each other. As Larry Bird admitted, "The first thing I would do every morning was look at the box scores to see what Magic did. I didn't care about anything else."

College roommates and childhood friends also have a shared history, which may explain why nothing produces as much social comparison agitation as a high school or college reunion. Because the people you will see at the reunion are the people you grew up with, every single person in the room serves as a salient point of comparison.

The most intense comparisons often occur when we are similar to others in ways that are "self-relevant." These are the skills or traits we care most about. Think for a moment about what really matters to you. Is your primary goal in life to make money? If so, you're probably prone to comparing yourself to others based on the size of their bank accounts.

Of course, the traits most self-relevant to one person may be of little or no importance to another. For an engineer, winning a coveted engineering prize may matter most. For gardening enthusiasts, the ability to grow prize-winning petunias may be critical. And for triathletes, their finishing time for a recent race may be an intense point of pride. For others, the success of their children may be the most important measure of their own accomplishment. Are you driven to climb to the top of the corporate ladder? Or grow the biggest tomato in your neighborhood? The areas that matter most to you are the same areas where you are likely to feel most threatened—and most motivated—by competition from others.

The most intense social comparisons are rivalries. Rivals, like

Larry Bird and Magic Johnson, emerge in meaningful domains, among closely matched competitors who are similar (or "psychologically close") in any number of ways.

Individuals can be rivals, but so too can teams, companies, and organizations. For example, in collegiate basketball, the quintessential rivalry is between Duke University and the University of North Carolina (UNC). Both colleges share a similar history, identity, and location. The college teams play each other frequently, are only nine miles apart, and are closely matched. As a result, their successes can powerfully motivate one another.

After Duke won the national championship in 1992, UNC won it the following year. Then, after UNC won the national championship in 2009, it was Duke's turn to win the title the next year. Of course, it takes many ingredients to win a national championship, but motivation is a critical one, and social comparisons fuel motivation in the workplace, on the basketball court, and beyond.

Monkeys and the Slings and Arrows of Outrageous Social Comparisons

Scott Crabtree had worked his way up the ladder at a tech company. He was happy with his company and his work—until a new hire arrived. The new hire negotiated a salary that was just a few thousand dollars short of Scott's current one. In Scott's words, "I realized he was going to get a salary right out of school that took me decades to reach." The salary of this new recruit ruined his own experience. He *had* been blissfully happy with his salary and his job. But now he grew frustrated with this ever present comparison. Eventually, not unlike David Miliband, he became so upset by the situation that he left the company.

One reason comparisons are so pernicious is that we are hardwired to make them. Frans de Waal of Emory University demonstrated this with capuchin monkeys. In one clever study, de Waal trained his monkeys to use stones as a form of currency and trade them with the experimenter for food. The exchange worked like this: The experimenter would hold out an open hand, the monkey would drop a stone into the open hand, and the experimenter would then offer the monkey a slice of cucumber.

Is a stone a fair price for a slice of cucumber? To these monkeys, it was—as long as every other monkey was getting the same deal. When a solitary monkey exchanged a stone for a piece of cucumber, he ate it with delight and would happily repeat this exchange over and over. However, de Waal also ran a condition in which two monkeys in neighboring cages participated in the exchange simultaneously. In one cage, the monkey received the usual cucumber slice for a stone. But in the other, the monkey received a sweet, juicy grape for his stone. Monkeys, just like humans, value grapes more highly than cucumbers . . . actually, it turns out that monkeys value grapes a lot more than cucumbers!

Upon seeing this inequity, the monkey who was offered the regular cucumber deal went, well, apeshit. Not only did the monkey who saw his neighbor get a better deal stop "paying" stones for the cucumbers, but some refused to accept the cucumber, even throwing it back at the experimenter. In one case, after receiving the cucumber, a monkey who saw the adjacent monkey receive a grape for the same "price" threw the cucumber on the cage floor and sulked in the back of the cage. The other monkey reached into the first monkey's cage, snatched the cucumber, and eagerly consumed both the grape *and* the cucumber. What this experiment demonstrates is that our evolutionary ancestors did not evaluate their outcomes in isolation; rather, they evaluated outcomes in a comparative process.

Just as monkeys eating cucumbers care about comparisons, so too do modern humans. And no area demonstrates this innate competitive instinct more than the world of business. Consider what happened in 2003, as American Airlines faced the prospect of bankruptcy. To save the airline, the management team asked the unions to accept steep concessions. Through difficult negotiations, American Airlines convinced the unions to agree to $1.8 billion in annual labor concessions, including $660 million from the pilots, $620 million from the mechanics and ground workers, and $340 million from the flight attendants.

In accepting these terms, the unions choose cooperation over competition . . . until they learned new information.

The day after the unions agreed to these concessions, details of American Airlines' 10-K filing with the Securities and Exchange Commission came to light. In these filings, the unions learned that, eager to keep top management, American Airlines had offered the top 45 executives large retention bonuses if they stayed with the airline through 2005.

Imagine, for a moment, being one of the pilots. Your union leaders have just convinced you to give up $660 million. A day later, you learn that many executives would be earning retention bonuses, some as high as $1.6 million!

With this comparison information, the unions shifted to competition. They withdrew their concessions and fired their negotiator. Not unlike the monkeys, the unions had thought that they were getting a fair deal until they found out that others were getting something better.

This is essentially the same situation in which Scott Crabtree found himself. The comparison to the salary of his new colleague caused him to resent not only his colleague but, more broadly, his work. Scott was affected by the same psychological force as the monkeys who were happy eating their piece of cucumber . . . until they saw a peer eating a grape. For Scott, the comparison silenced his cooperative spirit and fired up his competitive impulses. So Scott left his job and started his own company. His new title? Chief Happiness Officer.

Both Scott's former company and the management team at American Airlines failed to understand the power of social comparisons. Often, in our zeal to achieve one objective, like retain senior management or hire that hotshot new employee, it is easy to overlook how our actions create social comparisons. So whether we're hiring a new employee, closing a deal with a client, negotiating the sale of our home, or deciding what clothes to buy for one of our children, we need to think about how powerfully social comparisons can shift people's attitudes, behaviors, and perceptions.

Why Twins Reared Apart Can Be More Similar Than Twins Reared Together

Tom Patterson grew up in Kansas, and was raised by janitors who practiced Christianity. His twin brother, Steve Tazumi, grew up in Philadelphia with a pharmacist father who practiced Buddhism. They were separated soon after their birth, following their mother's passing. The boys knew that each had a twin, but their records had been lost and they had no contact with each other for nearly 40 years.

Yet, as it turns out, Steve and Tom shared the exact same interests and pursued the exact same careers. As Steve explained, "It's phenomenal. He owned a bodybuilding gym and I owned a bodybuilding gym. We're both 100 percent into fitness." Tom said, "We connected from the first time we met because we're so much alike."

Genetic factors profoundly shape who we are, but the social comparisons we make as we grow up help to explain this peculiar anomaly: Twins separated at birth and raised in different households are often as similar and sometimes more similar to each other than twins raised together. By all accounts, twins reared together should be more similar than twins raised apart. After all, twins reared together have the same social experiences, are exposed to the same parenting style, and grow up in the same local culture. But here's the catch: Twins reared together have a constant comparison. And when they engage in similar activities, one of them will inevitably come in second. Without a twin nearby to compare him- or herself with, individual twins reared apart are free to pursue their true passions without the vexing experience of having to look up at the superior performance of a twin.

It is this understanding of social comparisons that has even influenced guidelines for adoption agencies. In the world of adoption, the term "artificial twins" refers to adopting a child who would enter a family that already has a child very similar in age. At first glance, artificial twins sounds like a fantastic idea. There is a built-in playmate, and the parents can enjoy economies of scale—one pick-up at school, one drop-off for soccer practice, and so on. As adoption expert Sam Wojnilower explains, however, adoption agencies understand the problem of artificial twins. When an artificial twin is introduced into a family, the social comparison is constant and so corrosive that adoption professionals seek to avoid them altogether.

The power of social comparisons even extends to adult siblings. Consider two sisters. One sister works outside the home and the other does not. What influences their decision whether or not to enter the workforce? Surprisingly, the total amount of household income does not matter much. What really matters is *whether their household income is more or less than their sister's household income.* David Neumark of the University of California, Irvine, found that a wife whose husband earned less than her sister's husband is far more likely to feel compelled to work. Why? Because without her participation in the job market, her household income would be less than her sister's household income! We want to keep up with the Joneses, especially when Mrs. Jones is our sister.

Doing Better and Feeling Worse: The Benefits of Graduating in a Recession

Everyone knows that winning a silver medal is better than winning a bronze medal: Second place, of course, is better than third place. And so, second place finishers should be happier than third place finishers, right? Except for the research showing that they aren't. Silver medalists are often miserable.

Just ask Abel Kiviat, who lost the gold by just one-tenth of a second in the 1500-meter race at the 1912 Summer Olympics in Stockholm. Even at 91 years old, the pain of the silver medal had not receded. As he told his interpreter at the time, "I wake up sometimes and say, 'What the heck happened to me?' It's like a nightmare."

Victoria Medvec at Northwestern University studied the facial expressions of medalists at the Olympics. She had raters watch footage of Olympic athletes, both immediately upon completing a competition and on the medal stand. She found that bronze medalists were happier than silver medalists: on the raters' 10-point "happiness" scale, the bronze medalists averaged a 7.1; silver medalists averaged a mere 4.8. Even when the researchers controlled for different types of sports and expectations of athletic performance before the competition, this effect persisted.

In a follow-up study, David Matsumoto and Bob Willingham analyzed the expressions of judo competitors in the 2004 Athens Games. And again, they found the same effect. Not surprisingly, nearly all of the gold medalists smiled (93 percent). Most of the bronze medalists smiled (70 percent). But *none* of the silver medalists they studied had smiled. (These researchers termed their findings the "Silver Medal Face.")

Why might a bronze medalist be happier than a silver medalist? Like most of us, athletes compare their achievements to those of their nearest neighbors. For silver medalists, the most salient comparison is the gold medal winner. Gold isn't just a little better than silver, it is a lot better. The gold medal is the holy grail. But even though a silver medal is objectively a huge achievement, silver medalists feel vastly inferior to the gold medalists *in comparison*. Their proximity to the gold winner makes it easy for silver medalists to imagine what would have happened had they come in just one place higher.

The story is very different for bronze medalists. A bronze medalist is more likely to be influenced by the downward comparison with the fourth-place finisher. There is no prize for fourth place and no place on the medal stand. Thus, the bronze medalist feels lucky to have narrowly avoided that steep drop from "medalist" to mere "participant." Sure, second place would have been better, but both second and third are *medalists*.

This effect also explains why people are happier, on average, with the jobs they get right out of college when they graduate during a recession. Objectively, it is terrible to graduate during a recession. Take the recent recession of 2009. If you graduated from college in the spring of 2009, you faced bleak job prospects. In the United States, the probability of finding a job had dropped by almost 40 percent from the year before, and there were six job seekers for every job opening. Because of these competitive pressures, even if you did find a job, it would likely be in a lower-tier industry, and you would probably be paid substantially less than a graduate from the year before. And sadly, these economic effects continue to shadow graduates years later. Studies reveal that graduating in a recession lowers your lifetime earnings. Even 10 years later, graduates from a recession period make as much as 15 percent less than someone who graduated before or after the recession.

Despite this unhopeful picture, Emily Bianchi of Emory University found that people who graduated during a recession were actually *happier* with their jobs than those who entered the workforce during a period of economic expansion. And this effect persisted for years. Long after the recession was over and the economy had improved, people who graduated during a recession remained more satisfied with their jobs. Why?

During a recession, competition for jobs is fierce. When you finally get your first job, you are likely to compare your outcome with the outcomes of many of your peers who did not find a job right away. Thus, you feel grateful and fortunate that you did not suffer a worse fate.

Social comparisons can also help explain the puzzle of what gives rise to revolutions and civil uprisings. Many believe that the trigger is the despondency of the downtrodden as they are carried on a descending escalator to greater poverty. But it turns out that revolutions often occur after prolonged periods of *increasing* prosperity. Imagine that the world has become a better place . . . until suddenly, there is an abrupt downturn, a swift and unexpected reversal of fortune. Now, we compare our current state of financial struggle and deprivation to the prior years of abundance and plenty. This pattern of improving conditions followed by a sudden and sharp decline has preceded a large number of historical revolutions including the French, Russian, and Egyptian revolutions as well as the American Civil War and the American civil rights movement. In these cases, we can see how the unstable and dynamic nature of scarce resources can cause individuals and groups to pivot from cooperation to competition.

Social comparisons are also at the root of the reverse phenomenon: schadenfreude, taking malicious pleasure in another's misfortune. Schadenfreude is what seizes us when people we envy fall from their high perch. It is why we delight at the mistakes of former rivals, even long after the rivalry has played itself out, and it's why we're fixated on learning the details of the public meltdowns of celebrities like Martha Stewart and Britney Spears.

Neuroscience research led by Hidehiko Takahashi of Japan's National Institute of Radiological Sciences finds evidence that the experience of schadenfreude is more pronounced the more similar the person experiencing the misfortune is to us. His research found that when misfortune befalls others who are similar, but slightly superior to us, one of the major reward parts of the brain (the striatum) lights up.

Sports are a breeding ground for schadenfreude. When Colin Leach of the University of Connecticut studied fans of World Cup soccer, he found that people experience malicious joy when their rivals lose—especially when their own teams are no longer in the tournament. Fans who are no longer able to root for their own national team throw some of their fan energy behind whichever team is playing their rival. As a result, the rival's loss feels almost like a victory. This shows us that there is scientific basis to the phrase that "the enemy of my enemy is my friend."

Social comparisons not only determine whether we smile on a medal stand or harbor feelings of schadenfreude. They can also motivate us to work longer and harder.

Sputnik Moments and Halftime Scores: Behind by a Little, but Not for Long

In 1992, a lot was at stake for Duke's basketball team. Duke was trying to record back-to-back championships, a feat that had not been accomplished for almost 20 years. But in the NCAA national championship game against Michigan, Duke found itself down by one point at the half. Imagine the coach's speech in that Duke locker room at halftime.

In the second half of the game, a remarkable thing happened. Duke exploded. What had earlier looked like a tight contest became a rout. Duke prevailed over Michigan and won the game by 20 points, 71–51.

It turns out that Duke's performance that night was not an anomaly. Wharton professor Jonah Berger and University of

Chicago professor Devin Pope analyzed 18,060 professional basketball games played between 1993 and 2009 to determine the relationship between halftime scores and the final outcomes of games. They found that when a team is trailing by one point at halftime, they are actually *more* likely to win than the team that is ahead. Why?

A halftime score offers an intense social comparison for the trailing team. At halftime, the players stew with frustration at being so close, yet still behind. And so they emerge from the locker room full of motivation. This is likely why Jonah and Devin found that teams down by one point outscore their opponents significantly more in the first four minutes after halftime.

The experience of feeling behind is so unpleasant that most people—not just athletes—will do extraordinary things to regain a lead. Consider the race into space that was fueled by the rivalry between the United States and the Soviet Union in the years following World War II. The United States and the Soviets were locked in fierce competition in both military and civilian domains. The race to space, however, was particularly furious. Space exploration represented a new frontier that held both scientific and military importance.

It was with this backdrop that, on July 29, 1955, President Dwight Eisenhower boldly announced that the United States would do something that had never before been done: launch a satellite to orbit Earth. So imagine how he felt when, on October 4, 1957, the Soviet Union beat him to it and launched the world's first satellite: Sputnik.

But rather than discourage President Eisenhower, the Sputnik launch, or what he termed the "Sputnik Crisis," lit a fire under the Eisenhower administration. In short order, his administration enacted the National Defense Education Act to provide hundreds of millions of dollars for scholarships, student loans, and equipment; expanded support for the National Science Foundation; and created two new agencies: the Advanced Re-

search Projects Agency and the National Aeronautics and Space
Administration (NASA).

Eisenhower described this new legislation as "an emergency
undertaking . . . to strengthen our American system of education." But the endgame wasn't simply to invest in education for
the sake of education; it was to improve our system of education
in order to beat the Soviets. In the years that followed, the United
States continued to increase the percentage of the federal budget for the space program from 0.1 percent in 1958 to a record
4.41 percent, almost $6 billion, in 1966 (an amount that would
equal over $32 billion today).

The experience of falling behind the Russians was so trau-
matic that its specter even continued to hang over the presidential campaign of 1960, when Senator John F. Kennedy took to
the campaign trail vowing that if he was elected, the United
States would outperform the Soviets in almost every aspect. And
after winning the presidency, Kennedy upped the ante when he
famously declared his ambition to put a man on the Moon. In
an address at Rice University in Houston in 1962, President Kennedy described the competitive position of the United States in
space and the commitment he planned to make to the space
program:

> To be sure, we are behind, and will be behind for some time
> in manned flight. But we do not intend to stay behind, and in
> this decade, we shall make up and move ahead . . .

The feeling of being behind led America to invest a staggering
sum of money in its space program. We suspect that this expen-
diture would have been hotly contested had it not been for the
upward social comparison. After all, President Kennedy's vision
was not merely to put a man on the Moon, it was to put a man on
the Moon *before the Soviets could.*

Social comparisons can motivate teams and countries, but

how might it motivate individuals? When Gavin Kilduff of New York University set out to empirically capture the motivational benefits of rivalry, he found that people perform better on effort-based tasks when they compete against their close rivals versus other competitors. And importantly, these effects occur independently of how high the stakes are in the competition. In one study, Gavin analyzed data from a running club and found that the mere presence of a rival in a race—someone who was demographically similar, whom the runner had repeatedly raced against, and was relatively evenly matched with—caused people to run faster. And the more rivals present in a race? The faster the runner ran.

So, in many cases, comparisons can motivate us to run faster, play harder, or rocket to the Moon. But can they become *too* motivating? Could a fear of falling behind push us to engage in very risky actions or even unethical behavior?

When Comparisons Go Wild

Figure skating has always been a majestic sport filled with artistry and pageantry. Sure, it is competitive too, but the competition has always been dignified. That all changed on January 6, 1994, as the U.S. Olympic figure skating team prepared to select its two female representatives for the Winter Olympics in Lillehammer, Norway. Nancy Kerrigan and Tonya Harding, the two leading contenders, were fierce competitors and rivals.

Everyone following U.S. skating knew that the competition between Nancy and Tonya would be intense, but nobody was prepared for what happened after practice on that January afternoon. An assailant wielding a metal baton attacked Nancy, striking her right knee. Even more shocking was the news that the assault had been orchestrated by Nancy's rival, Tonya.

What could have driven Tonya to such a drastic action? Reports from the media circus that followed offer some insight. For one, Tonya had always felt that Nancy was treated with greater respect than she was. Although neither was from a wealthy family, Tonya appeared less graceful in her demeanor, dress, and style than Nancy. One skating expert called Tonya "an ugly duckling with frizzy hair from the wrong side of the tracks." Tonya herself referred to Nancy saying, "She's a princess. I'm a piece of crap."

Moreover, while Tonya and Nancy were fierce rivals, they were, in many ways, similar. Each could point to one major professional achievement: Nancy had already won an Olympic medal and Tonya was the only American woman to ever land a triple axel in a competition. And in 1994, both had excellent chances of making the U.S. Olympic team. Yet Tonya felt inferior to Nancy, and as we have seen, feeling inferior to a rival can be a powerful motivator. It certainly was in this case. Tonya poured herself into skating and practiced long hours. But she still felt that her path to success was blocked—by Nancy. She feared that simply practicing harder would not be enough. And so, Tonya orchestrated "the whack heard round the world."

Our own research conducted with NYU professor Gavin Kilduff confirms that feelings of rivalry, if left unchecked, can lead to violent behavior. For example, in one study, an analysis of 2,788 soccer matches played between 2002 and 2009 in Serie A, Italy's top league, we found that when teams located in the same city played each other, the games were rougher and players received more yellow and red cards for unsportsmanlike and unethical behavior.

Athletes aren't the only ones who fall prey to the pressure of social comparison. Even corporations resort to dirty tricks as they struggle to best their rivals. Take, for example, what happened as the airline Virgin Atlantic began to take market share from British Airways: British Airways responded by calling Virgin's customers and informing them that their flights had been canceled (even though they had not been canceled). The competition became so nasty that British Airways even circulated false rumors that Virgin's CEO Richard Branson was HIV positive.

Social comparison pressure even fuels cheating within the ivory tower of academia. A clever study led by Ben Edelman of Harvard University investigated cheating behavior within the Social Science Research Network (SSRN): a website that allows faculty to post their research and broadcast their findings well before they appear in print. One feature of the site displays the number of times an article has been downloaded. This number conveys a sense of how interesting and anticipated an article is; frequently downloaded articles are given special distinction, and some universities even use SSRN download counts as a measure of research quality.

But here is the problem. Download counts are easy to manipulate. Faculty can download their own articles—or even write computer programs to do this—which impacts their relative ranking. When Ben analyzed suspicious downloads (e.g., rapid downloads that occurred across fixed-time intervals), he found some obvious relationships. For example, professors hoping to get tenure at prestigious institutions are more likely to engage in suspicious downloads than are other professors. More interestingly, and more pertinent to our discussion of social comparisons, professors were much more likely to engage in suspicious downloads when their peers had high download counts. The lesson is clear: When those near to us are outshining us, we seek to increase our own apparent performance—and sometimes we are willing to resort to underhanded means to do it.

Social comparisons can also explain why we sabotage and exclude others. Consider Rhonda, age 34, who worked as a secretary in a midsize legal firm. Her boss, sensing her potential, encouraged her to take classes to develop her computer skills. Rhonda and her boss worked out an arrangement to accommodate her class schedule under the condition that she remain at the firm for at least a year after she completed her courses. This agreement represents the best face of cooperation: Both the employee and the firm can benefit.

The interesting part of the story is how Rhonda's coworkers reacted to her arrangement. At first, they congratulated her. But as time went on, according to an account by Cheryl Dellesega, "the emotional climate of the office grows noticeably cooler. Within a month of starting classes, Rhonda is no longer invited to lunch with the other women, and they frequently 'forget' to pass on important messages to her that arrived while she is in class."

Though Rhonda's boss initiated a cooperative move with Rhonda, it triggered an invidious social comparison that undermined cooperation from Rhonda's peers. And, not unlike Tonya Harding, they resorted to sabotage.

Finding the Right Balance: How to Make Comparisons Work for Us

We are hardwired to seek social comparisons. They help us make sense of our world, and their effect on us can be profound. Sometimes they are a source of comfort. Other times they can make us feel perfectly miserable. Social comparisons can propel us to land a man on the Moon, but they also cause us to abandon our career or cheat to get ahead of a rival. So how can we harness the power of social comparison to work *for* us, rather than bring us down? Consider these two opposing examples.

When John Kennedy ran for president of the United States in 1960, his brother Robert Kennedy put his own political ambitions on hold to stand by his side. In fact, Robert became John's campaign manager, and Robert helped his brother win the presidency.

What enabled the brother politicians John and Robert to cooperate so effectively, but caused David Miliband to leave England because of invidious comparisons with his brother Ed?

There are many reasons to be sure, but we highlight one key distinction: Robert helped his *older* brother win the presidency. But, Ed the *younger* brother challenged—and beat—his older brother. Why does this matter? Because the latter example challenged what we perceive as the natural order of things—we *expect* to see an elder brother achieve success before the younger, and when the opposite occurs, discontent can follow.

Moreover, Robert's status was enhanced by his older brother's victory, so much so that Robert would go on to launch his own run for the White House. But David's status was severely diminished when his younger brother beat him in a head-to-head competition.

Or consider the Williams sisters we discussed earlier. As the Williams sisters rose in the world of tennis, they went in order: Venus, the older sister, rose first. And when Serena reflected on the early years, she accepted the prominence of her older sister: "It was a lot about Venus—it needed to be about Venus." Venus was ranked No. 1 before Serena was, and in their first matchups, Venus beat Serena. Years later, Serena eclipsed Venus's accomplishments, but because the sisters went in order, the two sisters went on to collaborate seamlessly as one of the world's most dominant doubles teams.

So the first principle of making social comparison work *for* us is to assess whether or not the social comparison is "in" or "out" of order. If we expect our peer to win—and they do—the social comparison can be unpleasant, but it is unlikely to be toxic. If, however, we expect to beat our peer and they win, we need to anticipate a charged emotional reaction.

The second principle of finding the right social comparison balance is providing new opportunities to compete, so that disappointment can be turned into motivation. In other words, will we have the chance to channel regret in a constructive direction?

Athletes who come in second at the Olympics may never get a second shot at the gold. But for most of us, whether we're competing for a job, a promotion, or a position on the neighborhood council, we *will* get a second (or even a third or fourth) chance. So instead of licking our wounds at our defeat at the hands of a rival, we would do well to take matters into our own hands; to get back on that horse and try, try again.

A third key principle to remember about managing social comparisons is to anticipate the possibility that our successes will upset others, even if those around us don't voice their frustration. After buying a new car or renovating a house, we are often excited to share our new purchases or renovations with other people. But we should err on the side of modesty. This means thinking carefully before we post pictures on Facebook of our new purchases, our renovations, and our exotic vacations. People may congratulate us, but keep in mind that when people feel envy, they rarely admit it. As a result, we may easily miss signs that we have triggered social comparisons.

One way to be modest is to share *negative* information. Sure, when you get back from your vacation in Fiji, your coworkers and friends will ask you how it was. So, instead of simply showing them 100 photos of the beautiful vistas and meals, and regaling them with tales of your once-in-a-lifetime experience in a shark cage, try telling them about the day it rained and how you had to stay indoors, or how the airline lost your luggage. You'll be surprised by how satisfied people will be when you allow them to indulge in some schadenfreude.

And finally, when it comes to using social comparison to boost your own motivation, here is the key rule to keep in mind: *Seek favorable comparisons if you want to feel happier, and seek unfavorable comparisons if you want to push yourself harder.* In other words, when you want to feel better about yourself, consider those who are less fortunate. (Or better yet, spend time volunteering for those less fortunate.) Conversely, when you want to light a competitive fire, consider those who have accomplished a bit more than you have.

Even people who have to endure the uncertainty of a serious

disease and the trauma of treatment can make comparisons work for them. Consider breast cancer patients. Those who cope well with their illness show a particular pattern of comparisons: They focus on less fortunate peers to make themselves feel better about their own condition, but shift their focus to more fortunate peers to draw inspiration.

This same principle also works in negotiation. Our research with Thomas Mussweiler of the University of Cologne found a way to do well and feel well at the bargaining table. Before we negotiate, we want to find upward comparisons that motivate us to attain the best deal possible. But right after we strike a deal, we want to shift our focus to downward comparisons such as worse deals we could have gotten to maximize our satisfaction.

We close with a Russian parable. The beginning of the story will sound familiar, but like most stories, it is the ending that drives home its moral.

A man stumbles across an old lamp. He raises it for closer inspection and wipes away the dust. As he rubs the lamp, a genie appears. The genie offers to give the man anything he desires, but there is a catch. His neighbor will get double.

The man paces back and forth, thinking furiously. Finally, after several long moments of deep thought he lights up with his answer: "I know what I want! I want you to poke out one of my eyes."

o

We've seen how we rely on social comparisons to help us understand where we fit in our social world. But here's one element we haven't yet talked about: the fact that often the most important comparisons we make relate to power. Those with the most power lead, those with the least power follow. We next explore how relative differences in power influence our ability to compete and cooperate, and how we can manage power dynamics to be both a better friend *and* a more formidable foe.

2
═══

It's Good to Be the King . . .
Until It Isn't

In the satirical film *History of the World, Part I*, King Louis XVI of France traverses his day without inhibitions, indulging his every whim. He uses his staff for chess pieces, and when skeet shooting he has peasants, instead of clay disks, thrown up into the air as targets. Whenever he needs to urinate, he calls over a "piss boy" (his term, not ours) who carries a bucket for him to relieve himself. Each time he engages in one of these indulgent actions, he turns to the camera and says, "It's good to be the king."

But the story didn't end well for King Louis XVI; the people revolted and he was murdered. It was good to be the king . . . until it wasn't.

Mark Hurd, former CEO of Hewlett-Packard, understands what it feels like to ascend to power, only to fall from grace. After all, Mark started at the bottom. He began his career at NCR Corporation as a junior sales analyst and steadily moved up the ranks over the next 20 years until he was named the company's president and chief operating officer in 2001. A few years later, Hewlett-Packard stole Mark away and promoted him to chief executive officer. Under Mark's watch, HP became the top seller in desktop and laptop computers, its revenues rose, and its stock price doubled.

Mark enjoyed all the luxuries of being a CEO, and then some.

In the fiscal year of 2008, Mark earned $25.4 million in cash. He and his wife had access to the company jet, and when he asked for it, HP even gave him extra money to cover the taxes involved in using the jet. For Mark Hurd, it was good to be the CEO . . . until he met Jodie Fisher.

When Mark first saw Jodie on the reality television show *Age of Love*, he was immediately drawn to her. As a CEO, he was a man who was used to getting what he wanted, and he acted on his desire for Jodie. Mark handpicked Jodie to host various HP events in order to be in close contact with her. Even though Jodie resisted these advances, Mark was undeterred. He insisted on taking Jodie out to fancy dinners that had no business relevance but were charged to HP. In an attempt to woo Jodie, Mark pointed out all the women who were clamoring to be with him, including Sheryl Crow. When celebrity lawyer Gloria Allred detailed Mark's solicitations in a letter to HP, it became clear to the company that Mark had made a habit of using company money to wine, dine, and fly women around the country. Because Mark failed to properly report these expenses, it cost him his job in 2010. It was good to be the CEO, until it wasn't.

What caused Mark to behave so recklessly? Why did he risk everything?

We propose that the answer lies in one word: *power*. As the great British philosopher Bertrand Russell once stated, "The fundamental concept in social science is *Power*, in the same sense in which *Energy* is the fundamental concept in physics." In other words, how much power we have at any moment in time drives how we think and how we behave.

When people hear the word power, they immediately understand what it means. Formally, power is the amount of control that one person has over another. The powerful have greater access to scarce resources, and they can control the behavior of those with less power by offering or withholding resources, or meting out punishments.

The classic example is the difference between a boss and an employee. The boss can offer raises and promotions, or threaten demotions and termination. Yet power is not static and fixed; it is dynamic and subjective, and it changes across contexts. For example, an associate in a law firm has power over summer interns who are trying to get hired for full-time work. But this same associate has less power when dealing with partners in the firm. But you only have power over another person when that person values the resource you control. In our law firm example, the associate has power over the interns only to the extent that they want a full-time job or a reference letter, and the partners have power over the associate, especially when the associate covets partnership.

Power, in other words, is driven by the three factors that we detailed in the introduction: the fact that we are social beings vying for scarce resources that are unstable and dynamically fluctuate.

To understand the effects of power it is helpful to consider a story involving a magical lock of hair. Samson was a biblical figure whose hair gave him unparalleled strength; he could rip apart a lion with his bare hands and escape any bonds of chain or rope. He was invincible, that is, until his head was shaved. Without his mane, Samson lost his power, and he spent the rest of his life in servitude. It was good to be Samson . . . until it wasn't.

In today's modern world, power is a lot like Samson's hair—it may not make us invincible, but it makes us *feel* invincible. It is an elixir of strength and confidence that gives the powerful a psychological leg up on their competitors. But it can also blind us to the consequences of our actions, producing egocentric, selfish, and uncooperative behavior, as we saw with Mark Hurd and King Louis.

The interesting thing about power is that it's often not how powerful we are, but how powerful we *feel* that determines how we think and how we act. In other words, your experience of your own power can matter as much or even more than how much power you actually have. Indeed, our research shows that across a wide range of situations, from interviewing for a new job, to asking someone out on a date, to impressing our boss in a meeting, we can gain a competitive advantage by increasing our *feelings* of power.

By understanding how power affects everyone, we will show you how to harness the positive effects of power and mitigate its pitfalls. You will learn how to get power and how to keep it—how to remain the king even when others are vying to take your crown.

.

It's All in Your Head

Let's try a little experiment. Close your eyes and think about a time in which you had power—a time in which you controlled an important resource that others wanted or a time when you were in a position to reward another person. Really relive that experience and *feel* what it was like to have that power. Go ahead and take your time, we'll wait.

How did that memory make you feel? If you are like the tens of thousands of people who have done this exercise, it probably gave you a psychological dose of power—a feeling, at least temporarily, that you could accomplish anything. It may have made you feel more confident and more willing to take a chance you wouldn't have taken just moments earlier.

We stumbled upon this technique almost 15 years ago when we found that simply thinking about moments when someone had power actually made that person act as if they were more powerful. What we had done was to "prime" power in people's minds. Once we realized that a key element of power was simply *feeling* powerful, it opened up the door for new ways of creating power.

It was with this insight in mind that Dana Carney of the University of California, Berkeley, came up with another way to instill a sense of power. Simply stand up and put your hands on your hips. Stay in this position for a moment and think about how it makes you feel. Or sit down on a couch and lean back and spread your arms across the back. These are called expansive postures—your body is expanding out and taking up space. Now let's try a different posture. Sit on the edge of a chair, hunch your shoulders forward, and put your hands under your legs. How do you feel in this position? In this posture your body is constricted and confined. In which one did you feel more powerful?

Expansive postures are intimately tied to power. Indeed, dominant individuals across species often expand their postures and take up more space: Northern elephant seals rise up to ward off competitors for mating, the peacock expands its tail to signal its authority, the chimpanzee puffs out its chest by holding its breath to assert its power. Similarly, we've all witnessed how the executive sits back in their oversized chair or stands tall before the board to signal and assert who is in charge.

But these postures can be used to help people *feel* like they have more power. Dana found that simply putting people into one of these expansive postures (which she aptly named a power pose), like sitting back in a chair, standing up straight like Wonder Woman or Superman, or leaning forward on a desk like a boss barking orders, made people feel more powerful.

These are radically new ways of thinking about power. We intuitively know that how we feel influences our physical behavior—that when we feel proud, we stand up a little straighter, that when we feel strong, we grasp someone's handshake a little tighter, etc. But what this research shows is that this relationship also works in reverse; our physical behavior also influences how we feel. In other words, just as we can start a manual transmission car by rolling it down the street, putting the car in gear, and releasing the clutch, we can "roll start" feeling powerful by directing our body in a high-power "gear."

Some of our most recent research shows that even music can produce feelings of power. In a project led by Dennis Hsu of Northwestern University, we found that songs with strong, powerful beats and bass sounds—like "We Will Rock You" by Queen, "Get Ready for This" by 2 Unlimited, and "In Da Club" by 50 Cent—made people feel and act more powerfully. This may explain why so many athletes, from Colin Kaepernick in football to Serena Williams in tennis, walk into the stadium wearing headphones. Or why, the season after the Miami Heat lost in the NBA finals to the Dallas Mavericks, LeBron James prepared for a rematch by blasting Wu-Tang Clan's "Bring the Pain" (with its lyrics of "Basically, can't fuck with me") through the locker room. That night, Miami routed Dallas.

Any of these methods—recalling an experience with power, taking on a powerful posture, listening to powerful music—can increase your sense of power. The key is finding the one that works for you. Personally, we favor the recall task. What is nice about recalling an experience when you had power is that *everyone* has had such an experience—anyone can relive those feelings and produce a long-lasting and authentic sense of power. The power of recall also has the most scientific evidence behind it, with hundreds of studies documenting its effects. But again, you can use whichever route—memories, poses, or music—that best helps you kick-start your sense of power.

So now we know what power is, and how to feel more of it. We next turn to how this feeling of power fundamentally alters how we interact with our friends and our foes.

Speeding Down the Highway with Samson's Hair Blowing in the Wind

We first became interested in power when our collaborator Deb Gruenfeld, a professor at Stanford University, stepped on a plane in the late 1990s. As she settled into her seat, a man in a suit sat down next to her. The overhead fan was blowing in his face, and he immediately took action to remedy the annoying situation. Rather than simply turn the fan off, however, he redirected it right into Deb's face. In response, Deb just sat there, doing nothing, shivering in frustration. This man had felt entitled to adjust the temperature conditions at will, but Deb felt paralyzed. For months after, Deb stewed: Why had this man acted so quickly and confidently while she dithered?

Now imagine that you walked into a room with five other participants. You all sit down around a table and write an essay. Half of you are asked to write about a time when you had power, while the other half are instructed to write about a time when someone had power over you. When you are done with the essay, you are placed in your private room to fill out some surveys. The door closes behind you, and as you settle into your chair, you realize that there is a fan blowing directly into your face. What do you do? Remember, it is unclear whether or not you are allowed to adjust this annoying fan; whether you can turn it off or redirect it.

In one experiment, we purposely created this situation to see who would tinker with the fan and who would sit there getting colder and colder. In other words, we wanted to re-create the psychological experience that Deb had experienced on the plane.

It turned out that those who had been randomly assigned to think about a time they had power were 65 percent more likely to turn off or redirect the fan than someone who had thought about having little power. Simply recalling an experience in which they had power in one room led these individuals to assert agency and power to make their world a more comfortable place to be in the next room.

Being primed with power even changes our voice. In a project led by Sei Jin Ko of San Diego State University, we had participants read a passage to measure the baseline acoustics of each

participant's voice. We then had participants recall an experience with power. Finally, we had participants read their opening statement in a negotiation, and measured whether power
changed their acoustic properties. Here is what we found: Participants conveyed a steadier pitch and a greater shift between
being loud and quiet—that is, they varied their pitch less and
their volume more—after imagining they had power. Like our
subjects, Margaret Thatcher, the former British prime minister,
learned to speak with greater authority by varying her volume
more but her pitch less. (Thatcher went through vocal training
to express this authority in her voice.)

But were these effects noticeable to the naked ear? To find
out, we later played the recordings of all of our speakers to listeners at a different university. Without knowing that power had
been manipulated in the experiment, these listeners reported
that those primed with power *sounded* more authoritative and
more powerful.

As it turns out, there is a neurological explanation behind
these effects of power. When Maarten Boksem and colleagues
from Tilburg University used an EEG to measure brain activity in
people who had been primed to think about power, they found
that recalling an experience with power actually increased brain
activity on the frontal left side of the brain.

This finding tells us something fundamental about why power
produces all of the effects we just described, like feelings of authority and confidence. Much of human behavior is driven by
the interplay between two brain systems. One is the inhibition
system, which helps people avoid negative outcomes. The other
system is the approach system, which directs our attention toward achieving positive outcomes. The approach system resides
in that frontal left side of the brain, the side of the brain that gets
activated in those who feel powerful. It is this left-hemisphere activation that causes us to behave like the man on the plane and
take action to achieve the outcome we want.

Evidence of these effects of power can even be seen in our blood. Dana Carney has found that power leads individuals to experience decreased cortisol, a stress hormone that serves as a psychological inhibitor. Similarly, in our research with Jennifer Jordan of the University of Groningen, we have found that power reduces physiological stress as measured by heart rate and systolic blood pressure.

Neurologically, hormonally, and physiologically, it feels good to be the king. And when we *feel* like a king, we are more likely to act like one.

So, recalling an experience with power can temporarily change how we feel and act. But are there longer-term effects?

How to Nail a Job Interview and Become the Boss

In 2004, one of our former grad students, Gillian Ku, got a highly coveted interview for a professorship at London Business School (LBS). In general, academic interviews are long, arduous affairs that have tremendous amounts of stress built in. You typically have a series of 30-minute one-on-one interviews with each professor in the department throughout the day, culminating with the crucial job talk: a 90-minute presentation in which you present your research while being mercilessly grilled by a faculty that is searching for any flaw. When Gillian interviewed at LBS, she was given 30 minutes to prepare before her talk. She spent a full 10 minutes of that time completing our power prime— writing out an experience she had had with power. This simple task surged confidence into Gillian. As she gave her talk, she was in complete command of the room and situation. She handled every question with aplomb and captivated the audience with her persuasive responses. And better yet, she got the job.

This anecdote was so striking that we wanted to scientifically test whether activating that feeling of power can give someone a competitive advantage in landing a job. In a project led by Joris Lammers of the University of Cologne, we conducted an experiment that involved mock face-to-face interviews with a two-person committee for entrance into a prestigious French business school. During these selection interviews, applicants had to convince two expert interviewers (typically professors) that they had the motivation, skills, and experience to be successful. Unbeknownst to the interviewers, we randomly assigned these applicants to one of three conditions: a high-power recall prime, a low-power recall prime, and a baseline condition with no prime.

The result? Astoundingly, interviewers accepted 68 percent of the candidates in the high-power-prime condition but just a mere 26 percent in the low-power-prime condition. A later study replicated these effects with written job applications: Applicants who had been primed with power got higher ratings.

Why did these remarkable results occur? Because in both cases—the live interview and the application essay—those applicants primed with power displayed greater confidence, and were thus viewed as more capable and competent.

Now, you might think this effect is ephemeral, floating away after a few minutes. And you would be right if the power prime existed in isolation. Indeed, in a vacuum, the effects of priming only last for an hour or two. However, if the prime *alters behavior* in those couple of hours, it can have a lasting effect.

We demonstrated the enduring nature of power primes in a study we ran over a three-day period with Gavin Kilduff of New York University. We split participants into three-person, same-sex groups, and primed one person in each group with high power, one person with low power, and one with a neutral level of power. These three-person teams then worked together on a task and went home. Two days later each team came back to the lab and did some new tasks. Then came the interesting part: We asked each team member who they thought the leader of the group was. We found that the participants primed with power on the first day of the study were perceived to be leaders *two days later*.

Why did effects that seem so ephemeral persist here? Well, when we analyzed videotape of the conversations on the first day, we found that the individuals primed with power initially *acted* as though they were the leader. They spoke earlier and with greater conviction at the beginning of the group's meeting. Then two days later, they continued to be seen that way, even when their contributions were equal to those of others on the team. In other words, this power prime influenced short-term behavior, which then had enduring effects.

Thus, to be perceived as powerful, it helps to be not only in the right place at the right time, but also in the right *frame of mind*. A small change in our mindset—activated by something as quick and easy as thinking about a prior experience when we had power—can have a significant impact on our long-term success. Put simply, we can all achieve significantly higher status if we adjust our psychological states at the outset of a group interaction.

Now that we know that power helps us speed down the highway toward a brighter future, we need to be aware that power can also cause us to drive too fast. And when we speed down the highway, we become more likely to crash—sometimes literally.

Powerholics: Invincibility and Invisibility

On June 15, 2013, Ethan Couch was driving his truck at a speed of 70 miles an hour down a highway in Fort Worth, Texas. A mere 16 years of age, Ethan and a group of friends had stolen beer from a Walmart earlier in the evening. Severely drunk, with a blood alcohol content three times the legal limit, Ethan lost control of his vehicle and crashed into a group of pedestrians, killing four and injuring five others. Compounding the tragedy, many of the pedestrians who were struck were good Samaritans, people who had stopped to help out a motorist with a flat tire.

What caused such a horrific accident? According to Ethan's defense lawyers, it was a disease, one that required treatment, not imprisonment. What was this mysterious disease? It was "Affluenza," and it is caused by having too much wealth and too much power. Individuals who suffer from Affluenza, according to Ethan's defense, lose the ability to see the link between their behavior and consequences. Ethan, his defense argued, had been so indulged by his parents that he lost his capacity to engage in moral thinking and responsible behavior!

The judge in the case was apparently swayed by this argument, sentencing Ethan to just 10 years of probation and ordering that his parents pay for him to attend an intensive therapy program.

Whether or not you agree with this ruling, the judge got one thing fundamentally right: Power and privilege are intoxicating. Left unchecked, they can turn individuals into optimistic risk-takers who don't heed the boundaries that normally constrain our behavior. Often, the powerful only see the rewards in their behavior and not the risks or even mortal consequences.

This may be why, as we found in a study with Cameron Anderson of Berkeley, power makes people less likely to want to use condoms during sexual intercourse. And not just men—we found the same effect for women when they had been primed with power.

Or why the powerful are more likely to cheat and break the rules, even rules they themselves have created and imposed on others. In research we conducted with Joris Lammers of the University of Cologne, we had participants roll a set of dice to determine the number of lottery tickets they would receive—for example, a roll of two would earn them two tickets—and to report the roll of their dice. Would the powerful be more likely to overreport their outcomes? We found that indeed they were. So why do the powerful speed down the highway and end up hurting themselves and others? Part of the reason is because, like Mark Hurd and Ethan Couch, they assume they are the only ones on the road. Let's look at why.

The Powerful Think They Are the Only Ones on the Highway

Are people in power really *that* oblivious to the plight of others, or is that just something the less powerful say to feel better about themselves? We designed an experiment to find out. Here is what we asked our participants to do: Hold up the index finger of your dominant hand and draw a capital "E" on your forehead. Do this as quickly as possible, without stopping to think.

What does your E look like? Does it look like a normal E, or is it backward? It turns out that to draw an E on your forehead correctly requires that you think about what the E looks like from the *vantage point of others* (see left photo). In contrast, a self-focused E looks like an E from *your* vantage point, but is backward for others (see right photo).

 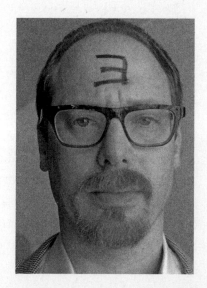

Here is why you should care about the direction of your E. Power, as it turns out, dramatically increases the tendency for people to draw the E backward, from a selfish perspective. In a study we conducted with Joe Magee of New York University, almost three times as many people drew the backward E when they had been primed with power compared to those primed with low power. (We even replicated these findings in our first meeting with our publisher, when we asked everyone in the room to draw an E on their forehead. Just as in our experiment, the senior editors drew backward E's. The junior editors drew them correctly.) Again and again, we see that power makes people more focused on their own unique vantage point and oblivious to the perspectives of others.

So why do the powerful seem to forget that other people are in the room, like the man who redirected the annoying fan into Deb's face? Our neuroscience research offers clues; in a project led by Keely Muscatell of UCLA, we found that individuals who feel a sense of power are less likely to activate the prefrontal cortex and cingulate cortex, which represent the neural circuitry that pays attention to others. Other research shows that the powerful display less neurological mirroring of other people, and thus less awareness of others around them.

Interestingly, even in nature, the more powerful species have a narrower field of vision. The distinction between predator and prey offers an illuminating example of this. The key feature that distinguishes predator species from prey species isn't the presence of fangs or claws or any other feature related to biological weaponry. The key feature is *the position of their eyes*. Predators evolved with eyes facing forward—which allows for binocular vision that offers exquisite depth perception when pursuing prey. Prey, on the other hand, often have eyes facing outward, maximizing peripheral vision, which allows the hunted to detect danger that may be approaching from any angle. Consistent with our place at the top of the food chain, humans have eyes that face forward. We have the ability to gauge depth and pursue our goals, but we can also miss important action on our periphery.

This focus on the self also explains why stinginess has been linked to power. Consider two famous Christmas tales. In Charles Dickens's *A Christmas Carol*, the character Scrooge is introduced as a man of extraordinary wealth who hoards his money for himself and scoffs at the thought of spending it on others. In stark contrast, O. Henry's "The Gift of the Magi," tells the tale of an impoverished couple, Jim and Della, in which Jim sells his prized pocket watch to purchase combs for Della's beautiful hair only to learn that she has cut and sold her hair to buy a gold chain for his watch. The characters of these stories vary on two dimensions. The first is their willingness to spend on themselves versus others. Scrooge hoards his money only for himself, whereas Jim and Della sacrifice their own prized possessions to buy gifts for each other. Second, they differ in terms of their power and wealth. Scrooge is a man of unlimited means whereas O. Henry's characters have very little.

In research we conducted with Derek Rucker of Northwestern University, we found that these stories echo a scientific truth. In one study, we manipulated power by having people take on the role of a Boss or an Employee. Afterward, all participants were given an opportunity to buy Hershey's Kisses at a cost of five cents. Some were asked to buy the chocolates for someone else, while others were buying only for themselves. Here is what we found: The powerful bosses acted like Scrooge—they bought 32 chocolates when buying for themselves but only 11 chocolates when buying for others. In contrast, those in the less powerful role of an employee acted like Jim and Della—they bought 37 chocolates when buying for others but only 14 when buying for themselves!

Other researchers have found that wealthier individuals donate a smaller percentage of their income to charity. Even though the powerful have more resources to share with others, power ironically makes people more Scrooge-like.

The key insight from all of this research is that power blinds us to the plight of others. And this "blindness" can have serious consequences: It can lead the powerful to lose their kingdom.

The King's Downfall

As we mentioned at the outset, there is a scene from the movie *History of the World, Part I* in which King Louis XVI shoots peasants instead of clay discs during his target practice. While shooting his subjects into the air, he is told that "the people are revolting . . . the peasants feel you have no regard for them." King Louis XVI responds with absolute shock, "I have no regard for the peasants??? They are my people . . . I love them." The very next moment, he yells "Pull!" and a peasant flies up in the air. King Louis XVI forgot to attend to the people and they ultimately beheaded him. He overestimated their loyalty and suffered as a result.

One modern-day version of King Louis XVI is James "Jimmy" Cayne, who resigned as CEO of Bear Stearns in January of 2008, just two months before the entire firm collapsed. Although he never fired rifles at peasants, he was similarly out of touch with his shareholders and employees. Rather than focusing on the welfare of the company, Cayne spent an inordinate amount of time playing bridge; in fact this is what he was doing the day when two of his firm's hedge funds collapsed and began bankruptcy proceedings. His departure was described as the "Cayne Mutiny" and characterized as "not a fond farewell." He was later named by CNBC as one of the "Worst American CEOs of All Time." But Cayne saw the emotions expressed during his departure differently. "When I left on January 4 . . . there wasn't a dry eye. Standing ovation. I was crying . . . Standing ovation, of the whole auditorium."

Whether in business, in government, or anywhere else, a lack of attention to others frequently contributes to powerful people's eventual downfall. But like Jimmy Cayne, the powerful never see it coming. Sebastien Brion of IESE Business School has documented this blindness scientifically. He found that the powerful are often overconfident in the support they have from others, and as a result they neglect to tend to those around them. Eventually, they lose the support of their subordinates and ultimately lose their power. Alexander Haig knows just how this can happen.

Alexander Haig liked being in charge. He slowly rose up the ranks of the Army, eventually becoming the vice chief of staff in the early 1970s. At the height of the Watergate scandal, Haig served as the White House chief of staff for the final year of President Richard Nixon's term. Given the immense pressure that President Nixon was facing with the Watergate investigation, Haig essentially ran the government—he was seen as the "acting president," and special prosecutor Leon Jaworski even called him the "37½ President."

A few years later, President Ronald Reagan appointed Haig as secretary of state. Just months into his presidency, on March, 30, 1981, President Reagan was shot. On that fateful day, Haig rushed into the briefing room and seized the reins of the presidency. He famously stated, "Constitutionally, gentlemen, you have the president, the vice president, and the secretary of state in that order, and should the president decide he wants to transfer the helm to the vice president, he will do so. He has not done that. As of now, I am in control here, in the White House."

There was a big problem with the statement: The 25th Amendment to the Constitution states that the line of succession goes from the vice president to the Speaker of the House to the president pro tempore of the Senate, before landing on the secretary of state. There was immense backlash to Haig's seizing of control, and he lasted only another year as secretary of state before resigning. His colleagues, who had long bristled at Haig's exaggerated sense of power, turned on him: "The public beating Mr. Haig received at the hands of the White House was virtually unprecedented." He became defined by this one moment and most of his obituaries when he passed away in 2010 led with his infamous phrase, "I am in control here."

When the powerful act selfishly and ignore others, they often veer into hypocrisy. As a leader, this is the last place you want to be. Hypocrisy involves holding a double standard—espousing and demanding strict moral standards for others while violating those same standards in one's own behavior. Indeed, our research with Joris Lammers shows that power increases hypocrisy—power licenses people to break laws and act freely on their desires while creating strict laws for others.

Consider two U.S. governors who made news for their dramatic and tragic downfalls: Eliot Spitzer and Rod Blagojevich. As attorney general, Spitzer targeted any organization with links to prostitution, even travel agencies that he said promoted sex tourism. He also targeted the male customers of prostitutes and signed into law the "anti–human trafficking" bill that increased the penalty for patronizing prostitutes. But on March 10, 2008, Spitzer was famously discovered to be a frequent customer of prostitutes. Two days later, Spitzer resigned as governor of New York.

Similarly, Governor Blagojevich had positioned himself as a reformer and campaigned against what he called a "legacy of corruption, mismanagement and lost opportunities." It was later discovered that Blagojevich had tried to *sell* the rights to a vacant United States Senate seat to the highest bidder (this was the seat that Barack Obama vacated when he was elected president in 2008 and resigned from the Senate). In recorded comments, Blagojevich said, "I've got this thing, and it's fucking golden. I'm just not giving it up for fucking nothing."

Hypocrisy is Spitzer passing laws that targeted prostitution cli-

ents, while patronizing prostitutes himself. It is Blagojevich cam-
paigning as a reformer, condemning corruption in others, while
flagrantly violating these standards himself. And it ended badly
for both of them.

Hypocrites are intolerable; they boil our blood and leave us
salivating at the prospect of revenge. And, often, we get it. This
is why hypocrites don't remain in power for very long. It's the
combined curses of selfishness and hypocrisy that bring the king
down.

Hubris and overconfidence can explain why many powerful
people act with selfishness and harshness. But it turns out that
powerful people also act badly when they feel threatened and
disrespected. In fact, power and low status are a particularly
toxic combination. Nearly all of us have suffered at the hands
of an official who holds power over us in one domain, but would
command little respect in the outside world. These individuals
are prone to using their power to make life difficult for others.
We call these people Little Tyrants.

A particularly notorious example of this toxic combination
involved the American prison guards in the Iraqi prison Abu
Ghraib. In 2004, these guards were caught on film celebrat-
ing their power over inmates. On a smaller scale, consider the
sometimes egregious bullying of security guards, DMV officials,
reimbursement administrators, or bouncers at nightclubs. Like
knowledge, a little power can be a dangerous thing.

Research we have done with Nathanael Fast of the University
of Southern California has shown that when we put people in
positions that are not well respected but command power over
others, those people become prone to turning into Little Tyrants. In one study, for example, we gave everyone a chance to
assign tasks to another person. When participants had power but
felt disrespected, they were almost twice as likely to assign tasks
that were particularly demeaning to others, like having someone repeat "I am filthy" five times or bark repeatedly like a dog.

These Little Tyrants demean others to compensate for their own wounded egos.

Power is precious but precarious. Whether it is hubris and hypocrisy or low status and threat, there are many paths people can take to abuse their power. When the powerful demonstrate little concern for those around them, they make themselves vulnerable to losing their power. So how can a king hold on to his crown? The key is finding a way to capture the benefits of having power without falling prey to the temptations that lead to the loss of power.

Finding the Right Balance: How to Speed Without Crashing

As we've seen, power acts almost like a wonder drug, giving you agency and confidence and optimism. But it's important not to get *too* high on your own power. For these benefits to emerge, you need to know your place in the power hierarchy and act accordingly. Those who act as if they have more power than they do, like Alexander Haig did, get ostracized. And this is bad news for the powerful, for as we saw in our introduction, the greatest form of torture is social isolation.

So, how do we reconcile these two points—the fact that power can be primed and lead to power, and the finding that if you act too powerfully for your position you will be socially punished?

To resolve this seeming contradiction, we need to understand two truths about power and social behavior. First, for each person at any point, there is a *range* of acceptable power that you can display relative to the actual power that you have. If you exceed that range, you are likely to be punished, but within the range, you can express more power than you actually have . . . but only up to a point. That is, you have some latitude, but don't get too cocky.

Second, we need to recognize that confidence and deference are not mutually exclusive, and it's usually a lack of deference rather than excess of confidence that gets powerful people into trouble. Take the job interview—the most successful candidates are those who display confidence but *also* show appropriate deference to the interviewer. Thus, the key is to be confident but also deferential. You need to find the right balance.

We mentioned that power is a psychological accelerator that encourages people to speed down the highway; it makes us more confident and optimistic, and helps us reach our destination faster. But to accelerate without endangering ourselves and others, we also need some mechanism for keeping our egos in check and preventing us from careening off the road. We need a steering wheel.

Our steering wheel is something we call perspective-taking, which is simply the ability to see the world from the perspective of others. Indeed, as we will discuss later in this book, our research has shown that the ability to take another's perspective is a critical ingredient for managing both our friends and our foes.

A crucial element to finding this balance is to know and consider the perspective of your audience. Take the power pose: Standing in front of your boss with a power pose may not go over so well; your boss may feel threatened and feel as though you are challenging their authority. This is why the power pose is best done *before* the interaction. It gives you a dose of confidence while still allowing you to appear deferential.

The ability to take the perspective of others helps the powerful see the others on the highway and fosters more cooperation from those with less power. Thus, the ability to see the world through the eyes of others can help the powerful stay in power—and be effective as well.

Research we have done with Joe Magee of NYU has established a number of benefits of combining power and perspective-taking. For one, it helps us solve problems more effectively. We have found that when the powerful member of the team is primed with an exercise in perspective-taking, it increases the team's ability to share critical information. In one study, when we gave the powerful a dose of perspective-taking, these individuals led their group to make better decisions by increasing the amount of information the team discussed and shared.

Just as a car needs both acceleration and a steering wheel to reach its destination, people need power *and* perspective-taking to be successful . . . and to hold on to their throne.

So how can we get the powerful to become more effective perspective-takers? One way is to direct their attention toward team objectives. Leigh Tost of the University of Michigan found that she could get the powerful to integrate and consider the perspective and advice of experts when she directed their attention toward the team goal of making the best decision. When powerful individuals focus on team goals rather than their own selfish goal of retaining power, they are more likely to realize that others have something unique to contribute.

Another method is to hold the powerful accountable for their decisions, to make the powerful explain their policies and articulate their rationale behind their actions. Indeed, our research has found that accountability steers the powerful to consider the perspectives of important stakeholders.

One final tip for harnessing power without its side effects of hubris and selfishness is to select leaders who already have a pretty good psychological steering wheel. An old piece of advice for those on first dates comes into play here: Watch how your date treats the waitstaff at dinner. They may be on their best behavior with you, but how they treat those with less power can portend their treatment of you when you are weak or vulnerable. Indeed, Roos Vonk of Radboud Universiteit found that people who kiss up but kick down are considered to be the slimiest of them all.

This kind of test is especially important when selecting leaders because it helps to expose who is most prone to abusing power. Because the powerful are less dependent on and less constrained by others, how they choose to use their power reveals their true nature. A quote by Robert Green Ingersoll when describing Abraham Lincoln eloquently captures this point: "If you want to test a man's character, give him power." With power, the constraints that normally govern how we act and behave recede and we become the truest form of ourselves.

So yes, it is good to be the king. And it is good to remain the king. Our research suggests that when the powerful develop the ability to see the world through the perspectives of others, they are more likely to retain their throne. Power paired with perspective-taking leads to stronger and more enduring kingdoms.

Here, we have considered how power influences our behavior at the individual level. Next, we turn to the question of power in groups and explore when having a steep hierarchy wins . . . and when it kills.

When Hierarchy Wins . . .
And When It Loses

F ather Michael Pfleger, a Catholic priest located on the south side of Chicago, committed a cardinal sin. His sin wasn't betraying his oath of sexual celibacy. It also didn't involve financial fraud, embezzlement, or corporate malfeasance. No, his crime was simply speaking up and publicly defying a direct order of the Catholic Church.

Father Pfleger was barely in his 30s when he became the youngest full pastor in the Chicago diocese. Armed with this early rise to power, Father Pfleger gained notoriety for his strident language and actions. He railed against—and even vandalized—billboards advertising alcohol and tobacco, ultimately persuading the city to eliminate tobacco and alcohol ads from certain neighborhoods.

However, in 2011, Father Pfleger spoke up at the wrong time, in the wrong place, and against the wrong people. It began when his superior, Cardinal Francis George, asked him to move as pastor of St. Sabina to take a new position as president for Chicago's Leo High School, a Catholic school near St. Sabina.

Not wanting to leave the diocese where he had served for 30 years, Father Pfleger not only resisted the transfer order, he defiantly and publicly challenged it, declaring on a radio show that he "would rather leave the Catholic church" than accept a position outside of St. Sabina. This did not go over well with his superiors. Dwight Hopkins, a theology professor at the University of Chicago, described the severity of the infraction: "If a priest disobeys the cardinal, the highest representative up to the pope, they disobey a direct line back to Jesus Christ."

On April 27, 2011, Father Pfleger was suspended from his ministry. He had violated the church hierarchy, and was severely punished for it.

Ten months earlier and 7,000 miles away, a similar dynamic played out in a very different but no less hierarchical organization. On June 22, 2010, *Rolling Stone* published an exposé, entitled "The Runaway General," about General Stanley McChrystal, the commander of all United States and NATO forces in Afghanistan. The article described how General McChrystal had publicly expressed disdain for the civilian leadership of the United States and of President Obama in particular. The *Rolling Stone* article described how "McChrystal likes to talk shit about many of Obama's top people" and how General McChrystal had specifically mentioned how unimpressed he was with his commander-in-chief.

In the hierarchy of the United States military, generals are subordinate to the president, much in the way Catholic priests are subordinate to their bishops. Like Father Pfleger, General McChrystal had violated this social contract. As a result, just one day after the article was published, McChrystal resigned. In the military, as in the Catholic Church, when it comes to criticizing your superiors, it is best to forever hold your peace—especially in public.

Both the Catholic Church and the military have some of the most clearly defined hierarchies in our society. In the Catholic Church, after the Holy Trinity, the pope sits at the top of a chain of "command," followed by cardinals, bishops, priests, deacons/nuns, and finally the laity. In the U.S. Army, generals sit at the top, followed by lieutenant generals, major generals, brigadier

generals, colonels, lieutenant colonels, majors, captains, 1st lieutenants, 2nd lieutenants, sergeants, corporals, and finally privates; even within the rank of general there are multiple rungs.

All of which makes one wonder, why are these two very different institutions, one paving a path to heaven and the other designed to send people into the afterlife, so similar in their rigidly
hierarchical organizational structures?

An examination of this question illuminates many of the reasons why hierarchy is the most ubiquitous form of social organization across all groups, countries, and cultures in the world: It
helps us navigate the shifting sands of our dynamic and unstable
social environments.

As we've discussed, humans are inherently social beings. Some
researchers believe humans evolved into an ultra-social species
because cooperative groups enabled our ancestors to outcompete our evolutionary rivals. However, group living also presents
numerous challenges. How do we coordinate our efforts? And
how do we keep individuals from pursuing personal interests
that compete with those of the group? The answer is simple: hierarchy.

Hierarchy helps us solve the dilemma between cooperation
and competition. This is why hierarchy is the predominant form
of social organization, why it emerges quickly, and why, once established, it is surprisingly resilient. Hierarchy is literally everywhere, from the corporate "ladder" to high school hallways to
the animal kingdom.

There are times, however, when hierarchy is *not* the surest
path to success. One critical weakness of hierarchy is that rigid
structures limit the opportunity for low-power individuals to
contribute wisdom and creative insights. Hierarchy can be costly
and at its worst, it can kill good ideas . . . and even people.

After extensively studying when hierarchy wins and when it
doesn't, we have discovered an important insight: The more
human the task, the less hierarchy helps. We will explain what

makes a task truly human. And we will share examples of how too much hierarchy contributed to a $182.3 billion government bailout, a failed invasion, and deaths on Mount Everest.

What we need is to find a way to make hierarchy work without holding us back. So in the pages that follow, we provide insight into how to harness the benefits of hierarchy while mitigating its downsides. Armed with this knowledge, we can create hierarchies that lead to victory with the fewest casualties along the way.

The Rise of Hierarchy

To understand why hierarchy has evolved to be the most dominant form of social organization across all species, including humans, it helps to look at one of its simplest forms: the beehive. The beehive is a well-known symbol of cooperation; it is even emblazoned on the Utah state flag to represent the state's commitment to social harmony. A beehive's members work so seamlessly together that the beehive has been described as its own living, breathing organism, as "a mammal in many bodies." Each member of the hive has its specialized tasks to complete—some clean, others build, some forage, others guard. But together, the bees' individual actions produce a symphony of coordinated activity.

It is this precision of coordination and seamless integration that has earned the beehive a rare distinction: It is considered to be a *superorganism*. Species that evolve into superorganisms are extremely rare, but once they emerge, they are extraordinarily successful. In fact, no species that has achieved superorganism status has ever gone extinct! Superorganisms are so successful because they are quintessentially hierarchical. Within a superorganism, every group member performs a role in synchrony with others, and any individual competitive desires are suppressed for the betterment of the collective.

As the beehive so elegantly demonstrates, hierarchy creates

a division of labor. In humans, this division of labor is often attentional, as leaders and followers direct their focus in different directions. Leaders view the forest while those with low power focus on the trees. A general needs to consider broad and abstract questions of readiness and strategy, and not get entangled in the intricacies of how to operate a tank or jet engine. The CEO needs to consider a firm's financial standing while the accountants crunch the numbers. And U.S. presidents are supposed to focus on the big issues of the economy and foreign affairs and not get lost in the details of something as trivial as managing a tennis schedule (which President Jimmy Carter apparently did). This division of labor allows all necessary tasks to be distributed and accomplished.

The invisible hand of hierarchy also allows for coordination among group members. Hierarchy helps people know who does what, when, and how. These rules promote efficient interactions by setting clear expectations for the behaviors of people of different ranks. Essentially, hierarchy facilitates social interactions by simplifying them.

Google thought they could succeed by creating a hierarchy-free workplace. They were wrong. Early on, Google founders Larry Page and Sergey Brin conducted what they thought would be a revolutionary experiment: They eliminated managers and created a completely flat organization. The experiment was indeed eye-opening, but only because it was a failure. The lack of hierarchy created chaos and confusion, and Page and Brin quickly realized that Google needed managers to set direction and facilitate collaboration. As they learned, even Google needs some hierarchy.

As we saw in the last chapter, it is good to be the king. As a result, hierarchy functions as an incentive system and creates motivation. Since those with greater rank receive greater rewards and face fewer threats, we have an incentive to work hard and contribute to the group in order to rise up the hierarchy and reap the accompanying rewards—a raise, a better job title, the bigger office, the closer parking space.

This reasoning suggests that cooperating and contributing to a group today can lead to a higher rank tomorrow. Indeed, Robb Willer of Stanford University has found that cooperative members of a group rise up the hierarchy more quickly: Those who sacrifice for the good of the group have greater influence and receive more social rewards. Deferring to and cooperating with high-ranked members of the organization indirectly benefits low-ranked members by promoting group success. When a team succeeds, everyone shares in the rewards. Thus, cooperation can lead to competitive benefits.

So now we can see why hierarchy governs two places—the military and the Catholic Church—where humans sublimate their own desires for the betterment of the group. The military epitomizes self-sacrifice for the collective; its members willingly risk their own lives for the sake of their group. Similarly, in the Catholic Church, members of the priesthood sacrifice their most individual desires—sex, family—in service to the Church. The Catholic Church is the longest continuously running organization in human history, and the Church's intense commitment to hierarchy helps to explain why.

Hierarchy offers one other benefit to humans, but this one is purely psychological. To appreciate this benefit, think about a time when you wanted your group to have a clear hierarchy, when you just had to know who was in charge. What made you crave a well-defined hierarchy in this situation?

If you are like most people, you embraced hierarchy when you were trapped in a threatening situation, or felt little control over your environment. In these situations, people desire a sense of order and control. Hierarchy offers much-needed structure. Thus, when we lack control, hierarchies become psychologically appealing because they offer clarity in the face of chaos. In a project led by Justin Friesen from York University, we found that when people don't feel in control, they are more likely to endorse hierarchy as the most appropriate form of social organization. In these situations, people want to be led, and willingly follow.

This makes sense when we look at political history. It explains why, in the terrifying days after the attacks of September 11, 2001, many Americans were willing to give more authority to the government. On an even larger scale, it also helps to explain the rise of authoritarian states in Germany and Italy during the period of great economic uncertainty after World War I.

The psychological benefits of hierarchy also extend into the heavens. Stephen Sales analyzed church membership in the United States over a 20-year period (1920–1939). He divided this period into two segments: one characterized by economic certainty and growth (the 1920s) and one beset by economic up-heaval and declining per capita income (1930s). Stephen then divided churches into two categories: hierarchical churches (e.g., Roman Catholic Church, Church of Jesus Christ of Latter Day Saints) and nonhierarchical churches (e.g., Protestant Epis-copal Church, Presbyterian Church). He defined "hierarchy" ac-cording to levels of hierarchy. For example, the Roman Catholic Church has 17 different levels of authority from the layman to God, whereas the Presbyterian Church has only seven.

Sales found that in the period of economic security, people were more likely to convert to nonhierarchical churches than to hierarchical ones. However, in the period of economic un-certainty, this pattern reversed, as more hierarchical churches dominated the recruitment of members. In studies with Aaron Kay of Duke University, we found the same effects at the individ-ual level: After people thought about a time in which they lacked control, they put greater faith in a more hierarchical God, one who is omniscient and omnipotent.

The idea of turning to hierarchy in times of threat can also explain why some countries have steeper and firmer hierarchies than others. When Michele Gelfand of the University of Maryland analyzed 33 countries around the world, she found that any force that put pressure on a society or threatened its security significantly increased the development of hierarchy. When a country historically faced the problems of population density, scarce resources, natural disasters, wars, and diseases, it tended to structure itself more hierarchically.

Why You Want to Play a Game with Your Boss Rather Than Your Best Friend

We have seen, in humans as in bees, that hierarchy facilitates a division of labor, increases coordination, maximizes motivation, and offers psychological comfort.

These benefits are most apparent in situations that would normally inspire conflict: when resources are scarce. Remember that scarcity is one of the foundational principles that create the tension between cooperation and competition. But hierarchy offers an easy heuristic for solving the perplexing dilemma of how to distribute scarce resources within a group: Those at the top receive the best spoils.

A series of studies conducted by Erik de Kwaadsteniet help us understand how hierarchy both facilitates social coordination and reduces conflict. These clever experiments use a stylized game to demonstrate an important point.

Imagine that you and your boss are playing a game and you have to coordinate your actions to earn money. The rules of this game—known as a Coordination Game—are such that you and your boss will each receive a monetary reward, but *only if you both choose the same option*. Unfortunately, you have to make your own individual decisions without being able to communicate with each other. There are two options in this game. Option A benefits you more than your boss. If you both pick A, you get eight lottery tickets and your boss only gets four. Option B benefits your boss more than you. If you both pick B, your boss gets eight lottery tickets and you only get four.

Which option would you choose? Option A or Option B? Remember, you only earn lottery tickets if you and your boss pick the same option.

Now, imagine playing the same game with your best friend. Which option would you choose?

Normally, most of us would prefer to play a game with our best friend more than we would with our boss. But in this game you are actually more likely to win money if you play with your boss. Why? Because with your boss, the clear status difference will help you coordinate your actions. Hierarchy dictates that you would both choose the option that benefits your boss more than you. As a result, you and your boss would coordinate your actions and both earn lottery tickets, though your boss will get a bit more.

Now consider playing the same game, but with your best friend. Here, you might pick the generous option, but your best friend might be generous too: In this case your mutual generosity would leave both of you with nothing. Or you might expect your friend to be generous, in which case you pick the selfish option. But your best friend might use the same logic and also pick the selfish option; again, you would both get nothing.

The point is that when playing with someone of equal status and power, the "obvious" option is unclear. Absent a clear hierarchy, coordination is difficult. So, in a Coordination Game like this one, hierarchy helps. It is better to be paired with your boss than your best friend.

For a similar reason, it wouldn't be a good idea for two bosses to play this game: The actions of two equally powerful people can be especially difficult to coordinate. This may be why, when Michael Eisner was recruited by Disney to be a co-CEO with Frank Wells, a former Warner Bros. executive, Eisner said no thanks. He felt being a *co*-CEO wouldn't work. He was right. As our own studies demonstrate, co-leadership is a bad idea, and we've found this to be true from fashion houses to mountain sides.

In one project led by Eric Anicich of Columbia University and Frédéric Godart of INSEAD, we collected industry-wide data on the global high-end fashion industry. We studied over 20 fashion seasons between 2000 and 2010. To evaluate the creative performance of the fashion houses, we used the industry standard: the ratings in the French trade magazine *Journal du Textile (JdT)*, which constructs its ranking by asking 70 industrial buyers to evaluate and rank the creativity of each fashion collection in each season.

The data were clear and strong: Fashion houses that had co–creative directors were consistently rated as less creative than houses with individual directors. And this isn't unique to fashion. We have found similar effects among Himalayan climbing teams: Co-led teams are more likely to have one of their members die on the mountain.

Co-leadership can kill both ideas and people, because it creates uncertainty over who is really in charge. Of course, co-led teams are not always ineffective and dangerous. But when there is not a clear division of labor among these leaders, coordination becomes difficult, patterns of deference can disappear, and conflict can erupt.

We began to wonder whether teams of superstars would suffer the same fate as co-led groups. Could more talent become too much talent?

When There Is Too Much Talent: Pecking Chickens and Squabbling Basketball Players

The Miami Heat basketball team shocked the basketball world in the summer of 2010 when they landed the two most coveted free agents on the market—LeBron James and Chris Bosh—to join their superstar Dwyane Wade. They now had a team stacked with an overwhelming amount of top talent. The Heat threw a lavish celebration for their new superstars. When predicting how many championships they were going to win, LeBron boasted during this party that they would win not just one, "not two, not three, not four, not five, not six, not seven . . ."

But hints of the Miami Heat's impending troubles were evident even at the celebration. When the announcer brought the three star players out on stage together, he mused, "So it's Wade's house, LeBron's kingdom, and Bosh's pit." At that moment, it became evident that it couldn't be all three, and that no one knew who the leader would be—would it be Wade, the proud resident who had already won a championship with Miami, or LeBron, the reigning MVP who was the most unstoppable force in the game?

Immediately, basketball insiders started wondering if the Heat had too much talent, and whether they would suffer from the absence of a clear leader. In the fall of 2010, sportswriter Bill Simmons articulated this sentiment: "They believe two alpha dog superstars . . . can reinvent themselves as co-CEOs of a basketball team. My gut feeling when LeBron took his talents to South Beach? 'That can't work.'" During that same fall, Phil Melanson echoed these concerns in a blog post: "If the Heat have one shot to win the game, who gets the ball . . . There's no synergy between these players and until they figure out a concrete pecking order, there won't be any order."

The concern about Miami's lack of a clear hierarchy turned out to be well founded. In late-game situations, the Heat's execution and coordination were disastrous. In the 2010–2011 season, their record in close games (those decided by five points or less) was an atrocious 32 percent, ranking them *29th* out of 30 teams. In comparison, the year before, when the Heat had an objectively worse team, but had a clear leader in Wade, their winning percentage in close games was 58 percent. When the new talent came on board, they fell out of sync because they didn't have a clear hierarchy.

A year later, the Heat won the championship. Ironically, critical injuries to Wade and Chris Bosh may have contributed to their success. With his fellow starters injured, James emerged as the clear leader of the team. Bill Simmons articulates this idea: "Dwyane Wade injured his knee . . . inadvertently solving the 'dueling banjos' dilemma. Less talent became more."

Intrigued by this idea, we set out to analyze 10 years of NBA performance with Roderick Swaab of INSEAD. Our analysis revealed exactly what we saw with the Miami Heat: At a certain point, adding more top talent caused teams' winning percentages to go down rather than up. These teams had *too much* talent!

It turns out that for basketball teams, steeper hierarchies lead to better performance. Why? Teams with a clear pecking order pass the ball more effectively, and as a result, players take higher percentage shots. As any good manager or athletics coach knows, getting a group of talented individuals—egos and all—to coordinate their behaviors effectively is easier said than done. A group of all-stars can easily tip the balance away from coordination and cooperation to competition and petty rivalry. When individual interests take precedence over what is best for the collective, group performance declines. It no longer functions like a superorganism.

The United States Olympic basketball committee came to appreciate the problem of "too much talent." Though the United States had dominated international competition in basketball in prior years, they stumbled in 2002 and 2004. In the 2002 FIBA World Championship, the United States finished a shocking sixth, and in the 2004 Summer Olympic Games, they settled for the bronze medal.

Then, in 2005, Jerry Colangelo took over as czar of the U.S. men's international basketball teams. He immediately signaled his intention to recruit *less* talent and focus on coordination and suppression of individual interests: "The first thing I wanted to establish was a real national team, not just an all-star team . . . That means a commitment from coaches and players for three years. I wanted to build an esprit de corps, camaraderie, and team unity . . . It's no longer about you, but about Team USA. You walk in the door here and you check your ego at the door . . . Basketball is the consummate team game . . . we wanted players who could complement [the stars]."

Colangelo put his money where his mouth was when he asked Andre Iguodala to join the team in 2010. As *Bleacher Report* put it: "Iguodala isn't one of the best players on the team. But Iguodala is a perfect fit for team USA . . . While most of the guys on the team play good defense, they need a player focused almost fully in their half of the court. That player is Iguodala. Iggy is great at stealing the ball, contesting shots, and starting fast-breaks."

Lo and behold, the new approach to selecting members for the Olympic team worked! The United States won the gold medal in the 2012 Olympics and again won the world championship in 2014.

The "too-much-talent" effect persists well beyond the basketball court. In business, companies and firms compete fiercely to attract the most talented individuals, presuming that ever higher levels of talent will produce better performance. But Boris Groysberg of Harvard University has also found the too-much-talent effect on Wall Street with sell-side equity research analysts. Here too, top talent was beneficial for performance . . . but only up to a point: The effect of more talent turned negative and started to harm performance.

When there is too much talent, the stars and high-status individuals compete among themselves to establish who the alpha dog is. As Corinne Bendersky of UCLA has shown, these status conflicts hurt group performance. With too many people at the top, individual competition dominates, and cooperation and coordination break down. It is like two bosses who can't agree on how to play the Coordination Game we described earlier.

The idea that a pecking order is critical for success comes from, well, chickens. As you could imagine, egg sellers want to produce a lot of eggs. So it makes sense that they would selectively breed the highest-egg-producing chickens. But something goes terribly wrong when you place a high number of the best egg-producing chickens in one colony. Total cage-wide production plummets! Even worse, chicken deaths skyrocket! Why? Because, the best egg producers also happen to be the most competitive birds, and when they are brought together, they begin fighting over food, space, and territory. They peck each other to death. For chickens, businessmen, and basketball players alike, high levels of performance come with high levels of competitive spirit. These status conflicts drive performance down.

The fact that too many dominant people in a group can impair performance is related to our earlier discussion about power. Remember we showed that simply having people think about a time in which they had power increased their confidence and assertiveness. But we've all witnessed conflicts when there are too many assertive people in a room. So we wondered what would happen if we primed *everyone* in a group with power: Would they end up squabbling like chickens and peck at each other?

To find out, we ran the following experiment. We had groups engage in a task that required coordination: create sentences where at least one word had to come from each group member. To succeed, group members had to successfully integrate their individual efforts.

Before the sentence task, we manipulated how many members of each group felt powerful: In the all-high-power condition, each member of a three-person group reflected on and wrote about a time in which they had power. In the all-low-power condition, each of the three members thought about a time in which they lacked power. In the hierarchy condition, we had only *one* of the group members think about a time in which they had power.

Our findings confirmed our suspicions: Groups in which all three members felt powerful descended into fierce battles for control—like the high-egg-producing chickens and basketball teams with too much talent—and thus performed worse. The groups in which no one felt powerful didn't fare any better. Here the group members all lacked agency, with too many followers milling around in search of a leader. Instead, it was the hierarchical group—the group where only one member was primed with power—that performed the best out of the three.

We then conducted a follow-up experiment with a biological marker of power and dominance—testosterone. If you want to know how much testosterone you were exposed to when you were in your mother's womb, take a look at your hand and focus on your ring and index fingers. It has been shown that the ratio between the length of the ring finger and the index finger is a marker of in utero testosterone exposure. If your ring finger is considerably longer than your index finger, you were exposed to greater levels of testosterone back in your mom's womb. If your two fingers are similar in length, it indicates that you were exposed to less testosterone in utero. It may seem ridiculous to use finger length to determine anything about a person's behavior.

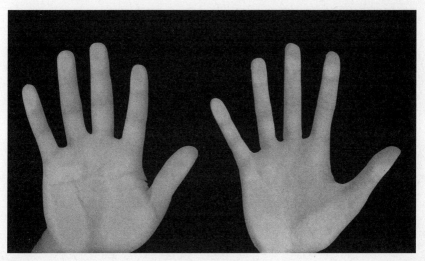

But there is evidence that high levels of prenatal testosterone exposure makes people sensitive to threats to their place on the hierarchical ladder. High-testosterone people, in other words, are more likely to feel disrespected.

We used this measure to create groups of all high-testosterone, all low-testosterone, or a mix of high-, low-, and average-testosterone individuals and had them do the same sentence task we just described. The results mirrored our first study—the all-high-testosterone groups did worse than the groups that had a range of testosterone because they spent more time embroiled in conflict.

This same effect has even been documented in baboons. When two baboons are both high in testosterone, they move toward each other in a competitive and assertive way that can promote conflict. When two baboons have different levels of testosterone, the one with lower testosterone yields and moves away.

So we can see that too much talent can derail groups by eliminating the necessary pecking order that helps produce effective coordination. Whether it's winning the NBA title, securing a victory on the battlefield, or building and sustaining a beehive, a group of individuals are most effective when they are integrated into a seamless whole. Hierarchy helps achieve this collaborative coordination by suppressing individual desires and synchronizing behavior.

But sometimes more talent *is* better. Consider baseball. When we studied the relationship between talent and performance on baseball teams—for the same 10-year period we studied talent and performance on basketball teams—the benefits from attracting top talent were linear: the more talent, the better. The "too much talent" effect didn't exist! In baseball, you can never have too much talent.

How do we explain this finding? As we have seen, hierarchy is most useful in situations where coordination is the key to success. Thus, the key to whether or not you can have "too much talent" hinges on how much the group performance requires coordination between the team's members.

Baseball and basketball differ markedly in terms of their need for coordination. A baseball team's offense plays sequentially rather than simultaneously. Each player bats individually. As a result, each batter gets approximately equal opportunities to hit. Of course, there are opportunities to cooperate on offense in baseball, but the extent of coordination between offensive players in baseball pales in comparison with basketball. In basketball, the number of shots a team can take is necessarily limited, and teams need a mechanism to efficiently allocate and reduce conflict over this scarce resource. Team members also depend on each other to create opportunities for high-percentage shots. Team defense is also more interdependent in basketball than it is in baseball. In basketball, defending requires all five players to constantly coordinate their actions and to support each other.

These differences were best expressed by two quotes uttered within three days of each other in the spring of 2010. In one, the sports columnist Bill Simmons referred to baseball as "an individual sport masquerading as a team sport." In the other, President Barack Obama referred to basketball as "the quintessential team sport" on CBS's March Madness broadcast.

In other words, whenever individuals perform largely independent tasks, like baseball players, you can never have enough talent. But in interdependent settings like beehives, Wall Street research groups, and basketball courts, more talent can lead to lackluster performance.

The basketball, Wall Street, chicken, and testosterone data offer cases where hierarchy wins. The baseball data suggest that sometimes hierarchy doesn't really matter. But in some cases hierarchy can actually hurt, killing performance and people.

When Hierarchy Hurts

In studying when hierarchy helps versus when it hurts, we began to realize that the more *human* the task, the less useful hierarchy appeared to be. So what makes a task human?

Humans, more than any other species, have the capacity to learn from each other and produce insights that build off each other's knowledge. For us, the coordination required is often intellectual.

So when we say a task is human, we mean that it is cognitively complex. In these cases, the number of things that have to be attended to is so great that no one perspective can capture all of the necessary information. In complex tasks, from flying a plane to performing surgery to deciding whether a country should go to war, people need to process and integrate a vast amount of information while also imagining myriad possible future scenarios.

And the more complex the task, the more likely we are to make a mistake or miss something critical. The costs of hierarchy can exceed its benefits in tasks like these—tasks that go beyond instinct and physical coordination, and instead require intellectual integration. Why? Because to make the best complex decisions, we need to tap ideas from all rungs of the hierarchical ladder and learn from everyone who has relevant knowledge to share.

Often, the best insights come from the least powerful. But as we have seen with Father Pfleger and General McChrystal, strong hierarchies silence voices that upset the chain of command. When we need insights from disparate members of a group, hierarchy can be a barrier to success.

Steve Jobs understood the tension between voice and hierarchy. In 2010, he declared, "You have to be run by ideas, not hierarchy. The best ideas have to win." In the companies he ran, Jobs tried to reduce hierarchy structurally. While at Pixar, he designed its headquarters to promote encounters across the rungs of the company; the front doors, stairs, corridors, all led to a central atrium that also contained the café and mailboxes. Contrast this with General Motors' headquarters, the Renaissance Center, in which executives had a separate elevator that also connected to their own private parking garage.

No firm appreciates the importance of empowering everyone at all levels of the organization to speak up better than IDEO, a top design firm in Silicon Valley. IDEO is considered to be one of the most innovative companies in the world, and they have won more *Business Week*/International Design Excellence Awards than any other firm.

IDEO wants ideas and lots of them. To produce groundbreaking innovation, IDEO limits the role of hierarchy in their brainstorming sessions. Founder Dave Kelley even went so far as to declare, "At IDEO, there is no corporate hierarchy and no management structure." Despite wide ranges in rank and pay, the title on every business card simply reads "Engineer." In their brainstorming meetings, there are no titles, only ideas.

IDEO's culture promotes something that Anita Woolley of Carnegie Mellon University identified as critical for a team's ability to be collectively intelligent: equal opportunities for sharing ideas. Woolley's research found that groups make more intelligent decisions when members participate equally in the conversation. Intelligent groups, in other words, benefit from the diversity of opinions of their members, whereas less intelligent groups are weighed down by a few individuals who dominate the conversation. When speaking time is concentrated in a few, a team becomes less intelligent.

There is a lot to be learned from cases in which hierarchy has silenced individual voices. Take the financial crisis of 2008. As we now know, the housing bubble that led to the economic meltdown in 2008 was fueled in part by a financial innovation called credit default swaps, financial instruments that function a

lot like insurance. Investors could insure themselves against the
risk of default by paying an annual premium that would protect
them against the failure of their investment.

One company that offered this financial insurance was
American International Group (AIG). AIG made unbelievable
amounts of money insuring mortgage-based securities—as long
as housing prices went up, they would get their premium checks
and have to pay no claims. But as AIG was making a huge profit,
storm clouds loomed on the horizon.

Unfortunately, the head of their Financial Products division
was Joe Cassano, a man who suppressed the voices of employees
who spoke out about the looming crisis. Cassano would express
rage and bully people into submission when they presented information that challenged his position. He was especially critical of anyone who suggested that AIG's strategy of providing
credit default swaps was no longer sound. Because he had so
successfully suppressed alternative voices, Cassano's team was
overexposed and completely unprepared for the financial crisis
of 2008. As mortgage-based securities fell into default, AIG was
responsible for honoring their insurance claims. Ultimately, the
federal government had to bail out AIG, lest the entire financial
market collapse, to the tune of *$182.3 billion.*

And it wasn't just Cassano at AIG who suppressed concerns
about the housing bubble. As chairman of the U.S. Federal Reserve from 1987 to 2006, Alan Greenspan was devoted to low
interest rates and limited regulation, and was convinced that
there was no housing bubble. He was also devoted to letting his
colleagues know exactly where he stood on policy recommen-
dations. When he met with bank presidents, Greenspan would
open with an in-depth soliloquy about his own views. Greenspan
would then open up the floor for comments, but few dared to
challenge this economic savant. In contrast, his effective succes-
sor, Ben Bernanke, chose to offer his perspective *last*, after all
other members of the committee had had a chance to speak first.

President John F. Kennedy learned the hard way to appreciate the importance of ensuring hierarchy didn't prevent the sharing of ideas. At first, he got it wrong with the disastrous invasion at the Bay of Pigs. Early in his presidency, Kennedy approved a CIA-orchestrated plan to overthrow the Cuban leader Fidel Castro. It involved training Cuban exiles to invade Cuba, with the aid of U.S. forces. On April 17, 1961, Cuban exiles landed at the Bay of Pigs, but after just two days of fighting, their forces were decimated; all 1,300 were either killed or captured. As a result, President Kennedy, only months in office, found his reputation severely compromised—the bungled affair made him seem young and inexperienced.

A major reason why the plan failed so spectacularly was a strong hierarchy that suppressed diverse perspectives. In deciding whether or not to launch the invasion, President Kennedy was present at all critical meetings and expressed a clear preference at the outset. That doesn't sound so bad on the surface, but his presence and strongly worded preferences served as subtle barriers that prevented others from expressing their own. Even his top aides held their tongues: Both the secretary of state and the deputy director of the CIA did not reveal their concerns to the president. Kennedy's advisors *felt certain that* the plan would fail, but no one spoke up.

A mere 18 months later, a more experienced Kennedy prevented nuclear apocalypse by changing the group dynamics that had crippled his planning for the Bay of Pigs invasion. The Cuban missile crisis was a high-stakes, fast-moving international drama—the epitome of complex, dynamic decision-making. As history buffs will recall, his first idea was to bomb the nuclear installations before they became operational. Yet, had the United States done so, the Soviets may well have countered with bombings of their own, possibly leading to a third world war, and a full-scale nuclear one at that.

Luckily, this time, Kennedy loosened the hierarchy reins, deliberately making himself absent from preliminary meetings and refraining from revealing any initial preferences. In describing the meetings held during the crisis, Robert Kennedy said: "We all spoke as equals. There was no rank, and, in fact, we did not even have a chairman." Lower-level officials with relevant knowledge and expertise were given the floor and there was periodic involvement of outside experts and fresh voices.

By reducing hierarchy, novel solutions emerged. The president eventually decided against air strikes and instead set up a blockade that prevented offensive weapons from being delivered to Cuba. The United States and the Soviets eventually reached an agreement—the Soviets would remove any missiles from Cuba and the United States would promise to never invade Cuba. Nuclear war was averted.

We can learn similar lessons about hierarchy from mountain climbers who have attempted to summit Mount Everest.

Everyone knows that climbing Mount Everest can be deadly. More than 200 people have died attempting to summit its peak, which sits at 29,029 feet (8,848 meters) above sea level. In fact, part of the mountain is even called the "Death Zone." But what many people don't realize is that high-altitude climbs are dangerous not only because they are so physically challenging, but because they also require a great deal of complex and dynamic decision-making. In order to be successful and avoid fatal errors, leaders and expedition members need to communicate frequently and coordinate not only physically but also intellectually. As a group, climbers need to assess the physical condition of each climber, monitor supplies, and navigate extreme and dynamic weather patterns. In other words, mountain climbing is the kind of activity that can suffer from hierarchy.

In May of 2006, when a storm hit during their descent, and two teams, one from the United States and one from New Zealand, lost five of their members, including the leader of each team, one factor that contributed to the fatalities was hierarchy.

As one climber noted, "there was not . . . a sense of individual responsibility, rather, clients were encouraged to see the leader and guides as saviors." The members relied too heavily on the leaders, never questioning their plan or contributing their own vantage point. Tragedy resulted.

Or consider the disaster that struck a ferry in South Korea in April of 2014. Things began to go wrong when the ferry began to list after making a sharp turn in the face of a strong current. All told, 302 people perished on the boat, and 250 of them were high school students. Many of these individuals could have been saved. Instead, as the ship began to sink they obediently followed orders from the crew to stay put . . . until it was too late. "A real tragedy of the disaster was that those students who followed the instructions died," said Bark Soon-il, head of the Korea Social Policy Institute. In cultures that emphasize obedience to authority—like South Korea—hierarchy can be particularly deadly.

We conducted a study to test whether hierarchical cultural values would predict fatalities in a high-stakes situation. Along with Eric Anicich of Columbia University, we analyzed over 30,000 Himalayan mountain climbers from 56 countries on over 5,000 expeditions. We found that members of expeditions hailing from more hierarchical countries were more likely to die in the Himalayas. Why? Because in countries and cultures that are hierarchical, decision-making tends to be a top-down process. People from these countries are more likely to die on difficult mountain climbs because they are less likely to speak up and less likely to alert leaders to changing conditions and impending problems. By not speaking up, these climbers preserved order but endangered their own lives. Importantly, we isolated the role of *group* processes by showing that the higher fatality rate occurred for group, but not solo, expeditions. It was only when a group of individuals had to communicate effectively that hierarchical cultures produced disaster.

The Himalayan context highlights a key feature that creates complex decisions: a dynamic and changing environment. When the environment can change dramatically and suddenly, people have to adapt and come up with a new plan. In these cases, we need everyone's perspective brought to bear and hierarchy can hurt by suppressing these insights.

Even the military appreciates that in fast-paced situations that involve significant consequences, hierarchy must be minimized to prevent disaster. Consider the now famous, cover-of-darkness helicopter ride on May 1, 2011. Two helicopters carrying 23 members of SEAL Team Six flew into Pakistan with the mission to capture or kill Osama bin Laden, the mastermind behind the 9/11 terror attacks. This was an incredibly risky mission, and disaster nearly struck when one of the helicopters crashed as they approached the bin Laden compound. This elite team had to improvise in that moment: They needed to complete the mission, they needed to limit the amount of classified information they left behind in the downed helicopter, and they needed to get out alive.

The combination of complexity and unpredictability made the bin Laden raid a quintessentially human task. Because they had to make fast-paced decisions on the ground, they were empowered to act. Speed and adaptation, flexibility and improvisation—not top-down leadership—are what characterize SEAL Team Six.

For much of our discussion on hierarchy, we have described how the military is the epitome of a strong hierarchy because hierarchy helps it solve the problem of massive physical coordination. But SEAL Team Six, and the Special Forces in general, stand out for their *lack* of hierarchy. Because there are no privates or corporals, the hierarchy in Special Forces is, by definition, flatter than it is in other areas of the military. The Special Forces represent "a leadership organization, where you invite participatory involvement in decision-making; where people at every level, from the sides and the bottom, have a voice and a view, and are permitted and encouraged to provide feedback."

The key lesson is that for human tasks that require knowledge to be shared and integrated in fast-paced, dynamic environments, hierarchy can contribute to catastrophic failure. In these environments, anyone in the team, even the lowest-ranked member, may have the critical insight that tips the balance.

Finding the Right Balance: How Psychological Safety Helps Hierarchies Win Without Killing

As we've seen, hierarchies can help teams and organizations collaborate more effectively and operate more efficiently. But at the same time, steep and strong hierarchies suppress the voices of the less powerful and can lead team members to their tragic death. So how do we leverage the benefits of hierarchy without the downsides?

Johns Hopkins Hospital tried to find a way to do this when they explored how to reduce critical mistakes during surgery. Every surgery carries risks, especially those of infections. A particularly problematic infection is a central-line infection because it spreads the infection through the whole body and massively increases the risk of mortality. So in 2001, Johns Hopkins implemented what they *thought* would be a simple but effective solution: a straightforward five-part checklist of sterilization to prevent infections when putting in a central line.

Their solution was a failure. The checklist did little to stem the tide of infections. Why? The problem was that for more than a third of patients, the doctor skipped one of the crucial steps *even while using the checklist.*

So, Johns Hopkins Hospital turned to a radical approach. They authorized the lowest-ranked members of the surgical team—nurses—to intervene if a doctor skipped a step on the checklist. They also empowered the nurses to ask questions about the timing of the central line removal. By getting nurses to speak up and share their concerns, the hospital prevented numerous infections and saved many lives.

Amy Edmondson of Harvard Business School popularized a simple yet revolutionary phrase to describe the conditions within a group that encourage the less powerful to speak up: *psychological safety*. In psychologically safe environments, team members feel encouraged to ask for clarification, to point out critical errors, and even to share new and challenging ideas. These psychologically safe environments produce fewer errors and more innovative ideas.

Psychological safety is particularly important in hierarchies without any prospects of advancement. Even in the military and the Catholic Church, lower-ranked individuals have a path to move up. But nurses will almost never become doctors. This rigid barrier between nurses and doctors makes communicating across professional boundaries difficult, and ultimately limits the quality of care. This steep hierarchy can lead to alarming errors, such as when a doctor used the shorthand R.EAR to indicate that a medication should be put in the *right ear,* but an unsure nurse didn't feel comfortable asking for clarification. Instead, she administered the medication, uh, rectally. Of course, it is easy for medical errors to happen, but they become *more* likely when individuals defer without seeking clarification. The fear of being marginalized and punished for asking questions of those in charge all too often guides people to pursue the seemingly safe and silent route. At Johns Hopkins, psychological safety was created structurally and officially: They put nurses in charge of the checklist, which empowered them to insist that the doctors follow the proper steps.

Often it is the day-to-day behavior of the powerful that determines whether psychological safety exists in an organization. With simple steps, the powerful can diminish barriers and create a sense of inclusiveness. By openly soliciting the input of others, the powerful can curtail the fear of speaking up. Small gestures can also provide people with an unexpected sense of inclusion. For example, when surgeons invite nurses to seminars previously reserved for physicians, it not only elevates the status of the non-surgeons, but it also expands their knowledge and scope.

We can start to understand when and how we need hierarchy to be successful. To solve complex, dynamic problems and make the best decisions, leaders need access to the most complete and varied information. To ensure that the perspectives and wisdom of the less powerful are brought to light, leaders and institutions need to promote psychological safety for their lower-status members. And for complex tasks, these efforts can generate tangible benefits.

But we still need to know who is in charge. In the operating room, we still need the surgeon to lead and direct the operation. When deciding whether or not to go to war, we still need the president to rally the troops or call them off. And once a decision has been made, we need hierarchy to produce the coordination necessary to successfully *implement* that well-conceived decision.

So, for a group or organization to achieve the highest level of success, we need to learn how and when to fluctuate between more versus less hierarchy. We need to figure out what type of hierarchy will enable our team to cooperate so that it can compete effectively.

By understanding a few basic principles, you can make hierarchy win with the fewest casualties along the way. Whenever we use a hierarchy, we make a trade-off between coordination and voice. Hierarchy creates a fundamental tension between suppressing individuality to achieve synchrony and denying key insights from those below.

So here are some key rules that can help you decide when to have more versus less hierarchy. For interdependent physical tasks, we need coordination and therefore hierarchy can win here. But for complex, dynamic decisions, ones that require the involvement of different perspectives, hierarchy can lose and even kill. To make the best decisions, leaders need to create psychological safety that encourages broad participation. And finally, almost every group still needs a leader, someone who sets the vision and the course and integrates all the different perspectives to make the final decision.

We see these rules play out at the design firm IDEO that we discussed earlier. When the tasks are intellectual, IDEO minimizes hierarchy to promote equal opportunity participation in the service of developing new ideas. Even in this stage, there is a leader, but this person merely facilitates the generation of ideas. But when the best idea needs to be identified, implemented, and produced, IDEO turns back to hierarchy. As intellectual integration turns into the need for physical coordination, IDEO reinstates hierarchical order through a division of labor that is well synchronized. And the leader turns from facilitator to general. Collectively, IDEO knows when to have more versus less hierarchy. And, as a result, it wins again and again and again.

Earlier, we described how comparisons and power regulate much of human psychology. Here, we have articulated how and when hierarchy within a group can help it operate more effectively. Next, we integrate these ideas to explore hierarchies *between* groups, and how our group's standing within a society can constrain the type of behavior we are allowed to engage in. We will show that it is good to be the queen. But because women have less power than men in society, queens face many more constraints than kings do.

It's Good to Be
the Queen . . . But It's Easier
Being the King

Iris Robinson was used to getting her way. She had quickly
climbed the rungs of the political ladder in Northern Ire-
land: First, as a borough councilor, then as the first female mayor
of her borough, and then in 2001, she entered parliament. Once
there, she took on one leadership role after another, eventually
rising to become the deputy whip for her Democratic Unionist
Party.

In her private life, she lived in style. In addition to her lavish estate in East Belfast, she and her husband had a house in
Florida and an apartment in London. She drove around in her
MG and Audi convertibles and freely shared details about her
extravagant lingerie purchases.

For Iris, it was good to be the queen.

Like Mark Hurd of HP, 60-year-old Iris had a wandering eye
for someone much younger than herself: 19-year-old Kirk Mc-
Cambley. So smitten was she with Kirk that over the course of
their affair, she arranged £50,000 in funding from two property
developers to help refurbish her lover's café.

And just like Mark Hurd, it was expense reports that brought
her down. Not only had she duplicitously obtained funds to help

support Kirk, but she had consistently double-claimed expenses when she was with her husband, who was another governmental official. She even used state funds to employ her two sons, daughter, and daughter-in-law.

Iris was expelled from her political party in disgrace. It was good to be the queen . . . until it wasn't.

We have already learned about the benefits and costs of being a king. We've looked at how power can corrupt, and make us feel invincible and above the law. Well, as Iris's story shows us, power can affect queens in much the same way as it affects kings. In fact, our research shows that power affects men and women in nearly identical ways.

After extensively studying both power and gender differences, we have observed that *many gender differences are actually just power differences in disguise!*

But there's a catch. Although power affects men and women similarly, research shows that it's a lot *easier* to be a king than it is to be a queen. No story illustrates this better than the story of Ann Hopkins.

After years of grueling work, it was finally time for Ann to be promoted to partner at Price Waterhouse. *Time* magazine reported that Hopkins "looked like a shoo-in," and it was easy to see why. As an associate, she had billed more hours and generated more business than any of the 87 other candidates up for promotion to partner. On her first assignment, a project for the Department of the Interior, one partner described her performance as "outstanding," and went on to say that her "project management skills are excellent." Another client called her "competent, intelligent, strong, and forthright." And she so impressed one of her clients at the State Department that he sought to hire her away from Price Waterhouse.

Yet, when all the votes were cast, *less than half* of the partners recommended Hopkins for promotion to partner. Her candidacy was put on hold, pending further review. Within months she quit the firm.

Why did Ann, who had so excelled at Price Waterhouse, fail to become partner?

Well, it turns out that she had "irritated" some of the senior partners. How? By being too assertive and being too aggressive. As one of her colleagues summarized it, she was too . . . masculine. In fact, the head of her department advised her to "walk more femininely, talk more femininely, dress more femininely, wear makeup, have her hair styled, and wear jewelry." She was told to relax, "take charge less often," and to "soften her image in the manner in which she walked, talked, and dressed."

In 1983, Ann filed a lawsuit claiming sexual discrimination. The landmark case went all the way to the Supreme Court, where Hopkins won, and she was reinstated as a partner at Price Waterhouse in February, 1991. In writing the court's opinion, Justice William Brennan stated that "an employer who objects to aggressiveness in women but whose positions require this trait places women in an intolerable and impermissible Catch-22: out of a job if they behave aggressively and out of a job if they don't."

The Supreme Court decision captured the double bind that women face in the corporate world today: They can't get ahead if they don't act assertively, but if they do act with confidence, they are often punished. Ironically, the very same behaviors that enabled Ann to secure more business than any other associate— ambition, confidence, drive, assertiveness—were also the same behaviors that annoyed so many of her colleagues . . . but only because she was a woman.

Sheryl Sandberg of Facebook has recommended that women "lean in" to secure positions of power and leadership. But she also acknowledges that when women act assertively, they often get pushed back. Our society rewards confident men but punishes assertive women. We *expect* and *demand* that women be warm and cooperative. Yet this expectation makes it harder for women to compete effectively.

How can we—organizations, men, and women—eliminate this double bind?

Here, we answer this question by looking at how many gender differences are really just power differences in disguise, and exploring just how closely intertwined gender and power really are. As we describe the fundamental challenge women face when they lean in and act with power, we offer specific advice for what organizations, men, and women can do to end this double bind.

One final note as we wade into this area: We are keenly aware that we are tackling this topic from a male perspective. We have tried to report the science in a way that is sensitive, and we hope we have been successful.

Men Aren't from Mars and Women Aren't from Venus

In 2005, the president of Harvard University, Larry Summers, created a firestorm when he answered a question about why there were so few women in engineering and science at the very best universities. He pointed to the "different availability of aptitude at the high end" and suggested that ability, rather than issues of "socialization and patterns of discrimination," could account for gender imbalance in the sciences. In short, he conjectured that men might have what it takes to do well in science, while women don't.

Larry Summers is not the first to suggest that there are biologically based gender differences in aptitude; this idea has been posited countless times and in countless ways for centuries. It is telling that perhaps one of the most common and popular conceptualizations of gender—epitomized by John Gray's mega-bestselling book, *Men Are from Mars, Women Are from Venus*—is that men and women are essentially *different species of people.*

This depiction of gender is wrong.

We're not claiming that biological differences between the sexes don't exist. Rather, we offer three fundamental insights. First, gender differences are far more subtle than we commonly believe. Gender differences are not categorical—black or white. Instead, they are shades of gray. Indeed, after examining the data from over 13,000 participants, Harry Reis of the University of Rochester found that men and women are far more similar than they are different.

Second, there is one clear difference between men and women in the United States and through most of the world: the amount of power each has in society. Despite the great strides that have been made in promoting gender equality, women and men are not currently competing on a level playing field. So to understand gender differences we need to understand *power* differences, and the fact that men have so much more of it in just about every modern culture.

Building off this power difference brings us to our third point: Gender stereotypes are deeply ingrained and impose constraints on the behavior and actions of women. To understand differences in how men and women behave, we need to start with an understanding of how men and women are *expected* to behave.

To put these issues into perspective, let's consider some numbers. In the United States in 2013, women earned only 77 cents on the dollar compared to what men earned. And if we look at those at the top of the corporate ladder, the picture looks even bleaker. In 2012, only 4.2 percent of Fortune 500 CEOs were women, and women made up only 17 percent of the corporate boards of Fortune 500 companies. And the imbalance isn't limited to existing organizations: Even starting a business is tougher for women. Alison Wood Brooks of Harvard University studied 90 entrepreneurial pitches from three competitions for investors. Even when the content of the pitch was identical, she found that 68 percent of the investors funded male entrepreneurs but only 32 percent funded female entrepreneurs.

You could turn to gender differences in competencies and skills, as Summers did, to explain these differences. If men are better at math and science than women are, then maybe they get the jobs that pay more. And in fact, if you look at standardized test scores, men do outperform women in math. For example, in the United States, males have scored between 33 and 36 points higher on the Scholastic Aptitude Test (SAT) than women in every year since 1994. At first blush, it looks like Larry Summers might be right, that "different availability of aptitude" could explain why women don't succeed as often as men do in math and the sciences.

But to really understand what's going on we need to dig deeper into the data. That is what Luigi Guiso of the Einaudi Institute did when he set out to test whether this math gap that Larry Summers so famously attributed to biology could be attributed instead to power. He collected data from the 2003 Programme for International Student Assessment (PISA) that reports results for a quarter of a million 15-year-old students from 40 countries. If you look at that data set overall, you would find the typical gender gap.

But when Luigi looked more closely, he found that the size of the gender gap varied considerably across countries. And when he looked at different factors to try and understand what could explain where the gap was largest and where it was smallest, it turns out that the gap was closely related to the level of *gender equality* in each country (as measured by the political empowerment index and an index of women in the labor market). In countries with the highest levels of gender equality, the gap in math performance disappeared. In fact, in Iceland, the country with the highest level of gender equality, females actually *outperformed* males in math. In other words, women only demonstrated inferior math ability in societies where they lacked power. But why?

To find out, we can take Luigi's investigation one step farther. If power plays a role in the male advantage in math, we wondered, could we improve women's math abilities simply by manipulating power? And indeed, work conducted by Joan Chiao of Northwestern University has found that simply having women recall an experience with power can increase their scores on a math test. As we saw in our discussion of power, feelings of power help buffer people from experiencing stress and build confidence and focus. Power reduces the anxiety women feel during a math test and allows them to perform at their best.

What these data tell us is that gender differences in performance are not hardwired. Rather, the differences in performance often reflect power disparities and not differences in competence.

Cultural disparities in gender equality impact far more than math performance. Take the most popular sport in the world, soccer. Since 1993, the Fédération Internationale de Football Association (FIFA) has ranked all member countries each year in terms of performance and quality. In research we conducted with Roderick Swaab of INSEAD, we found that gender equality predicts women's FIFA rankings, even after controlling for population size and per capita GDP. When women have more power and opportunity in a country, that country's female soccer team has a competitive advantage.

So, if power differentials underlie some of the gender differences in aptitudes, in everything from math to sports, we couldn't help but wonder whether power can account for two other widely accepted gender differences: the willingness to negotiate and the decision to engage in infidelity.

Salaries and Sex

Imagine that you just landed a new job. Your employer welcomes you and offers you a salary. Do you accept that salary or do you ask for more?

And does the answer to this question hinge on whether you are a man or a woman?

This is the very question that Linda Babcock of Carnegie Mellon explored. As she has eloquently written in her book, *Women Don't Ask*, one reason that women make 77 cents on the dollar compared with men is because women are less likely to negotiate their salaries after getting an initial offer. In one survey she found that 52 percent of male MBA students negotiated for a better offer, while only 17 percent of female MBAs negotiated; the remaining 83 percent simply accepted their offers without asking for more.

Linda then created a clever experiment to test whether women would be less likely to ask for more even when they were in the exact same situation as men. So she told participants that they could earn anywhere from $3 to $10 for playing a game of Boggle. After each person finished the game, she paid everyone exactly $3. She did not mention at any time that they could negotiate and ask for more. She also didn't inform them why they received the amount they did or provide any feedback on their performance. If people *asked* for more, she gave them what they asked for, up to the $10 limit. And as suspected, the gender difference in people's willingness to ask was striking; *men were seven times more likely to ask for more money than women*. This was not a fluke; in our own work, we've replicated these shocking results.

Interestingly, it turns out that manipulating feelings of power can actually produce these same gender disparities. In a study we conducted with Joe Magee of New York University, we gave people of both genders the following scenario: "You have been asked to be bumped off your flight. How likely are you to ask for a voucher of greater value and/or amenities like an upgrade to first class?" We found that when participants—men or women—were primed with power they were more likely to say they would negotiate and ask for more. That is, by merely priming people with power, everyone behaved the way men did in this setting.

But perhaps the most notorious gender stereotype is that men have a greater propensity to be unfaithful. And this isn't just an unfounded stereotype merely propagated by movies. Numerous studies have found that men cheat more often and with more partners than women. There are lots of theories for this pronounced effect, but most lead back to the idea that women engage in less infidelity because they bear greater reproductive costs than men. In other words, they are the ones who have to deal with the consequences of accidentally getting pregnant. As a result, the theory goes, women have evolved to be more selective in terms of sexual partners in general and with regard to infidelity in particular.

Yet, *power* can increase infidelity—for both men *and* women. Just ask Iris Robinson. Or, better yet, consider a study led by our colleague Joris Lammers of the University of Cologne. He surveyed 1,561 professionals and asked them to rank their position in their organization's power hierarchy on a scale of 0–100, then asked respondents how often they had been unfaithful to their partner (i.e., how often they had secretly had sex with another person).

Across the board, higher-power individuals reported more instances of infidelity. And, consistent with our thesis that many perceived gender differences are in fact power differences, this effect was the same for men and women.

Over and over again, we and others have found that *many well-known gender differences can be reproduced by manipulating power.* In other words: The suggestion that men and women come from different planets is wrong. Men aren't from Mars and women aren't from Venus. Instead both are from Earth, and how each behaves is profoundly influenced by how much power they have.

So, if these gender differences reflect power differences, can we solve gender inequality by making women feel more powerful? Can't we simply utilize some of the strategies we identified in Chapter 2—recalling experiences with power, listening to high-power music, power posing—to help women improve their outcomes by making themselves feel as powerful as the men around them?

Unfortunately, it's not that simple. Changing how powerful we feel only solves half of the problem. Because women as a group have less power than men, they face an additional barrier to acting with power. What the experience of Ann Hopkins shows us is that women are expected to be communal, caring, and submissive. These expectations produce the unfortunate double bind: When women *do* feel and project power, they are punished for it.

The Double Bind

Women need to act with confidence and agency to get ahead. But when they do so they face a potential backlash. They are dammed if they do and damned if they don't.

To understand this double bind that women face, we first need to understand that there are two types of stereotypes. One is called a *descriptive* stereotype. These are stereotypes about what one *is likely to* do. The other is called a *prescriptive* stereotype. These are stereotypes about what one *should* do. Women are particularly burdened by prescriptive stereotypes. They are *expected* to be warm and deferential and they are *not expected* to be demanding and to ask for more money. These sentiments were exemplified in the comments that Microsoft's CEO Satya Nadella gave during the 2014 Grace Hopper Celebration of Women in Computing conference when he remarked, "It's not really about asking for a raise, but knowing and having faith that the system will give you the right raise. That might be one of the initial 'super powers,' that quite frankly, women [who] don't ask for a raise have. It's good karma. It will come back." Although he quickly issued an apology—"If you think you deserve a raise, you should just ask"—the implication of his initial comments was clear: Women shouldn't ask.

This prescriptive stereotype, and the double bind that it creates, limit the ability of women to compete effectively.

Consider the act of negotiation. We mentioned that women are less likely to ask for a higher salary when they accept a job offer. Hannah Riley Bowles of Harvard has found that women are right to be cautious about asking. Across multiple studies, she explored what happens when men and women behave assertively. Even when men and women engage in the *exact same* behavior, women are the ones who get punished for not accepting first offers and asking for more.

Consider what happened when one female academic recently tried to negotiate her job offer. In March of 2014, after the professor was offered a tenure-track position in the Philosophy Department at Nazareth College in Rochester, New York, she did what many academics do: She wrote an e-mail proposing a counteroffer. "As you know, I am very enthusiastic about the possibility of coming to Nazareth," she politely wrote. "Granting some of the following provisions would make my decision easier." After listing her requests, she ended with this line: "I know that some of these might be easier to grant than others. Let me know what you think."

Much to her surprise, Nazareth College didn't respond with a subsequent counteroffer. Instead, they simply rescinded the offer altogether: "Thank you for your e-mail. The search committee discussed your provisions. They were also reviewed by the Dean and the VPAA. It was determined that on the whole these provisions indicate [a lack of] interest in teaching at a college, like ours . . . Thus, the institution has decided to withdraw its offer of employment to you." As a *Slate* article aptly summed up the moral of the story: "Negotiating While Female: Sometimes It *Does* Hurt to Ask."

The professor had the nerve to express confidence in her skills and talents and to ask for the compensation she felt she deserved, and she was immediately punished for doing so.

Imagine the following situation. You observe an interview. The interviewer asks, "Do you like performing in high-pressure situations?" And the job candidate responds, "I tend to thrive in pressure situations. For example, in high school I was the editor of the school paper and I had to prepare a weekly column under deadline all the time . . . and I always pulled it off—so well that sometimes I even surprised myself. My supervisors noticed also and were quite complimentary."

If you were watching this interaction, what would your reaction to the candidate be? Well, the research has found that it likely would depend on whether the job candidate was a man or a woman. Laurie Rudman of Rutgers University conducted an experiment using this exact wording and only varied the gender of the applicant. And she found that when a man delivered this response, he was seen as confident and competent; observers said they would want to hire him. But when a woman expressed the same words, she was viewed as less likable and judged to be not a good fit for the job.

This experiment highlights the double standard that women face. For the same behavior, men are characterized as confident, but women as arrogant; men take charge, but women are bossy; men are persistent, but women are pushy. In a *New Yorker* cartoon, a queen complains to a king, "But when a *woman* has someone's head cut off she's a bitch."

This double standard doesn't exist just in the workplace. It was also on display in the political trajectory of one of America's most visible power couples: Bill and Hillary Clinton. As

Bill Clinton geared up to run for president in 1992, it was clear that the career success of his wife was going to be a problem. A strategy memo from her husband's 1992 presidential campaign explained the campaign's dilemma: "While voters genuinely admire Hillary Clinton's intelligence and tenacity, they are uncomfortable with these traits in a woman. She needs to project a softer side—some humor, some informality." Or, in short: "What voters find slick in Bill Clinton, they find ruthless in Hillary." While her husband was lauded for his strength and tenacity, she was punished for exhibiting the same traits.

And it's not just men who discriminate against assertive women. Women do it too. In the negotiation study that Hannah Riley Bowles ran that we mentioned earlier, women punished other women who asked for more in a negotiation just as much as men did. And in the studies done by Laurie Rudman of Rutgers University, both men and women were less likely to hire assertive, self-promoting women. Women impose that same double bind on each other.

But no woman is as punishing to other women as the Queen Bee herself.

Queen Bees: When Women Exclude Women

Similarity attracts. Over a hundred years of social science research reveals that we prefer to associate with others who are like us. In hiring and promoting employees, we select people who went to the same schools as we did, grew up in the same town as we did, think like us . . . and are the same gender as we are. Sociologists call this homophily, the tendency to cooperate and bond with similar others.

Homophily is an almost universal truth. Except, that is, for the Queen Bee. In our discussion of hierarchy, we lionized bees

as the quintessential superorganism. Bees epitomize cooperation. But there is one exception. Queen Bees—the rulers of the
hive—don't cooperate, they compete. And as they compete, they
can sting, both literally and figuratively. When it comes to gender, women in positions of power—aka Queen Bees—can be the
most punishing toward other women below them in their organizations. Queen Bees tend to see other women not as friends but
as foes to be thwarted.

Kelly Smith knows what it's like to be stung by a Queen Bee.
She was a smart, ambitious young consultant who worked for
one of the few female partners in a major consulting firm. Initially, Kelly was thrilled to have a female partner as her boss.
Here was a woman whose accomplishments she could admire,
and who might even help Kelly avoid the obstacles and overcome
barriers that she had once faced. However, instead of feeling
nurtured or mentored by her role model, she felt as if she were
constantly under siege. In meetings, Kelly's ideas were summarily dismissed. And then there were the meetings she wasn't even
invited to attend. And it got even worse: It turned out her boss
was bad-mouthing her behind her back, calling into question
whether she had the skills to do the job.

Why would Kelly's boss be dismissive, exclude her from meetings, and engage in backbiting? Because Kelly's boss wanted to
be the only Queen on the throne. If she could shatter Kelly's
confidence and derail Kelly's path to partnership, Kelly would
pose no threat.

Obviously, not all powerful women behave this way. So what
turns someone into a Queen Bee? Michelle Duguid of Washington University has spent years studying the precise conditions
that turn a high-status woman into someone who prevents other
women from joining her on the throne.

Here are the conditions that Michelle has found that spawn
Queen Bees. First, Queen Bees only develop when they are alone
or surrounded by very few women in a group. Being the only fe-

male in a group makes a woman feel special, so she doesn't want another woman invading her privileged castle. Second, Queen Bees arise in *high-status* groups; being in the group has to be socially and materially valuable. Third, Queen Bees target only highly qualified women who are rivals to their throne.

What these three ingredients—solo women, in high-status groups, settled just above other talented women—tell us is that the catalyst of Queen Bee behavior is essentially a threat to one's power. It is the fear of losing one's footing on a unique, high-status perch to another female bee that brings out the Queen's stinger.

Michelle has conducted a number of clever laboratory studies to demonstrate how the rise of Queen Bees can occur in the workplace. In her typical study, participants take part in a selection committee. Some committees are high status (they work directly with high-ranking officials in the university), whereas others are low status (they work with student advisors). Some committees are made up of almost all men whereas other committees have more women. The committee is tasked with selecting a new member. They have two options: a male and a female. Sometimes the female is very competent and, importantly, has higher test scores than the female committee member. Other times, the female applicant lags behind.

Consistent with her theory, Michelle found that the female committee member was more likely to vote in favor of the man over the woman when she was a) the only female committee member; b) in a high-status group; and c) the female candidate had high scores. Interestingly, these women were often honest about the threat they felt. They readily agreed with statements like this: "If Samantha is a group member, my group might favor her over me."

Naomi Ellemers of Leiden University has found similar evidence for Queen Bees in academics. She found that it was women who had achieved their success at a time when few other female academics had been successful who were especially likely to be Queen Bees. These pioneering women had achieved something rare, and after achieving their success, they retreated into their castle—and put up a big wall to keep others out.

This may all sound depressing. But there is hope. Michelle Duguid found that when women were made to feel secure in their position, the stinger receded. Women who felt secure were more likely to support other women, even when those other women were potential stars.

The Queen Bee phenomenon appears to be diminishing. As more women emerge as leaders, the psychological forces that produce Queen Bees—solo women in high-status groups—start to recede. In time, we hope to see the Queen Bee effect become a psychological and historical relic.

Michelle's research starts to give us insights into how ambitious women can find the right balance between gaining power and being punished for being seen as *too* powerful.

Finding the Right Balance: It Takes a Village to Lean In Without Getting Pushed Back

Power affects women similarly to men. But because women have less power in society and face prescriptive stereotypes that prohibit assertiveness, these forces combine to give women less latitude to act with power. In other words, when women lean in, they often face a backlash.

To truly eliminate this double bind, we need the whole village to participate in the solution, not just women. And here's the good news. According to our research, when *groups* achieve greater gender equality, then everyone, including men, benefits. When it comes to gender equality, a rising tide lifts all boats.

The Organization

Imagine you are the male CEO of a company. You believe it is the right thing to do to create a culture that embraces diversity and creates equal opportunities for all of your organizational members, regardless of gender or race, to rise up the corporate ladder. What can you do?

Like leaders of so many organizations, you might propose a diversity training program. Your goal in creating such a program is to make every member of the organization, especially white men, aware of the subtle and often unconscious biases they harbor. Your hope is that your managers, armed with this awareness and some practical tools for dealing with bias, will help create a culture of equality that helps level the playing field, and ultimately get women and minorities promoted into management.

There's only one problem with diversity training programs. They often don't work.

When Frank Dobbin of Harvard University obtained data from the Equal Employment Opportunity Commission on 708 private sector organizations from 1971 to 2002, he found that the diversity training programs had *zero effect* on increasing the number of women in management. In fact, these programs actually *decreased* the number of black women in management. Why? Frank suggests it's because these programs create a reaction that triggers a backlash effect that outweighs any positive effects.

Well, if diversity training programs don't work, what does? It turns out there are a few things organizations can do to build the kind of workplace where women can lean in without getting pushed back.

First, there has to be a commitment and accountability from the top to support and encourage diversity. And this commitment can't be framed merely as a prosocial endeavor. Rather, the argument in favor of diversity needs to be presented as a business imperative. It can't be just lip service: Research shows that a commitment to diversity helps groups and organizations make better decisions and earn greater profits. For example, a 2012 study conducted by the Credit Suisse Research Institute found that the stock performance of companies that had both men and women board members outperformed those with all-male boards. And Sheen Levine of the University of Texas at Dallas has found that greater diversity in his experimental markets diminished speculative price bubbles, and that market prices fit the true values of stocks 58 percent better in diverse markets in both Asia and North America.

So, what can leaders do to increase diversity? Seminars alone don't help, but committees and formal roles can. For example, the consulting and accounting firm Deloitte created committees that were tasked not only with analyzing and addressing the gender gap, but also with monitoring results to ensure accountability. At PricewaterhouseCoopers, the chief diversity officer is a partner and a member of the leadership team that reports directly to CEO Robert Moritz. As Moritz notes, "Programs matter. While the ultimate goal of any diversity initiative is cultural change, formal programs send a powerful signal." In the employment data that Frank Dobbin analyzed, the introduction of these departments and committees had huge effects: They increased the number of white women and black women (and black men) hired into the organization.

Another factor that makes a difference is the availability of networking and mentoring programs to help women and minorities. But these programs only succeed when they are inclusive and engage senior leadership. For example, PricewaterhouseCoopers recently asked all 2,700 of its partners to serve as a mentor for at least three diverse professionals. These social connections not only help people build trust, but they also give people access to information and opportunities that may not publicly be available. By connecting aspiring female managers with both male and female senior executives, these programs help these managers gain tacit knowledge needed to navigate the organization. And the Frank Dobbin Equal Employment Opportunity data reveal that these programs are associated with an increase in the number of white and black women in management positions.

Finally, and critically, hiring and promotion systems should be fair and unbiased. This is easier said than done. A series of studies conducted by Eric Uhlmann of INSEAD offers us insight into how to get this right. In one study, Eric had people evaluate two candidates for the position of police chief. Each candidate was superior on one criterion: One had more education while the other had more experience in the field. He manipulated the gender of the applicants so that half of the evaluators saw a male name attached to the resume with more education and a female name attached to the resume with more experience. The other half saw the female name attached to the resume with more education and the male name attached to the resume with more experience. When evaluators saw that the male had more education, they picked the man and proclaimed that education was the critical criterion. But when evaluators saw that the female candidate had more education, they still picked the man, but now declared that experience was the more important criterion. Gender discrimination occurred because evaluators focused on whatever criterion benefited the man. But Eric then ran a new experiment in which evaluators had to commit to the criteria that they would use *before* seeing any information about the applicants: In this case, the gender bias disappeared! From these and related studies, we have learned the importance of establishing criteria *in advance.* And once we have these criteria, we need to consistently and transparently apply these to our decisions. If we can do this, we can reduce gender bias and promote diversity.

As we showed earlier, when women have greater economic and political participation in a society, the gender difference in math ability disappears. Similarly, when organizations create a culture that increases the participation of women, women prosper. We can see this in Frank Dobbin's data: The proportion of women in top management increased the probability that other women were promoted to management positions. Remember Michelle Duguid's work showing that Queen Bees disappear when there are many women in high-status positions? Having more women in higher ranks not only decreases bias by men, it also decreases bias by women.

And women shouldn't be the only ones pushing for gender equality. Even though gender equality can feel like a zero-sum contest—as women gain in power, men have to lose—this thinking is flawed. Gender equality can *expand* the pie of resources for women *and* men.

Recall the finding that countries with great gender egalitarianism had higher-performing female national soccer teams. Well, research we have done with Roderick Swaab of INSEAD has also found something even more remarkable: Countries with greater gender equality not only had better female teams, but they also had better *male* teams as well!

Why? A country that values women is also more likely to value other segments of society as well. This appreciation allows societies and their companies to tap the potential of a much wider pool of talent. And that is exactly what we found in our studies: Countries that had greater gender equality had higher-performing male soccer teams because they were able to field more talented teams.

Spain's recent promotion of women's rights highlights how a culture that promotes gender equality can help elevate not only women, but men, too. Francisco Franco, the dictator who governed Spain from 1939 to 1975, institutionalized gender inequality. Under Franco, women could not open bank accounts, apply for passports, or even sign a contract without their husband's permission.

After Franco passed away, gender equality started to ripple through the country. On the Gender Empowerment Index,

Spain jumped from a 40 (out of 100) in 1990 to a score of 70 only 12 years later. In fact, in 2008, Spain became the first European country whose cabinet had more women than men in positions of power (nine women and eight men, including Spain's first female defense minister, Carme Chacón). It is also notable that one of the cabinet ministers is the minister for equality, demonstrating a structural commitment to greater opportunity. This is a remarkable milestone in a country whose culture so glorified masculinity that it gave us the term *machismo*.

Indeed, these changes in gender equality may explain why the *male* athletes of Spain have exploded into a golden age of athletic dominance. In 2010, the Spanish soccer team won their first World Cup, Alberto Contador won his second straight Tour de France, and Rafael Nadal won three straight major tennis championships—the French Open, Wimbledon, and the U.S. Open. The average year of birth of the World Cup soccer team was 1984, Contador was born in 1983, and Nadal in 1986; all of these male performers were born after Franco's reign had come to an end.

Prime Minister José Luis Rodríguez Zapatero put it well when he said: "The most unfair domination is that of one half of humanity over the other. The more equality women will have, the more civilized and tolerant society will be."

There are simple actions that organizations can take to level the playing field. These actions may be designed to help women, but they can also benefit everyone, including men. Take this example described by Sheryl Sandberg and Adam Grant. In story pitch meetings for the television show *The Shield*, the producer Glen Mazzara became concerned when he realized that two female writers rarely spoke up during the meetings. When Glen pulled aside the female writers and encouraged them to speak up, they laughed at his suggestion. "Watch what happens when we do," they replied. At the next meeting, Glen quickly noticed the constant interruptions whenever the female writers spoke. So he introduced a new rule for pitch meetings—no interruptions. This rule applied to every writer, men and women alike. Not only did the women now have the space to express their ideas, but the group as a whole generated better pitches. The no interruption rule leveled the playing field and produced a group-level benefit.

So equality makes societies and nations not only more tolerant, but more successful as well. Whether it is in the classroom, on the athletic field, in the pitch room, or in the boardroom, a culture of equality can lead a group to have a competitive advantage over its less equality-minded rivals. When it comes to gender, it is the cooperative and inclusive approach that increases talent levels and predicts competitive success.

Making Ourselves Blind to Undo
the Double Bind

So we've seen that a company's and a nation's commitment to institutionalizing gender equality can help both women and men compete more effectively. But sometimes official government and corporate interventions aren't enough. After all, many gender biases exist on a deep, often subconscious level. So how do we, both men and women, undo this double bind in our minds?

The first thing we can do is blind ourselves to gender altogether. This is exactly what symphony orchestras have done. Today, when musicians audition for orchestras in the United States, they do so from behind a screen. By having musicians perform behind a screen, the evaluation process is devoid of any gender cues. Claudia Goldin of Harvard found that this type of blind screening process increased the likelihood of selecting a woman musician by 300 percent! Before 1970, women made up less than 10 percent of symphony orchestras, but today, after the introduction of blind auditions, they now compose nearly 50 percent of orchestras. And to be sure that judges are truly blind, applicants are required to remove a piece of clothing before they audition . . . their shoes! Why? The click, click, click of high heels would be a telling clue. So to make the selection process truly blind, aspiring musicians now audition behind a screen, without shoes.

Another way to blind ourselves is to focus on the data—rather than subjective measures of performance, such as likability and other interpersonal factors. If Price Waterhouse had only looked at the numbers, they would have seen that Ann Hopkins billed more hours and generated more business (over $40 million) than any of the 87 other candidates up for partnership that year. Stereotypes and double standards are less likely to influence evaluations when they are based on hard facts. By using objective, quantifiable criteria, we can help level the playing field.

But even looking only at the numbers sometimes isn't enough. Remember the police chief study we mentioned earlier? When people knew the applicant's gender, they (whether consciously or not) shifted the criteria they used to favor the man. But when they committed to a specific criterion in advance, before knowing the gender of the candidates, the bias disappeared. So setting up procedures and criteria can tie us to the right decision even when we cannot blind ourselves to gender.

If we combine these ideas, we can generate insight into what a company, manager, or team leader can do to increase the number of competent women (and men) in the ranks. When you are making promotion decisions, the first thing you want to do is identify the selection criteria in advance, long before you know anything about the candidates. Second, whenever you can, remove identifying features and focus on the objective criteria for all of the candidates. When we are blind to gender cues, we can truly focus on the music.

Of course, we don't always have the opportunity to be blind. If someone's giving a presentation, for example, it is hard to alter their voice and put them behind a screen. And sometimes the criteria are truly subjective: What makes a good presentation can be hard to quantify. What can we do to ensure that we aren't holding women to a different standard?

One solution is to mentally give the person a sex change! Specifically, ask yourself the following question: Would I have had the same reaction to that behavior if the behavior was performed by a man? This might seem silly, but Charles Lord of Texas Christian University has found that engaging in this mental simulation can help free us of the double bind.

Lawyers, Mama Bears, and the Power of Advocating for "Us"

Clearly institutions and observers need to take steps to reduce the tendency to hold back and punish women who exhibit signs of confidence and competence. But until the day comes when gender bias is eliminated, what can women do to reduce the likelihood of being caught in that double bind?

It's clear that women are constrained by the prescriptive stereotype that demands they act cooperatively and communally. But this stereotype can actually be leveraged: Women can be assertive without getting pushed back when they ask for things *on behalf of others*. As we've seen, women are less likely to ask for things for themselves—like a raise—but they are more willing to be assertive and aggressive when asking for something for another person. The famous humanitarian Mother Teresa was lauded for her ability to assertively raise money; a likely secret to her success is that she was asking on behalf of others.

Work done by Hannah Riley Bowles of Harvard University and Emily Amanatullah of the University of Texas discovered the same remarkable insight—when women serve as advocates for others, two things happen. First, they negotiate just as aggressively and successfully as men. Second, they avoid the backlash of being seen as overly assertive.

In some professions, like law, advocating for others is the essence of the job. So it might not surprise you to learn that assertive female lawyers avoid backlash more than women in other professions. In a study in which lawyers rated one another after a negotiation interaction, Andrea Schneider of Marquette University Law School found no gender differences. Women and men were perceived to be identical in their negotiation abilities. Andrea proposed that the nature of the law profession contributed to this result. Because lawyers are *expected* to be assertive and confident, and to advocate on behalf of others, female lawyers do not face backlash because of it.

And there's another natural setting in which women can be highly assertive without fear of backlash: moms protecting the interests of their kids. We even have a phrase for it: "Mama Bear." As a mother defending her cubs, a woman is given great latitude for assertive and even aggressive behavior.

Cathy Tinsley at Georgetown University has shown that women can use these techniques to advocate for themselves as well; the key is to advocate for others at the same time. Cathy calls this "us advocacy." Us advocacy allows for a woman to advocate for her own self-interest by arguing for the collective good of her group—say, by fighting to reinstate a bonus for her entire department—without suffering from backlash.

So we've seen that when it comes to competing for resources, less powerful groups, such as women, face subtle discrimination and backlash. Sometimes, however, less powerful groups face overt, public displays of discrimination like slurs and hateful terms. We next explore the power of names and show that the terms and nicknames we use can help us make friends but also create foes.

How Names Can Bond
and Bully

"Is our children learning?" When President George W. Bush asked this question, he reinforced an impression many people had: The 43rd president does not have a way with words.

But in fact, George W. Bush was quite the wordsmith. He had an uncanny ability to connect with people, and much of his skill derived from his facility with language. But his specialty wasn't in rhetoric (or, clearly, in grammar); it was nicknames. George W. Bush was a master of the moniker. For example, he called his vice president "Big Time," and his secretary of state "Guru." He called the two female senators from California "Ali" and "Frazier," in honor of the great heavyweight boxers. He even had nicknames for political leaders from across the globe, from friendly foreign leaders (Tony Blair was "Landslide") to those who were potential foes (Vladimir Putin was "Pootie-Poot").

For George Bush, nicknames were a tool for cooperation; when he bestowed one on a person, it brought him closer to them and cemented an important bond. The names we use can help us connect with our friends. They can be the glue that binds us together.

But not everyone uses names to make friends. In fact, many names are tools that our foes use against us. As children, we are told that "sticks and stones may break our bones, but words can never hurt us." But this isn't true. Words are often the preferred weapon of bullies—and they *can* hurt us. A lot.

In some cases, they can even kill. Consider the tragic story of Rachel Ehmke. The Minnesota seventh grader was bullied for months. Though she had never kissed a boy, her peers taunted her by calling her a "slut," and even sprayed the word on her gym locker. With just weeks to go before summer vacation, Rachel reached her breaking point. The 13-year-old hung herself in her room.

So sometimes names help us bond with others, and other times we are bullied by them. To navigate our social world, we need to know when and how to use names. And by the same token, when others call us negative names or use slurs against us, we need to know how to react and how to defend ourselves.

A key theme we develop is the idea that the meanings of names are not fixed. Rather, the meaning of a term can vary widely depending on who is using it, in what context, and why. And, of course, the meaning of a name can change dramatically over time. A slur that was once used with vicious derision can be transformed into a display of affection. Just consider how certain derogatory terms, like the "n-word," that are wildly offensive when spoken by a Caucasian, can signal camaraderie or affection when spoken by one African American to another.

Because the meanings of names are constantly negotiated and renegotiated, there is hope even when bullies use names against us. We see how even the hurtful word *slut* can be reclaimed and reappropriated.

The point is that words matter. The names that we give to objects, to emotions, to experiences, critically guide how we think, how we feel, and how we act. Here, we explore how names—from nicknames to professional titles to slurs—affect how we become friends and how we compete as foes.

Names as Cooperative Glue

It's difficult to give yourself a nickname. Why?

Because nicknames are inherently social. They signal membership in a relationship or group, and thus they are more likely to stick when they are bestowed on us by others.

Consider the nicknames Maverick, Iceman, and Goose, made famous by the movie *Top Gun*. (You can even go and get your own Top Gun call sign at http://www.topgunday.com/call-sign-generator.) But the idea for these now iconic nicknames didn't come out of thin air; in the actual military, pilots are actually given an aviator call sign that replaces the pilot's name; it's even stitched onto their flight suit. All branches of the military use nicknames to solidify common bonds and connect individuals to their platoon. These nicknames forge a unique group identity that promotes cooperation and loyalty.

And the military is not alone. Recall the parallels we drew earlier between the strong hierarchy in the military and the hierarchy in the Catholic Church. For both institutions, a cohesive identity is critical. And both groups use names to build that collective connection. In the Catholic Church, people are given a new name upon their confirmation; and popes, once appointed, are given a new name. In Judaism there is a tradition of changing your name when embarking on a new life chapter; in Islam it is customary to change your name after converting from another religion. And it turns out that when it comes to nicknames, fraternities and sororities are an awful lot like the military; they assign nicknames to members in a way that promotes group identity.

All kinds of groups use nicknames to promote bonding. Wharton undergraduates, for example, are assigned to groups with given names; they use names of currencies like the Rupee, Yuan, and Dollar. And Columbia MBA students are assigned to groups that are only given a generic alphabet letter when they arrive. Then, during orientation, each group invents its own name using that letter: Group "A" might become the Aviators one semester, while the following class might create a different "A" name, like Animal House. Here again, names promote bonding and help make friends out of strangers.

Nicknames even play a role in helping love bloom. They aren't just a kind of shorthand that develops over the course of a relationship; they actually breed affection—they help romance flourish by making the couple feel special and unique.

What do these intimate nicknames look like? We analyzed the 250 most common nicknames that romantic partners give to each other. Most fall into one of two categories: food and animals. As you might have guessed, names like "honey," "sugar," and "pumpkin" are very popular (so too is "waffles"). From the animal kingdom, we find names like "kitten," "bunny," and "honey bear." Why food and animal names? Because they connote sweetness on the one hand, and warmth and cuddliness on the other.

Whether among romantic couples, university students, or navy pilots, nicknames strengthen bonds by separating insiders from outsiders. But they aren't the only semantic tool groups use to separate themselves from others. Another is jargon, or some shared vocabulary that makes group members feel "in the know." By using jargon, we distinguish "the inner circle" from those outside it. One time-honored approach to inventing new terms is the use of acronyms.

Jargon, in other words, helps groups develop their own unique identity and allows group members to cooperate and coordinate more effectively within their groups. But jargon can also make communication more difficult with people outside the group and can leave others feeling left out. That is why some professors have an NAZ in their classrooms. Oh wait, you don't know what an NAZ is? It is a No Acronym Zone!

And jargon can also seem pretentious to those not in the inner circle. Two law school classmates studying for an exam would naturally use legal jargon with each other; it would sound authentic and natural. But if one of those law students started spitting out fancy legal terms in casual conversation with the building janitor, they'd probably sound like a pretentious jerk.

It may not surprise you to learn that nicknames are deeply connected to status and power. In romantic couples, where status is (hopefully) equal, nicknames flow both ways; even George Bush and his wife had nicknames for each other. But at work, it is the powerful who get to bestow nicknames on the less powerful. To understand this important idea, try a simple mental exercise: Think about what it would feel like to give your boss a playful nickname. Pretty awkward, right?

Of course, less powerful employees conjure nicknames for their bosses all the time. But they do so secretly. And rightly so; assigning nicknames (especially unfavorable ones) to those more powerful can have real consequences. For example, three employees, ironically from the Iowa Civil Rights Commission, lost their jobs and were even denied unemployment benefits after their boss discovered e-mails referring to the commission's director as "Knight Rider" and to their direct supervisor as "Teen Wolf."

So nicknames and jargon are often used as expressions of power and status. Yet some names can also be used to *acquire* power and status. We have a term for those names: We call them *titles*.

Why PhDs Want to Be Called Doctors

Who is a *real* doctor?

If you ask people to describe a doctor, they will invariably depict someone who can harness the wonders of modern medicine to cure people of physical ailments. In short, they will describe a medical doctor.

But this wasn't always how we defined a doctor. The Latin verb *docere* means to teach, and the first people referred to as doctors were the Apostles who taught others about the Bible. The use of the term soon spread to refer to scholars who had accumulated knowledge and were qualified to teach others.

At the same time that teachers and scholars were rising in status, there was another profession that had made surprisingly little progress since the time of Aristotle—the profession of medicine. For example, in 1348, England was ravaged by the Black Death. Nearly one in three people died. The real problem was sanitation, but medieval medical practitioners were still prescribing leeches and herbs.

Because physicians were not held in high regard during this period, they sought markers of status. So they began to call themselves doctors.

It would take centuries, but eventually medical practitioners abandoned the use of leeches and began to prescribe lifesaving antibiotics. And by the 21st century the medical profession had leveraged science to fundamentally transform the quality of health care. Because of the modern miracles that today's medical doctors perform, the term doctor became supercharged with status.

But if you have wandered around a college campus, you might have noticed that physicians aren't the only ones today who use the name "doctor." Colleges typically require their instructors to have a doctorate of philosophy, i.e., a PhD. Although most instructors are called professors, there are academics who insist on being called "doctor." Interestingly, this phenomenon is more common in some regions of the United States than in others. In the northeast part of the United States, where education is highly valued, the name "professor" is associated with high status and commands respect; Professor Galinsky or Professor Schweitzer works just fine. But in the South, "professor" doesn't carry the same gravitas. And so, professors prefer to be called doctor; only Dr. Galinsky or Dr. Schweitzer will do.

So why the difference? Research has shown that when people lack power and status, they are more prone to publicly display their titles. This phenomenon can be seen on the web pages of academic departments: Cindy Harmon-Jones of the University of New South Wales found that lower-status colleges list more professional titles on their departmental web pages than higher-ranked colleges do. Similarly, professors whose research is less frequently cited by their peers tend to display more professional titles in their e-mail signatures compared to professors with higher citation rates.

You can even see a difference in the use of status markers between male and female professors (remember that gender differences are often power differences in disguise). Carlotta Berry, an African American female engineering professor, explained this perspective in a *New York Times* op-ed: "When I introduce myself in the classroom, I'm Dr. Berry. And I insist on being Dr. Berry . . . I have colleagues who would prefer to be called by their first name . . . But they are mostly men, and almost all white, and they have that luxury. As an African American woman in a mostly Caucasian- and male-dominated field, I don't." Or consider the case of a four-person teaching team at a business school one of us once taught at that included two men and two women. The two male professors signed all their e-mails to students with their first names. The two female professors, however, signed their e-mails with "Professor (Last name)." In schools where female professors (sadly and unfairly) don't receive the respect their male counterparts do, the use of a title is one way to demand the respect that they deserve.

So we see how the word doctor started as a descriptive word for a profession and accrued status over time. Other times, this process flows in reverse; titles can take on negative meaning.

Take the term Nazi. Originally Nazi was just a term, like "Democrat" or "Republican," which simply described membership in a political party in Germany, the National Socialist party. But as that party's supremacist teachings and dictatorial policies became more widely known, the term Nazi became synonymous with authoritarian intolerance. And a short time later, it became associated with the atrocities of the Holocaust. Today the term has become one of the greatest forms of condemnation. There are few insults worse than calling someone a Nazi.

From these examples, we can see how the meaning of names can change over time and even across regions. We have seen how certain names—like doctor—may help us express status and feel more powerful, and in doing so they help us compete more effectively. We turn next to how names—slurs and epithets—can be used as harmful and searing weapons.

Banning the Word Bossy and Why
Philip Morris Became Altria

Slut. Bitch. N-word. Kike. Queer.

These are hateful words. One is so hurtful that we didn't even spell it out.

They are so hateful that some people will do anything to escape their curse and the associated discrimination. In a large-scale study of ethnic immigrants to the United States during the 1950s, Brian Mullen of Syracuse University found that when slurs were especially derogatory toward a group, suicide rates were higher among its members. Mullen also analyzed data spanning a 150-year period of American history and found that groups who were the targets of hurtful epithets were more likely to be socially excluded from fraternal associations, face housing segregation, and suffer employment discrimination.

But as we've seen, the meaning of words is fluid over place

and time. In fact, a seemingly innocuous term can become a slur overnight. This is what happened in a third-grade classroom in Iowa over 40 years ago. In this now-famous experiment, the teacher, Jane Elliott, separated her students into two groups based on the color of their eyes. She then privileged the blue-eyed students, giving them more recess time, greater access to the water fountain, and second helpings of food—all signs, to an eight-year-old at least, of high status. In contrast, the brown-eyed students were treated like second-class citizens.

Though we might readily recognize that a class distinction based upon eye color is wildly arbitrary, Jane's experiment produced incredibly powerful effects. What had been an insignificant and neutral physical marker only the day before became a justification for exclusion and bullying. When the teacher asked a student after recess why he hit another student, the boy replied "Because he called me brown eyes." Upon being asked what he thought the student meant by calling him "brown eyes," he explained: "That I'm stupid." The descriptor "brown eyes" had become a slur.

So, what should we do when we're connected to a derogatory term? One possibility is to simply ignore it. But this is unlikely to work. In spite of what our parents may have told us, ignoring the schoolyard bully is often *not* the best way to get them to leave us alone.

Another strategy is to eliminate the offensive word from our conversations altogether. Sheryl Sandberg, the COO of Facebook and author of *Lean In*, argued for this tactic in 2014 when she proposed banning the term "bossy" after she studied a 2008 survey conducted by the Girl Scouts. The study found that "girls between the ages of 8 and 17 avoid leadership roles for fear that they will be labeled 'bossy' and be disliked by their peers." It turns out that the term bossy is not applied equally across genders: In books, females are four times more likely to be called bossy than males. Our view is that Sheryl Sandberg is right to be concerned with the term "bossy." This term can hold women back from achieving their ambitions. So, we can sympathize with the call to stop using the word altogether. But is simply refusing to use a term enough to eliminate it from the vernacular?

Sometimes it is. Consider the name of Washington's National Football League team: the Washington Redskins. This term is offensive to Native Americans, and after a long and public debate about the name, *Slate* declared on August 8, 2013, that "this is the last *Slate* article that will refer to the Washington NFL team as the Redskins." Other news organizations have followed suit, including such eminent writers as Bill Simmons. Even though the owner of the team has proclaimed that "we will never change the name of the team," the tide is turning. The name Redskin may soon be headed for the history books.

But banning a word is difficult. It requires a broad consensus. So another option is simply to rename one's group. If we go back in time, we can see that African Americans were called "Colored," then "Negro," then "Black," until the present day's "African American." By rejecting prior names and creating new ones in their stead, African Americans distanced themselves from the negative associations of slavery and disadvantage.

Even businesses employ the tactic of changing their name to combat stigma. Take how, after a series of high-profile crashes, the airline Valujet became AirTran. Or, as smoking and cigarettes began to acquire a negative stigma, note how Philip Morris changed its name to Altria.

And of course, businesses have used the renaming strategy to better market their products for decades. In 1977, a young fish merchant named Lee Lantz discovered that Chilean fishermen had been catching a delicious fish with a somewhat unappetizing name, the Patagonian toothfish. He realized that this fish would be more appetizing if he simply renamed it. So, the Patagonian toothfish became "Chilean seabass." The U.S. Food and Drug

Administration eventually accepted this name change and con-sumption of the fish took off.

This "rebranding" tactic can work for individuals as well as companies. That's why Jeff Gillooly, the husband of Tonya Hard-ing, the skater who orchestrated the attack against her competi-tor Nancy Kerrigan, legally changed his name to Jeff Stone. And why Matt Sandusky and his family changed their last name fol-lowing the shocking revelation that his adoptive father, former Penn State football coach Jerry Sandusky, had sexually assaulted numerous boys.

Some people change their names proactively to appeal to mass audiences. Allen Konigsberg became Woody Allen. Carlos Estevez became Charlie Sheen. And Natalie Hershlag became Natalie Portman. We hope the stigma of ethnic names recedes and in the future Bruno Mars can remain Peter Hernandez.

Even lawmakers employ this tactic. For years, the American government levied a tax on the estates of individuals after they passed away. But, as it turns out, what we call this tax matters. Political consultant Frank Luntz realized that by changing the name of the "estate tax" to the "death tax," he could change how people viewed the tax. And so, he launched an aggressive re-branding campaign. As he explained, "Look, for years, political people and lawyers . . . used the phrase 'estate tax.' And for years they couldn't eliminate it. The public wouldn't support [its re-peal] because the word 'estate' sounds wealthy. Someone like me comes around and realizes that it's not an estate tax, it's a death tax, because you're taxed at death. And suddenly something that isn't viable achieves the support of 75 percent of the American people." The name made all the difference.

So as we see, renaming can be a powerful tool that can help us compete more effectively. But when slurs are hurled against us, renaming is not always an option and censorship may not work. So what else can we do?

Reappropriation: Turning Your Weakness into Your Strength

Just as slurs can be created, they can be reclaimed and reappropriated. Reappropriation happens when a stigmatized group takes a slur that another (dominant) group had used to demean them and uses the term *proudly* instead. It involves changing the meaning associated with the slur by taking the name for and by one's self.

Consider the hateful and vicious term "slut." Long hurled at women to imply promiscuity, the word's connotations are exceedingly negative. Yet Heather Jarvis is on the front line in the battle to reclaim the word slut. Galvanized to action after a Toronto police officer proclaimed that women "should avoid dressing like sluts in order not to be victimized," she started a movement to extinguish the mentality of blaming the victim. A key feature of her campaign has been to shift the connotation of the word slut from a hateful slur into a compliment! She founded the grassroots movement SlutWalk to encourage women to proudly embrace the word.

A similar mission has been advanced by the international sensation *The Vagina Monologues*. This play, a series of monologues billed as a "celebration of female sexuality," has been performed by women in front of countless audiences across the globe. One of the monologues is literally entitled "Reclaiming Cunt." Rather than accepting the derogatory connotation of the word, *The Vagina Monologues* empowers women by transforming the meaning associated with what is generally considered a highly offensive term.

So rather than banning offensive words, we can work to reappropriate them. This approach underscores some of the criticism that Sheryl Sandberg received when she proposed banning the word "bossy." According to Margaret Talbot of *The New Yorker*, women need to "reappropriate the word [bossy], mining it for its positive associations with assertiveness." And in fact, this is exactly the approach the "Black is Beautiful" campaign took in the 1960s. By changing the connotative meaning of the term "Black," this campaign aimed to change the value of being a member of the group.

In popular culture, examples of reappropriation abound. In a movie (*8 Mile*), Eminem declares, "I'm a piece of white trash, I say it proudly," and in *X-Men: First Class*, one of the persecuted mutants rallies others: "Let's reclaim that word: Mutant and proud." Reappropriation declares that the term is now *our* term, that we are stealing the term from the bullies.

Reclaiming derogatory nicknames can be an effective way to defuse negative associations on the national political stage as well. Consider how Republicans pejoratively called the Affordable Care Act (ACA) of 2010 "Obamacare." By calling this legislation Obamacare, the Republicans were derogating it. But by the time of his reelection campaign in 2012, President Obama had fully embraced the term: His campaign urged supporters to post Twitter messages that began, "I like #Obamacare because . . ." And in the first presidential debate with Mitt Romney, Barack Obama explained, "I like the term Obamacare. That's okay, I have grown fond of it." By owning the name Obamacare, the president reduced its power to stigmatize.

Reappropriation can even transform offensive or degrading symbols into badges of pride. The pink triangle, for example, was originally used as a Nazi concentration camp badge to stigmatize sexual offenders, most notably homosexual men. Years later, the gay community reclaimed it, but with their own literal spin; they flipped the triangle on its head to change it from a symbol of shame into one of empowerment. Rita Adessa, executive director of the Philadelphia Lesbian and Gay Task Force, explained her thinking about the pink triangle this way: "Why don't we turn this around? And it was so symbolically apt that that's exactly what we did, because that's what this movement is all about. It is turning oppression around." And over time, both the regular and upside-down pink triangle became potent symbols of gay pride.

The process of reclaiming a label can itself be a form of cooperative glue for a group. Working with Jennifer Whitson of the University of Texas at Austin, we have found that when people label themselves with a derogatory term for their group, they feel more identified and more connected to their group.

Of course, changing entrenched cultural associations doesn't happen overnight. It took some time for the Obama campaign to reappropriate the term Obamacare. And it took time for the gay community to reappropriate the pink triangle. But it can be done.

In some cases, however, groups can reappropriate slurs quickly. This happens when the negativity of a phrase hasn't yet been cemented. Consider Jessica Ahlquist, who successfully sued her high school in Rhode Island to remove a religious prayer from her school auditorium. The day after the ruling in January of 2012, state representative Peter Palumbo attacked Ahlquist and characterized her as "an evil little thing." In response, Ahlquist took ownership of Palumbo's phrase. She printed and sold T-shirts with the phrase "Evil Little Thing" to raise money for her college education. Within four months of selling T-shirts, she had raised $62,000!

Or consider how quickly a failed symbol can be reclaimed. During the opening ceremonies of the 2014 Sochi Winter Olympics, one of the five snowflake-like figures of the Olympic ring failed to unfold. The Russians had failed to create the universal five-ring symbol of the Olympics—at the opening ceremony no less! Global mockery and derision ensued.

How did the Russian Olympic committee respond? They might have gotten defensive. They could have pointed to everything else that they had done right. But instead, they owned their mistake! In the closing ceremony, a group of dancers stayed tightly packed together when the rest of the dancers recreated the Olympic rings; this effectively replicated the four-out-of-five Olympic ring motif of the snowflake from the opening ceremonies. The audience *loved it*. They laughed and applauded and worldwide tweets exploded: "The Ring!" The Olympic ceremony director Konstantin Ernst even designed a shirt with four interlocking rings—and a small satellite circle that refused to open.

It is important to note that once a name or symbol has been fully reappropriated, the stigmatized group "owns" it. What this means is that even if it has become a term of pride or endearment within the group, it is often still taboo for those *outside* the group to use it. For example, non-blacks still can't use the n-word. Period. The well-known actor who played Kramer on *Seinfeld*, Michael Richards, learned this the hard way on November 17, 2006. During a stand-up comedy performance, he used the term on hecklers and was so vilified afterward that he ultimately gave up stand-up comedy. But for African Americans, the sense of ownership of the name is a source of pride. As the African American sociologist Michael Eric Dyson demonstrated when he remarked, "We hijacked, or word-jacked, that word." Or as the writer Rembert Browne put it, "Saying [the n-word] in front of white people. I know some people who do, almost as a way of reminding white people that there is still something in this world a black person can do that whites can't."

And this phenomenon isn't a feature of that particular word; consider how, after the New York Knicks lost their first game with their new golden boy point guard, Jeremy Lin (who happened to be Chinese American), ESPN posted a headline on their website that read, CHINK IN THE ARMOR. But the word "chink" is a historically derogatory term for Chinese people. And so, the editor was immediately fired. Yet it turns out that when Jeremy Lin was in high school, he had used the screen name ChiNkBaLLa88. Lin could refer to himself with the derogatory term, but others could not.

Although not every stigmatizing term can be reappropriated, in general, taking back a term that has been used against us can blunt the attacks of foes and transform victims into victors.

The idea that names can be reappropriated actually represents a larger phenomenon—owning your weaknesses and turning them into strengths. We saw this in how the Russians took ownership of their failure at the opening ceremony at the Sochi Olympics. Similarly, networking guru Keith Ferrazzi, author of *Never Eat Alone,* encourages people to "own your weaknesses at work. Be powerful with them, be the first to admit them, and what follows may surprise you."

These examples illustrate how our foes will use opportunities to derogate us and exploit our weaknesses. However, by embracing our weaknesses, we can leverage them for our own advantage, both psychologically and materially.

Finding the Right Balance: Start Making Sense

When Shakespeare's Juliet says "What's in a name? That which we call a rose by any other name would smell as sweet," she is suggesting that names don't matter. But Juliet misses a key psychological insight. How we name something can profoundly change how we feel about it—even if the essence is unchanged. What we call something matters a lot.

Finding the right name can help us compete more effectively, and also shift us from competition to cooperation. Varda Liberman from the Interdisciplinary Center in Israel demonstrated this with a very clever experiment. She found that the mere words you use to call a game determine whether people cooperate or compete. In her study, participants played a two-person game in which each party would get a good outcome if both of them cooperated, but there was always a temptation to compete and exploit the other side's cooperation. She told half of the participants that they would be playing the "Wall Street Game." She told the other half that they would be playing the "Community Game." Importantly, the incentives were *exactly the same* in both games.

When the game was called the Community Game, over 72 percent chose to cooperate. When the game was called the Wall Street Game, just 33 percent did. The *only* difference between the games was the name she used to describe it. Names matter. The right name can move us to cooperation. And a different name can lead us into competition.

The right name can even help us make sense of and even gain control over our emotions. Many of us have felt performance anxiety. Public speaking, a job interview, and even singing karaoke can cause our chest to tighten. But Alison Wood Brooks of Harvard University has explored how names can help us manage this performance anxiety so that we can compete more effectively. In one study, she had people sing "Don't Stop Believin'" by Journey. In another study, she had people take a stressful math test. And in another, she had people deliver a videotaped speech. In every case, people felt anxious!

Think about the last time you faced a stressful task like this. What did you say to yourself? If you are like most people, you might have said to yourself, "Calm down" or "Take a deep breath." But lots of research has found that trying to "calm down" in the face of anxiety isn't very effective. In fact, it can even backfire.

So Alison came up with a different approach. She had some participants say a different phrase before they performed: These participants said out loud "I am excited" before performing. People who stated that they were excited were more likely to succeed at these stressful tasks compared to people who tried to calm down. The excited participants nailed the Journey classic (earning higher scores from the Nintendo Wii), they outperformed others on the math test, and they were more likely to

deliver persuasive and confident speeches (as rated by independent evaluators).

Notice what Alison is doing here. She is not trying to change
or eliminate the heightened arousal people feel. She is simply
getting people to reframe what that arousal means. When the
arousal is seen as excitement it becomes positive, something to
embrace. When the arousal is anxiety, it is negative and something to be avoided.

Here is the key insight. Choosing the right name to capture
an internal feeling can help you deal with that feeling, or even
harness it, rather than be defeated by it.

Finding the right name can also help us transition out of a
bad mood before it spirals into competitive feelings. Take the example of how one couple addresses the invariably cranky behavior that we all experience. When one of them is in a bad mood,
the other simply asks, "Are you having a fuss?" This couple has
found that by giving a name to this state, it takes the force out of
the bad mood and defuses the situation. By naming the situation
"a fuss," this couple moves from foe back to friend.

Matthew Lieberman at UCLA offers some insight into why
this strategy works. Giving a name to an emotion as we experience it reduces activation in the parts of the brain like the amygdala that light up under duress. In other words, identifying and
naming what we feel help us process and let go of our negative
emotions.

In fact, correctly naming our emotions is one of the most
powerful steps in dealing with those emotions. If we come home
frustrated and angry from work, we may take out our anger on
our spouse and kids. If, however, we identify our feelings and figure out what triggered those emotions (e.g., "I am angry because
of what happened at work"), we and other scholars have consistently found that we become dramatically less likely to displace
our feelings. By naming and attributing our feelings, we are less

likely to take our anger (triggered by our foes) out on undeserving others (like our friends).

By identifying our feelings, we become more cooperative with our friends, and save our fury for our foes. But in order for these bonds of friendship to hold, the relationship needs to include one critical component: trust. We turn next to how to forge cooperative relationships out of competitive ones by winning others' trust.

How to Get Others to Put Their Trust in You

Detective Marshall Frank had Paul Rowles just where he wanted him, in an interrogation booth. Paul's neighbor had been strangled to death, and Marshall was pretty sure that Paul had done it. But what Marshall needed was a confession—and he got it in just 30 minutes. How did Marshall get Paul to confess so quickly to a crime that Paul knew could earn him a lifetime in jail?

Well, you might think that Marshall intimidated Paul and scared him into confessing. But Marshall didn't take this competitive approach. Instead of approaching his suspect as a foe, he acted like a friend.

When Marshall sat down to interrogate Paul, he positioned himself physically close to Paul. As they spoke, Marshall would lean in toward Paul, just as a buddy might. Then Marshall began his line of questioning. In the movies, detectives cut to the chase with little pretext. But this is not what Marshall did. Instead, he asked Paul about his family, his parents, and his life in general.

In Marshall's words, "I made friends with him. . . . What you want to do is get the person talking and feeling good about talking to you," Marshall explained. "Eventually you just work your way into whatever the issue is." And so, after about 30 minutes, Paul started "blathering the confession out."

We typically think of trust as slow to build, yet Marshall did it in just half an hour with a suspected murderer—who *knew* he was a suspect as he sat in an interrogation room! And he did it simply by spending almost the entire half hour building rapport with Paul, rather than by asking hard-hitting questions that might have caused Paul to take a more defensive, competitive stance.

This story illustrates how fast trust can develop, even when there is every reason to be suspicious and fearful of being exploited. But trust can disappear just as quickly. No one knows this better than Elizabeth Cioffi.

Elizabeth started dating Peter Petrakis when she was 18 years old. She was so smitten with her beau that she converted to his religion and joined the Greek Orthodox Church. As she prepared their lavish wedding, she was floating on air.

But she was brought down to earth four days before the wedding when Peter convinced Elizabeth to sign a prenuptial agreement. According to the terms of the agreement, if they got divorced Peter would keep all of the assets they accumulated during their marriage. Elizabeth would get a consolation prize of sorts: $25,000 for every year they had been married.

For obvious reasons, Elizabeth hated that agreement. In fact, she hated that agreement so much that it eclipsed all of the other things that she loved about Peter. In her words, "He's a good father. He's a very successful businessman. But this prenup was a thorn in our marriage."

But her problem with the prenup wasn't the allocation of the assets. The problem was the very presence of the prenup in and of itself. She felt that the prenup signaled a lack of trust, and for her *that* is what killed her marriage. "I think without being forced to sign a prenup I'd still be married," she recalled. Emphasizing how little it had to do with the money, she explained, "I would rather live in a two-bedroom apartment with someone who loves me than live in a 14,000-square-foot mansion and not trust someone. I said I was done." And so when Elizabeth could no longer stand the thorn in her side, she ended their marriage.

Trust is essential for almost every social relationship: a happy marriage, a supportive friendship, and a successful organization. If we cannot trust our spouses, our friends, and our business partners, our relationships break down. In fact, almost every transaction we engage in requires some level of trust. When trust is high, these relationships are collaborative and friction-less. Trust, in so many ways, is a key social lubricant.

When trust is low, on the other hand, there is friction in every interaction. We are consumed with minimizing the risk of being exploited. And as a result, we become competitive, even combat-ive. It's tough to be a good friend *or* an effective foe when we're constantly suspicious and fear exploitation.

This isn't just true for individuals; countries and societies also cannot achieve the level of cooperation they need to succeed in the global economy without trust. Indeed, economists have linked the economic prosperity of countries to the levels of trust within them. In societies with high levels of trust, economies thrive. But where trust is low, growth is stunted.

Conventional wisdom tells us two things about trust. First, that trust is slow to develop. Second, that once broken, trust, like a vase, is almost impossible to repair. Here, we challenge the first of these blanket assumptions. And in a later chapter, we challenge the second. Taken together, we offer a guide for how to inspire and build trust quickly, and how to restore it when it has broken down.

Smile and Get a Dog

Ron Klein had a problem. As he campaigned to unseat Clay Shaw, the 13-time incumbent congressman in Florida's 22nd

District, he faced a formidable opponent. In his last election, Clay had beaten his opponent soundly: 63 percent to 35 percent. Perhaps unsurprisingly, early polls showed that Clay was likely to be reelected a 14th time. And as Ron campaigned, his chances became even worse—he was struggling to connect with voters.

What was particularly frustrating to Ron was that he knew the policy issues inside and out. As a member of the Florida legislature, he had expertise in education and criminal justice legislation, and he was energized to bring his ideas to Washington. When he got talking about policy issues, he sounded articulate and knowledgeable . . . but aloof. His problem was that he lacked the warmth he needed to connect with voters.

He knew that he needed help, so he reached out to a communication firm, KNP. In one meeting, the KNP team had Ron watch a TV interview he had given, and then asked him what he thought about his performance. Ron had ideas for a few additional points he wished he had added, but overall he thought he had done a good job.

Then the KNP team had him watch the video again. This time, they told him to notice how often he smiled. After watching the video the second time, Ron realized, "I never smile."

It seems obvious that Ron needed to smile more often. But just telling Ron to smile more wasn't the answer. Why? Because fake smiles look, well, fake. Ron needed to feel emotion on the inside. Only then, they explained, would he be able to express warmth effectively on the outside.

So the team came up with a strategy. They had noticed that whenever Ron talked about his son, he broke out into a wide authentic smile. In the words of his campaign manager, Brian Smoot, whenever he talked about his son, "He just lights up." And so, KNP got Ron to talk a bit about his son on the campaign trail. He would, after a few moments, transition right back to policy issues, but voters got to see Ron smile and they also got to see Ron as a warm and loving father.

As Ron's campaign headed into the final stretch, the tide began to turn. Ron was winning the trust of more and more voters. And lo and behold, on Election Day, against long odds, Ron won.

Research shows that people who inspire the most trust are those who exhibit two distinct traits: *warmth* and *competence*. Think of a friend or a coworker. Is this person warm or cold? And is this person competent or ineffective? We trust warm people, because we know they care about us; in contrast, cold people pose a potential threat to us. We trust competent people, because they are credible, effective, and efficient.

It turns out that there is a lot we can learn about trust once we know where people fall along these two dimensions: warmth and competence. In fact, Susan Fiske of Princeton suggests that warmth and competence are the key factors we use to understand anyone.

As you think about people who are naturally warm, the first people who come to mind are probably not world leaders. Many leaders are viewed as competent, but cold. This is exactly why politicians like Ron spend time on the campaign trail talking about their children and their childhood, or kissing babies.

It's also why, in the United States, every American president since the advent of television has consistently employed a specific public relations tool after moving into the White House: He's gotten a dog. Even the Obamas, who had never owned a dog and whose daughter Malia is *allergic* to dogs, felt compelled to get one. After all, there are few things that make someone look warmer than nuzzling with a cuddly, tail-wagging dog. The warmth these images project ultimately builds trust.

Perceptions of warmth and competence influence how much we trust other people as well as how much other people trust us. Ron Klein projected competence, but what he initially lacked, and what almost cost him the election, was warmth. Many of us inherently project either warmth *or* competence. But if we want to build strong relationships, we need to project both. And when it comes to making friends, the people *we* want to connect with are those who are high on both dimensions.

I'm Sorry for the Rain

If a complete stranger came up to you on the street and asked to borrow your cell phone, what would you do? Most people are, at least at first, reluctant. After all, these days, cell phones are expensive and often contain a great deal of personal information. You probably wouldn't hand your phone over to just anyone. You would have to trust them.

This is why we used this very scenario in an experiment we ran with Alison Brooks of Harvard to better understand the trust-building process. We had a research assistant approach people with the cell phone request as they entered the train station on a rainy day. (We spaced out the requests so that people would never see someone else who was approached.) Our research assistant would ask to borrow the person's cell phone in one of two ways. Half of the time he simply asked, "Can I borrow your phone? I need to make an important call." In this condition, only 9 percent of people were willing to hand over their cell phone.

In the other condition, the research assistant said, "I'm sorry about the rain! Can I borrow your phone? I need to make an important call." This opening statement is, on the face of it, a bit absurd. After all, it doesn't make much sense to apologize for something (like the rain) over which we have no control. However, this "superfluous apology" demonstrates concern and conveys warmth—and in turn, engenders trust.

When "I'm sorry about the rain!" preceded the request, 47 percent of people handed it over. That's a 400 percent increase over the normal request!

We found this same pattern of results for a whole set of scenarios (e.g., I'm sorry about your delayed flight; I'm sorry you were stuck in traffic). Regardless of how superfluous the apology was, as long as it conveyed care and concern, it boosted perceptions of warmth and increased trust. And with a dose of trust, people were willing to cooperate even when they were vulnerable and could have been exploited.

In these studies, the words themselves projected warmth. But words aren't the only form of communication that can help build trust. *How* we say things is often more important than what we say, and when it comes to conveying warmth, nothing works like nonverbal cues.

Let's return to our opening story of Detective Marshall Frank and the murder suspect Paul Rowles. It wasn't just *what* Marshall said, but *how* he said it that mattered. First, Marshall sat close to Paul and leaned in so they were almost touching. It turns out that physical connection is one of the best things we can do to build trust. We might think little of it, but actions like handshakes, an embrace, a pat on the shoulder, or even a light touch on an elbow can send a powerful cooperative message.

Detective Marshall also talked to his suspect face-to-face, and when it comes to trust, face-to-face meetings are critical. Being in the same place signals commitment to the relationship, heightens our focus, and allows for more complete communication—including the ability to project warmth.

As professors, we speak to a lot of students who ask for our advice about job offers. Part of the advice we give is always the same. If this is an employer you care about and you want your prospective boss to know that this is a relationship you value, go meet them in person. A phone call simply doesn't convey your concern for the relationship the way that a face-to-face meeting does.

So make the effort to meet someone face-to-face. Sometimes

this involves getting on a plane. Other times it involves walking down the hall. When we make this effort, we send the message that we care about the relationship, and we build trust.

When It Pays to Drive Rather Than Fly

When trying to win over others—whether it's the electorate, a murder suspect, a client, or a boss—warmth is clearly important, but competence also matters. It wasn't enough for Ron Klein to be warm; he also needed to be competent.

When we meet someone, we immediately assess their credibility, whether consciously or not. On the conscious level, we might look at obvious cues, like credentials—degrees, professional achievements, and so on. As we saw in our discussion of names and labels, one way we express confidence is with titles. This is why many professors want to be called "doctor."

But often enough people subconsciously look for more subtle hints as well as the obvious ones. So how can we learn to convey the kinds of subtle cues that will help us project competence, and in turn, build trust? One way is by using the right terminology— in other words, "talking the talk." When we tell our students they need to use the correct terms on their exams in our classes, they don't like it much. They think that when it comes time for a test, understanding concepts matters much more than what they deride as jargon. And they have a point. But terminology still matters. The correct use of terms and jargon identifies us as experts—whether as lawyers or real estate agents or financial wizards—and it in turn breeds confidence.

People pay attention to even more superficial cues than using the right jargon. Like it or not, in most domains, if you want to project competence, it pays to *appear* competent—in everything from the car you drive to the cufflinks you wear. One of our students took this advice so seriously that he rented a Rolls-Royce to impress important clients at a lunch meeting to convey the image that he was successful and had far more well-paying clients than he really did. Whether it helped him win the business, we don't know . . . But it certainly made an impression.

Of course, cues that project credibility in one context may fail to project credibility in another context. What's important is that the cue matches the situation. Take surgeons. When we are on the operating table, the woman who walks into the operating room wearing scrubs has instant credibility. But when we need a mechanic, and someone walks into the garage wearing scrubs, this doesn't inspire confidence that our car will be fixed. The scrubs are still a "cue," but in this case they don't match the situation—wearing scrubs in a garage is unlikely to build credibility the way it does in the operating room.

We also build credibility when our deeds match our words. Remember the example from our discussion of comparisons about how quickly American Airlines lost the trust of their pilots when executives asked the pilots to take massive pay cuts while simultaneously giving themselves retention bonuses? Nobody is less credible than a hypocrite.

Or perhaps remember how, in 2008, the three leading automakers in the United States came to Washington, D.C., to ask for a bailout? They explained that their companies were broke, that their financial situation was dire, and that their only way to survive was with help from the government. They needed billions of dollars in government support or they would go bankrupt.

Their request sparked a firestorm of criticism. But the public's anger wasn't focused on the amount of the request or whether the automakers were deceitful. In fact, they were being completely truthful: Their financial straits *were* dire. The problem was that each of the three executives had flown to Washington, D.C., on his own company's private jet. They were roundly condemned as hypocrites, and their credibility was at that moment totally shot. (In Chapter 8, on rebuilding trust, we'll learn about what they did to earn back that trust.)

And it is not just individuals who need to be credible. Institutions need credibility, too. And both people and institutions can gain credibility from each other. For example, researchers gain credibility by associating with universities, other scientists, and the prestige of the journals that publish our work. Professionals gain credibility by working at prestigious companies and joining exclusive associations. In turn, these institutions become more credible, and that credibility becomes a competitive advantage.

This is true not just in business; when countries have strong and credible legal institutions, for example, they enjoy greater economic growth. This is in part because trust in our legal institutions enables us to buy, sell, and trade effectively and efficiently.

In fact, the ability to trade has even been cited as an evolutionary advantage for humankind, and one reason some scholars think Homo sapiens were able to outcompete Neanderthals who had superior strength and even 10 percent larger brains. Consider for a moment the role of credibility and trust in one of the most significant inventions in human history: money. It used to be the case that people bartered for goods and services. But this was inefficient and limited. For example, a worker might get paid with food, but other people, like a landlord, might not accept that "currency." Money solves this problem.

But for money to work effectively, we have to *trust* the currency of exchange. And we need institutions to offer this security. Credible institutions, in other words, are necessary both for cooperating within one's society, and for competing in the global marketplace.

"They Did What They Had to Do"

Credible institutions are costly to build—and costly to maintain. They require our support even when, and sometimes especially when, they give us bad outcomes. And when it came to Alton Logan, the criminal justice system delivered an outcome that was shockingly bad.

In 1982, during a robbery at a McDonald's in Chicago a young man shot and killed a security guard. The scene was chaotic, but the police caught Alton Logan, who witnesses identified as the killer. Although Alton professed his innocence, he was sentenced to life in prison.

But two lawyers, Jamie Kunz and Dale Coventry, knew that Alton was innocent. They were sure of it. So sure, in fact, that they signed an affidavit swearing to his innocence and even had it notarized. Then they did something bizarre. They put that affidavit in a box and hid it away.

Why?

While Alton's case was going through the criminal justice system, the police arrested a man, Andrew Wilson, for murdering two Chicago police officers. Andrew confessed to the robbery and murder at the McDonald's to his lawyers, Jamie Kunz and Dale Coventry. This confession, however, was protected under the powerful institution of attorney-client privilege: the law that says when you meet with your lawyer, your lawyer can't share what you tell him with anyone else. Attorney-client privilege exists to protect the rights of defendants and to ensure that they get the best counsel possible; the only way to secure an effective defense is to be able to be completely open and honest with your attorney.

Jamie and Dale *knew* that Alton was innocent, but they could not reveal that information without violating the principle of attorney-client privilege. Had they done so, they would have failed to deliver the best defense they could muster for their client, Andrew Wilson, and they would have been disbarred, never to work as lawyers again. Of course, they pressed Andrew to come clean, but he insisted that they keep that information secret until his death.

When Andrew finally passed away (after serving a life sentence in prison for the murder of the police officers)—26 years later—Jamie came forward with the affidavit that would finally spring Alton, at age 54, from prison. As Alton walked out of the Cook County Jail, tears streamed down his face.

In reflecting on Alton's ordeal and the 26 years in which Jamie and Dale had locked away the secret information that could have freed him, Barbara Cannon, Alton's aunt, reflected, "We're not angry. They did what they had to do." Why was she so understanding of a system that had kept her nephew imprisoned for a crime he didn't commit? Quite simply, because she believed in the institution and she understood the principle that forced Jamie and Dale to keep their client's confession secret.

For institutions to work, they must command our respect. And in her statement, Alton's aunt reveals the reverence we can hold for our legal institutions—even when they delivered a devastating outcome.

So far, we've talked about the role of warmth and competence in building trust. But is there such a thing as projecting *too much* competence? Are there times when being vulnerable might hold benefits for us?

When to Spill Your Coffee: The Hidden Strength in Vulnerability

In their profession, psychiatrists face a daunting challenge. After meeting a new patient, they often have only a short period to get their patients to trust them with some of their innermost secrets.

The tools psychologists use to build trust quickly help us under-stand key insights about trust that can help us succeed not just in psychology, but in nearly every profession where building trust quickly can help secure a competitive edge.

So how do psychiatrists do it? Take the example of one of our former executive education students, Tom. He would employ some surprising strategies. Recall how, in the last section, we ex-plored how professionals build trust by finding ways to highlight and showcase their credentials? Well, Tom would do the oppo-site. When he met a new patient, rather than talking about his credentials or training, he would start off by dropping his pen-cil, telling a bad joke, or spilling his coffee. Other doctors, after meeting a new patient, point to their hearing aid and explain that their hearing isn't very good. Why would they do this? Why start a meeting by pointing out a weakness or making a clumsy mistake?

We can begin to answer this question by looking at a classic study led by Elliot Aronson at the University of Texas at Austin in the 1960s. Participants listened to a taped interview of a college student trying out for the College Quiz Bowl team (this was back in the 1960s, when representing your college in the College Bowl was very prestigious). As part of the interview process, the "can-didate" (who was really working for the interviewer) was asked 50 difficult quiz questions; they also shared some background information about themselves.

Unbeknownst to the participants, Elliot and his team created four versions of the interview. In one version, the "candidate" answered 92 percent of the questions correctly and had been an honors student, the yearbook editor, and a member of the track team in high school.

A second version had this exact same stellar performance of 92 percent correct, but tacked onto the end of the interview was a pratfall: The candidate spilled coffee. On the tape, par-ticipants heard the clatter of a cup and saucer, the scraping of a chair across the floor, and the candidate exclaiming, "Oh my goodness, I've spilled coffee all over my new suit."

In a third version, the candidate answered only 30 percent of the questions correctly, and had earned average grades, was a proofreader for the yearbook, and had tried out for, but not made, the track team in high school. And the fourth version replicated the interview of the less impressive candidate, but ended with the same coffee-spilling pratfall.

After listening to one of the four different interviews, participants rated the candidate. Here's the question: Whom did they like best?

As you might expect, participants liked the high-performing candidate better than the low-performing candidate. But what about spilling the coffee? Strangely enough, it turns out that they thought more highly of the high-performing person who spilled coffee than of the high performer who had been less clumsy.

A number of studies have since replicated these results and offered the same explanation: Highly competent people can make themselves appear more approachable by committing a pratfall. A small blunder makes them seem a little vulnerable, and this vulnerability makes them seem approachable and warm.

And so, when you enter a psychiatrist's office and see their fancy degrees and other trappings of modern medicine, you automatically perceive them to be competent and capable. Making themselves vulnerable by spilling their coffee or telling a bad joke is what helps them seem just a bit more human—and this projects warmth.

The effectiveness of this strategy debunks the common assumption that trust is something that can only be built *slowly* over time. By making yourself vulnerable, it is possible to build trust in less time than it takes to mop up a spilled latte.

Of course, there are many ways to make ourselves vulnerable. Instead of spilling coffee, we can reveal a secret or make a mistake. One of our executive students was seen at work as highly competent but cold, so she tried a new tactic: She purposely began to introduce typos and grammatical errors in some of her e-mails to colleagues, to make her appear more human, and thus warmer. And indeed, her workplace relationships *improved* after she started including typos.

But not all pratfalls are good. We want to emphasize a key finding from the Aronson study. To get the benefits of appearing vulnerable, you have to establish your credibility *first*. It was the high-performing student who benefited from spilling the coffee. And think back to Ron Klein, the congressman who beat the powerhouse incumbent. His competence was never in question. Without his credibility, talking about his son to make him seem warm would not have been effective in winning voters' trust. Or, take our former student who purposely placed typos in her e-mails. She only did this *after* she had demonstrated her competence.

The other side of that coin is that you must be careful not to make yourself vulnerable in a way that undermines your credibility. Again the context matters. Psychiatrists can build trust by spilling their coffee and saying, "I've never been very good with my hands." Surgeons cannot. It is essential that the vulnerable episode does not compromise your credibility or competence in a domain in which you are trying to inspire trust.

As long as you are already perceived as competent, embarrassing yourself can be another way to appear a bit vulnerable. We saw this firsthand with a former student, JP La Forest. Several years ago, he represented an American auto manufacturer as a liaison engineer in a Japanese company in Yokohama. He was the only American in the office, and he was frustrated that he was always listed as a visitor in the minutes of the meetings. One night, he went out on the town with his Japanese counterparts. They ate, drank, and sang karaoke. In all of the official documents issued from then on, JP was no longer listed as a visitor; instead, his name appeared along with the local office staff.

Why does singing off-key, revealing a secret, or making a mistake build trust? As most of us have learned the hard way, karaoke can be embarrassing. But it is precisely for this reason that it can help build trust. When you sing karaoke with your friends, sometimes the louder and worse you perform, the more you bond.

Embarrassing experiences—like off-key karaoke performances—are about shared vulnerability. Shared consumption of alcohol can build cooperation too, but just be careful to balance these benefits with the harm that alcohol consumption can cause. In addition to impairing our motor coordination, alcohol can blind us to issues that, upon sober reflection, seem utterly obvious. And this can lead to decisions with far graver consequences than an off-color comment to your boss. Consider this cautionary tale about the power of alcohol to both promote cooperation and put us at a competitive disadvantage.

As the Bosnian war raged in the former Yugoslavia, Richard Holbrooke led negotiations to broker a deal to end the war once and for all. The leaders of the different factions had failed to reach an accord in prior meetings, but Richard was determined. During the first three weeks of November, 1995, he sequestered the parties in Dayton, Ohio.

During two weeks of intense negotiations, they were able to resolve many issues, but they reached an impasse regarding access to the town of Gorazde. The final discussions came down to a land corridor that would connect Gorazde with Sarajevo. This corridor would be protected under international control; the key issue was how much land and control the Serbians would relinquish.

On November 17, Slobodan Milosevic, the Serbian president, and Richard Holbrooke sat down in a special room to hammer out this final point. This room had two key features. First, it was equipped with a hi-tech map of Bosnia. Second, it was stocked with scotch. As they navigated the virtual Bosnian terrain, they drank and drank and drank. Holbrooke commented five years later, "I can remember exactly where I was on Friday, November 17, 1995. At 2:00 a.m. that morning, after four hours of [virtually] 'flying' through Bosnia's terrain, we carved a corridor connecting Gorazde to Sarajevo . . . Finally, Milosevic stuck out his hand to me and said 'Okay, so this is it,' and he drank a toast and said 'Richard Charles Albert Holbrooke, we have found our road.'" In honor of the alcohol consumed, they named the corridor "Scotch Road."

Yet Slobodan Milosevic should have paid closer attention as he drank with Richard Holbrooke that night in Dayton, Ohio. In his scotch-induced haze, it did not occur to Slobodan to include amnesty for himself in the agreement. Not long after the deal went into place, Slobodan was extradited to the International Criminal Tribunal at The Hague where he was charged with war crimes. His trial lasted five years, and he died in his prison cell before the court reached a verdict.

From bonding over a few drinks to revealing a weakness, we have shown that making ourselves vulnerable can help us inspire trust. It turns out that the inverse is also true—avoiding vulnerability can shatter trust and weaken relationships.

This is the classic problem of the prenuptial agreement. People fear being financially exposed and vulnerable and seek to protect themselves. But in the process they undermine trust, as we saw with Peter and Elizabeth Petrakis. For Elizabeth, Peter's refusal to be vulnerable was a thorn that she could never get out of her side—until she ended their marriage.

Deepak Malhotra at Harvard has conducted experiments that echo Elizabeth's experience, when he found that contracts prevent trust from developing. And he has found out why: People use contracts to facilitate transactions, but when people with a contract behave in a trustworthy way, they don't get credit for their trustworthy actions. Observers assume that their trustworthy behavior must have been motivated by the contract, that they were merely being compliant, not trustworthy. Contracts in general, and prenuptial agreements in particular, are classic examples of how our attempts to protect ourselves can backfire and destroy the very thing we want—a trusting relationship.

So far, we have discussed factors that influence why and how we build trust with other people. But as we noted in the introduction, humans evolved as inherently social beings who live and work in *groups*. So, to successfully compete and cooperate in our society, we need to learn how to place trust not just in the right individuals, but also in the right *groups* of individuals. The most common rule of thumb we use—sometimes consciously, sometimes not—is to trust those who are "in" our group and be wary of those who are from other groups. Indeed, whether we realize it in the moment, many of our trust decisions are informed by a simple question: Are you "like me" or not?

Why Happy Families Produce Terrorists

Omar Hammami was raised in rural Alabama. The son of a Syrian immigrant and an Alabama native, he grew up in a loving family. He played soccer, he was close with his sister and parents, and he regularly visited his grandparents' farm, where he enjoyed lazy afternoons shelling peas and eating watermelon.

And at school, Omar was popular—very popular. He was the president of his sophomore class, he was always surrounded by friends, and he dated one of the most popular girls.

So how did someone like Omar come to join an Islamist rebel group known for beheadings, stoning people to death, and chopping off people's hands? According to Robert Pape of the University of Chicago, his transition from class president to foreign jihadist reflected "an altruism gone wildly wrong." Though Omar had attended Bible camp and church growing up, in his adolescence he found meaning in his Muslim roots. He began to identify as a Muslim, and it was through this prism that he viewed the invasion of Iraq and the events in Somalia with alarm. Despite having grown up in America, when Muslims in Iraq and Somalia were attacked, he identified with them so strongly that he was moved to act.

In contrast to the belief that terrorists are isolated loners, most terrorists were raised just like Omar—in caring families surrounded by friends. When the British Security Service, MI5, interviewed convicted terrorists and conducted long-term surveillance of terrorists, they found that most terrorists grew up in loving families and had lots of friends. In fact, fully 90 percent of the terrorists MI5 interviewed were characterized as "sociable."

The MI5 findings are completely consistent with former CIA operations officer Marc Sageman's research. As a foreign service officer, Marc worked with Islamic fundamentalists during the Afghan-Soviet war and studied terrorism extensively after he returned to the United States. Similar to the MI5 conclusions, he found that terrorists tend to come from middle-class, educated, religious, and supportive families. These individuals care deeply about their community, but begin to see outsiders as a threat.

And this is why it is sometimes the friendliest people within a group who come to see members of other groups as foes.

To succeed in our social world—whether in business, in our relationships, or in any other area of our lives—we cooperate within our group in order to compete effectively against other groups. Often, this means looking out for—and trusting—members of our own group, and distrusting members of other groups.

But how we define "our" group is often fluid. Across scores of studies of groups, two key results keep emerging. First, it is surprisingly easy for us to define ourselves as part of a group. Consider experiments where complete strangers are randomly assigned to either a "red" team or a "blue" team. It only takes a few moments before each team starts adopting favorable impressions of their teammates . . . and hostile views of the other team members. If we are assigned to the red team, we cooperate with other "reds" but compete against the "blues."

Second, trust within a group can fan the flames of hostility toward other groups. When Taya Cohen of Carnegie Mellon investigated conflict within and between societies by analyzing data from 186 societies across the globe, she found that the more loyal we are to our own group, the more we relish and approve of warfare against other groups.

These findings teach us something fundamental about cooperation and competition. It is often the most cooperative members of a group that can become highly competitive against other groups; when individuals identify very closely with their group, they see outsiders as a threat. At the same time, competitive individuals can also become highly cooperative—when they collaborate with members of their group to compete against others.

And how do we bring together two warring factions? Introduce a common enemy!

We know that perceived threats promote cooperation within a group and trigger competition between groups. The same principle applies to bringing competing groups together, and to this end there is really nothing that works more effectively than introducing a common enemy. From the diplomatic stage to the boardroom, a common threat can create some truly odd bedfellows as former adversaries shift gears to cooperate with each other.

In fact, the birth of the United States of America was made possible, in large measure, because of the shifting loyalties created by a common enemy. To appreciate how dramatically these forces changed, we need to start with a battle that preceded the American Revolution. In the mid-1700s, the French and British were locked in fierce competition for control over North America. The dispute between the two colonial powers had simmered for years and both the British and French had recruited the North American colonists to fight on their behalf.

The first violent conflict between the French and British in the colonies was fought in present-day Pennsylvania in 1754, when a small group of militiamen from Virginia ambushed a French patrol, killing many of them and capturing others. One of the people killed was a French officer, and his death enraged the French. As it turns out, the leader of that British militia was a little-known 22-year-old named George Washington. Washington was vilified by the French who accused him of assassinating their officer. And this battle ignited a seven-year war between the French and the British. Throughout this war, Washington remained a stalwart ally of the British and a reviled foe of the French.

Twenty years later, George Washington once again donned his military uniform. This time, however, to fight the British. And as he began his war against the British, things were not going well. The American colonists were outmatched by the British in almost every way.

George Washington realized that the colonists needed help. But who would come to the aid of his fledgling rebel movement? The French! Even though the French had vilified Washington, they hated the British even more. By coming to the aid of the Americans with money, weapons, soldiers, and even naval vessels, they were able to defeat their most loathed foe, the British. The French were able to gain a "victory" over the British, and the colonists were able to claim a new nation.

Of course, the story of shifting loyalties in the face of a common enemy doesn't end here. France and Britain were bitter foes for centuries. But in the twentieth century, in the face of a common enemy, first Germany and then the Soviet Union, the two foes became fast friends.

Finding the Right Balance: Reputations
and Relationships

Competence and warmth are the key ingredients for building trust. When it comes to conveying competence, there are many tools we can use, everything from credentials to jargon. But remember, competence alone is insufficient. Whether it's on the campaign trail or negotiating a high-stakes deal, we also need warmth.

As we've seen, one way to build warmth is to demonstrate concern for others or share information about our most important relationships. Another way is to take actions that make us vulnerable, from spilling coffee to singing off-key.

Both in business and in our personal lives, however, one of the *best* strategies we can undertake is to build long-term relationships. When we transform single transactions into repeated relationships, we promote cooperation and make friends out of possible foes.

To illustrate the importance of long-term relationships, let's travel to the commodity market for rubber in Thailand. When rubber is sold at market, the quality of the rubber is difficult to discern. Only after processing the raw rubber will the buyer know for certain whether or not the seller invested the time and effort to raise a high-quality crop.

In other words, at the time of the sale only the seller knows whether or not the rubber is high quality. Thus sellers have an incentive to compete: They could save time and money by raising a low-quality crop and telling potential buyers that their rubber is high quality. Over time, however, buyers would learn not to trust sellers. Ultimately, even sellers who did invest the effort to raise a high-quality product wouldn't be able to convince skeptical buyers that they had a high-quality product. In this case, the market would collapse. Sellers would produce low-quality rubber and the buyers would assume that the rubber is poor.

But this is not what happens. Why not?

Long-term relationships solve the problem. Rather than buying and selling with anonymous strangers, the buyers and sellers develop long-term partnerships. Buyers trust sellers to disclose the true quality of their rubber. And sellers do so because they know that if they mislead their buyers they will have a hard time selling rubber in the future. Long-term relationships create the trust that makes this market work.

Long-term relationships can also provide the foundation for trust in more complex business transactions. In 1963, Phil Knight thought he could build a better running shoe. He sent a few pairs to his former coach, Bill Bowerman, at the University of Oregon. Phil hoped that Bill might buy a few pairs. Instead, Bill offered to be his partner. The two shook hands in January 1964 and launched a shoe company. In the early years, Bill would rip apart running shoes to figure out new designs and Phil would sell shoes out of the trunk of his car. Bill and Phil trusted each other and with a handshake they built one of the most successful sportswear companies in history: Nike.

But what do we do when we don't have a long-term relationship? If we lack experience working with others, what can we do? We can rely on *other* people's experiences. And this is where reputations come in.

We recently saw a sign in front of a church that read, "If your friend gossips to you, you know they also gossip about you." We take issue with this quote. Not because we think it is untrue—we suspect that all of our friends, like us, gossip about everyone—but because it gives gossip a bad rap. Though gossip can be competitive and hurtful, it is also essential for building trust. Gossip not only conveys important information, but it also helps to solidify relationships.

Importantly, gossip serves to police and punish individuals who exploit others. It ensures that when people double-cross us, our friends will certainly hear about it. Matt Feinberg of the University of Toronto found that even when people can't formally punish those who exploited them, they can spread negative reputation information about them in the form of gossip. People use gossip to decide whom to trust and whom to avoid. In short, gossip helps us build reputations.

We are all familiar with old-fashioned gossip, the type that the church sign warned us about. But gossip has gotten much more sophisticated in the Internet age, and so too have reputation systems. To appreciate this, we only need to consider the now commonplace event of having complete strangers spend the night in our homes!

That is exactly what 17 million people have done since 2008 via Airbnb. As most readers are probably aware, Airbnb is a host site that helps prospective renters find short-term accommodations from private owners. When you post your property on Airbnb, in other words, you are opening your home to a complete stranger—and that requires a lot of trust! And Airbnb knows it. Trust is the foundational component of this enterprise and it is featured in their mission: "Airbnb is a trusted community marketplace for people to list, discover, and book unique accommodations around the world." They even have a web page dedicated to trust: https://www.airbnb.com/trust.

How do they create trust among complete strangers? Well, they have institutionalized the idea of gossip by using a reciprocal rating system. Every guest and every host rate each other after each rental. Your score becomes your reputation. If your ratings are low, it will be hard for you to secure accommodations or attract renters. And if your ratings become too low, you can be dropped from the system entirely. This system motivates both parties to be on their best behavior. More important, it enables hosts to trust a complete stranger not to steal their most valued possessions or trash their home.

In recent years there has been an explosion of peer-to-peer networks like these—from Airbnb to eBay to Uber. And each one runs almost entirely on trust and reputations. As we mentioned earlier, trust is the foundation of any economy, and when it comes to Internet ventures that connect strangers, trust is essential. Like gossip, reputation systems are not perfect, but they go a long way to help us solve the problem of trust.

We have discussed the importance of building trust. But although trust enables cooperation, unconditional trust—or blind trust—can make us vulnerable to competitive moves and exploitation by others. We benefit from trusting the *right* people, and we suffer when we trust the wrong people. Next, we offer a guide to help you discern whom to trust and whom to hold at arm's length.

When and How to Raise Your Guard

They finally caught her.

Before she could even speak, the detectives had her in handcuffs. When they brought her to the station, one of them shouted, "You know you did it. Just admit it!"

Seemona Sumasar was scared, terrified in fact. She was also confused. She had no idea what the police thought she had done. Nothing in her life had prepared her for this moment.

After working as an analyst at Morgan Stanley, Seemona had decided to leave the corporate world and start her own restaurant. It was difficult work for the 36-year-old single mother, but she enjoyed working for herself and being in control of her own destiny. Now, here she was imprisoned, cut off from her child.

When she found out that she was accused of committing *three* armed robberies *while impersonating a police officer*, she was flabbergasted. Not only was she innocent, she couldn't begin to fathom how the police could have even considered her a suspect.

Her claims of innocence were summarily ignored, and her bail was set at a shockingly high price of $1 million. Unable to come up with the enormous sum of money, she sat in prison . . . for seven months. She lost her restaurant and then her house. Her contact with her daughter was limited.

But as she sat in jail it hit her: "Jerry is behind this!"

Jerry, Seemona's ex-boyfriend, was a private detective. Seemona had accused him of rape following an encounter after they had broken up, and despite his insistence that she drop the charges, she was determined to have her day in court.

This had infuriated Jerry, who set out to destroy Seemona. Unfortunately for Seemona, Jerry was not only a detective but an avid fan of *CSI: Miami* and *Law & Order*. He used everything he had learned from both his career and these shows to devise a plot worthy of prime time. And in doing so, he managed to convince authorities that Seemona was a criminal and a true menace to society.

To fabricate a case against Seemona, Jerry had three witnesses make false statements to the police. Their statements were spread out in time, and each was increasingly specific. Jerry even showed his false witnesses photos of Seemona and had them drive by Seemona's house to see her car.

The first witness told police that an Indian woman disguised as a police officer with a gun had handcuffed him and robbed him of $700.

Six months later, Jerry had a second witness report that he had been robbed by two people impersonating the police. This witness was able to describe one of the robbers in detail—details that fit Seemona perfectly. This man also provided two other clues that pointed to Seemona: The getaway car was a Jeep Grand Cherokee, and he remembered that the first three letters of the license plate were AJD.

Months after that, a third person reported a very similar crime. This witness, too, claimed that she had been robbed by people posing as police officers, but she was able to provide even more detail; this witness overheard the two robbers refer to each other as "Seem" and "Elvis." As before, they had escaped the scene in a Jeep Grand Cherokee. And this time, the witness provided the clue the police really wanted, the complete license plate number.

After entering the license plate in their database, the police confirmed that it matched a Jeep Grand Cherokee, owned by a man named Elvis. Incriminating Seemona even further, the police learned that Elvis had transferred the title and plate of the car to Seemona's sister the day after the reported robbery. To the police it looked like Seemona had something to hide.

The case against Seemona appeared to be rock solid. The police had a wealth of evidence from multiple sources including specific descriptions of Seemona's car and the license plate. With this mountain of evidence on their side, it was easy to ignore her pleas, and almost impossible for them to believe anything she said.

It was only after one of the witnesses came forward to recant his testimony that the wheels of justice began to turn in the right direction. The informant revealed the deception and gave detectives Jerry's phone number, which would ultimately link him to the two other witnesses. And once the police began to take Seemona's protestations seriously, they uncovered surveillance and cell phone records that proved that Seemona couldn't have committed the crimes. For example, during one of the alleged robberies, there was video footage of Seemona at a casino in Connecticut.

And with that, the case against Seemona fell apart, and the case against Jerry came together. Seemona was released, and Jerry was sentenced to 33 years in prison with no possibility of parole for 20 years.

How was Jerry able to so easily persuade the police and the courts that this innocent woman was a hardened criminal?

Jerry's deception worked, to such great effect and with such tragic consequences for Seemona, because he cleverly hijacked the criminal justice system. Once the first false police report had been filed, Jerry set in motion a chain of events that he knew would focus like a laser on catching Seemona.

First, Jerry knew that multiple reports would make his deception more credible. A single report might have been dismissed. But *three* reports, spread over time, with increasing levels of detail, were impossible to ignore. He knew they would make the police feel as if they were building their case and getting closer and closer to catching their perpetrator.

Second, while police aspire to apprehend every criminal, they are especially keen to apprehend someone who makes their work more difficult and more dangerous. By describing Seemona as a robber who impersonated a police officer, Jerry knew that police would be particularly keen to catch this perpetrator.

In the preceding chapter, we described trust as a cooperative tool of friends. But by trusting others we also make ourselves vulnerable to deception and exploitation by the competitive intentions of our foes. In other words, deception sits at the intersection of competition and cooperation. Deceivers pretend to cooperate, but compete instead.

To find the right balance between cooperation and competition, we need to understand what deception is and how it works. On the following pages, we address two fundamental questions: Why do we deceive? And how can we detect deception and prevent being exploited by our foes or even taken advantage of by our friends?

We also introduce a new approach to thinking about deception: Deception can be a *cooperative* tool. Though we are taught that lying is unethical and harmful, we challenge this belief and explain why some lies actually help us build trust and cooperation—and can even be considered ethical.

In many instances, however, we are targets of unethical deception. To avoid exploitation, we need to raise our guard. So here we explore the dynamics of detecting deception and how to raise our guard. We identify the red flags that signal deception and we offer advice for how to spot them.

Deceptive Cuckoo Birds and Misleading Dating Profiles

Humans are not the only ones who use deception to get what they want. In fact, many animal species have learned how to exploit others to gain greater access to scarce resources, from reproductive opportunities to food to protection and safety.

Consider the European cuckoos, famous for inspiring the cuckoo clock. These birds look perfectly harmless on a piece of furniture, but out in nature they are masters of deception: They trick other birds into rearing their young for them.

Here's how. Female cuckoos locate nests of other birds that contain eggs. They wait until the expectant parents are away gathering food. Then, the mama cuckoo sneaks into the nest, removes at least one of the existing eggs, and quickly lays one of her own in its place. Female cuckoos can place up to 20 eggs in 20 different nests just this way. When the cuckoo egg hatches, the "foster" parent bird instinctively feeds the open beak of a young chick. Deception in this case succeeds because it plays on the bird's basic maternal instincts: Feed hungry chicks that hatch in your nest.

Many species use deception to feed themselves and their families. For example, antshrikes cooperate by raising an alarm with a special call (you might remember from our introduction that ground squirrels do this as well). However, sometimes these small birds use this cooperative tool to gain a competitive advantage. Biologists have observed antshrikes raising *false* alarms. When another bird is about to consume a tantalizing insect, a competing bird will sound the alarm. This grabs attention and distracts a competitor, and often gives the bird that raised the false alarm just enough time to swoop in for the meal. These birds have figured out how to "cry wolf" to gain an advantage over their competitors.

Examples like these abound. From birds to baboons, most animals use deception, both to compete with members of their own species for resources and to evade predators. Interestingly, deception can also be used as a form of cooperation, helping entire groups coordinate their actions to more effectively compete with predators. For example, when a predator is near a group of birds, one of the birds may pretend to be injured. This deceptive act is meant to distract the predator's attention, and buy others, especially their offspring, time to escape imminent doom.

Humans also use deception to claim greater resources, acquire better mating opportunities, or promote their family's or group's interests. With human deception, however, a few things change. For one, human deception is typically a bit more clever.

Drawing on prior work, we define deception as any action or statement that intentionally misleads a target. Our definition has two key features. *First, deception is intentional.* If you lead someone to believe something that turns out to be false, but you truly believe it, we wouldn't consider that deception. *Second, the statements or actions themselves don't need to be false.* Sometimes, individually truthful statements strung together can be misleading. For example, if I ask a car seller if her car has any problems, she could tell me that it always starts right up and that she can produce five years of receipts for routine maintenance. If the car leaks fluids and was involved in a serious accident, however, her statements might be true, but they would be misleading. We would call that deceptive.

We'd all like to believe that the majority of people are honest. But is that true?

When scholars study ordinary communication, the rates of deception they observe are astoundingly high. In one study, 60 percent of people lied to strangers within the first 10 minutes of meeting them. The vast majority of college students (86 percent) report that they lie to their parents on a regular basis. And surveys reveal that most of us lie to our friends (75 percent), siblings (73 percent), and spouses (69 percent).

But what about when the information we state is public and can be pretty easily verified?

To answer this question, Jeffrey Hancock of Cornell University analyzed profiles on dating websites like Match.com and then met dozens of people who had posted profiles on these sites. He weighed them, measured their height, and verified their birth date by looking at their driver's licenses. He then compared those values with what people had *claimed* on the dating websites. It turned out that almost 60 percent of people misrepresented their weight by at least five pounds. And almost half (48 percent) misrepresented their height. As you might expect, men were more likely to inflate their height, and women were more likely to underreport their weight.

The dating site study also tells something else about everyday deception. We often deceive by only a "small" amount. Sure, a few people on the dating site told some tall tales. For instance, one person claimed to be more than 20 pounds lighter than she really was. But overall, most of the lies were modest—an inch or two taller, five or six pounds lighter, and a year or two younger. Why are most lies so modest? Because we need to balance competing concerns. We want to look better to others online, but at the end of the day we need to look at ourselves in the mirror. As Nina Mazar at the University of Toronto has found, we can justify small lies, but the bigger the lie the harder it is to justify to ourselves. Plus, the bigger the lie, the bigger the consequences—*and* the easier it is to get caught.

When we tell lies, we fear getting caught, but we have other feelings as well. In fact, deception does not always make us feel bad. Sometimes it feels good to be bad.

Why Cheating Is Like Chocolate Cake

When pop star Britney Spears stole a cigarette lighter from a gas station, she was caught making a joke out of her petty crime. "I stole something. Oh, I'm bad. Ohhh," she said playfully.

This example raises two puzzles. First, why would a millionaire steal something as cheap and trivial as a lighter? To be fair, Britney isn't the only celebrity to behave this way. Actress Winona Ryder was arrested for stealing clothes and shoplifting, and the tennis champion Jennifer Capriati was once caught shoplifting a $15 ring from a mall.

Why do wealthy people steal? None of them *needed* these items, and each of them could easily have afforded them. The costs of engaging in these behaviors far exceed the benefits. So something curious must be going on.

The second puzzle, which helps us solve the first, is the fact that many of them were filled with glee as they engaged in theft. Shouldn't they feel guilt and remorse?

Not Frank Abagnale, Jr. He traveled the world conning people by impersonating such diverse characters as a Pan Am pilot, a supervising resident of a hospital, a lawyer, and a college sociology professor. In the end, he cashed a staggering total of $2.5 million in forged checks.

After Frank had committed his first con, here is how he describes how he felt:

> I was heady with happiness. Since I hadn't yet had my first taste of alcohol, I couldn't compare the feeling to a champagne high, but it was the most delightful sensation I'd ever experienced.

Intuitively, we assume that unethical behavior makes people feel guilty, remorseful, and full of regret. And it often does. However, our research has found that this is not always the case.

After engaging in unethical behavior, many of us, not just the rare individual like Britney or Frank, feel happy and even giddy. This isn't just true anecdotally. Across several experiments, we've found that those who cheated actually reported feeling much happier than those who refrained from cheating. We call this the "Cheater's High."

We have replicated this study across a range of conditions and situations, and each time we found that cheaters were happier. So we cannot assume that feelings of guilt will deter people from cheating or deceiving others. Some people, especially after experiencing the thrill of cheating and getting away with it, may even be more drawn to it.

This idea has an important practical implication. If people feel a sense of accomplishment from cheating, monitoring systems and greater deterrence can actually *encourage* some people to cheat. Consider a computer hacker looking for a challenge. The more secure the system, the more alluring the target. We suspect that this problem may be particularly acute for online security, where bragging rights represent a substantial part of the "reward." But the Cheater's High poses a challenge for *any* system: While tighter controls may deter some people, they may actually motivate others.

Of course, although cheating may give us an instant high, there are often negative long-term consequences. We may damage relationships, ruin a marriage, lose a job, or even get thrown in jail. And so, in the heat of the moment, we also need to tap into one of our most important capacities as human beings to not fall prey to the temptation to cheat: self-control.

Our research has shown us that cheating is an awful lot like chocolate cake. To resist temptation, we need self-control, and this is true not just for cheating but for nearly every long-term goal that we have—dieting, exercising, saving money, and so on.

There are two key things to understand about self-control. First, self-control is like a muscle that gets easily tired and worn out with overuse. Second, we use the same muscle every time we do *anything* that requires self-control. This means that we exert the same self-control "muscle" when we take the stairs instead of the elevator at work, when we skip the chocolate cake at lunch, and when we include only eligible expenses in our expense report. This is why during exam time it is so hard to study diligently while also eating well. With so much self-control expended on studying, there is too little left over to avoid the temptation of a junk food binge.

Consider a study we conducted with Nicole Mead of the Rotterdam School of Management. In the first stage of the experiment, participants watched a six-minute video of a woman being interviewed. The interview video, however, had no sound, and at the bottom of the screen we posted a series of short words like "play," "tight," and "greet" for 30 seconds each. We asked some people "not to read or look at any words that may appear on the screen." The video without sound is boring to watch, and for most people, it is a struggle *not* to read the words at the bottom of the screen. As we expected, our participants told us they found this task to be exhausting.

We then gave participants an opportunity to cheat. We had them take a math test in which they could earn money for each correct problem. The computer told them their score, but each participant was responsible for informing the experimenter. Participants had an incentive to cheat. Reporting a higher score would earn them more money. As we predicted, the people who had expended self-control by avoiding the words at the bottom of the screen were more than twice as likely to overstate the number of problems they had solved. Across many different self-control and cheating tasks we found the same result: After people expend self-control, they are more likely to cheat.

Here is the key lesson: When we are tempted to cheat, we need our self-control muscle to hold us back. Yet we only have a single muscle for self-control, and it is easily fatigued.

Our advice is to be mindful of your self-control muscle. If it's gotten a recent workout (whether by saying no to that slice of cake, or avoiding some other temptation), we may want to postpone important ethical decisions until that muscle is rested and recharged.

But as we noted earlier, not every lie is unethical. In fact, we use deception surprisingly often to *cooperate* with others. What are these prosocial lies like, and how do they work?

When Deception Builds Cooperation

"Every lie is a sin."
> —St. Augustine, fifth century

For centuries, parents, spouses, and religious leaders have echoed this sentiment. But is it always? Think about what you should do when your grandmother asks if you enjoyed her meatloaf, your friend asks if you enjoyed her wedding reception, your child asks if you liked his choral performance, or your spouse asks you if their new jeans make them look fat? In situations like these, deception might be exactly the *right thing to do*. It helps us keep our friends and prevents acquaintances from becoming our foes. In other words, sometimes we use deception to build cooperation.

In a project led by Emma Levine at Wharton, we studied the benefits of *prosocial* deception; by prosocial we mean lies that *benefited* other people. In some of our studies, we asked people to judge the morality of different types of lies. Some of these were prosocial lies. In other studies, we had people make decisions after receiving advice from a partner. After making their decisions, they learned two pieces of information: a) whether or not their partner had misled them and b) how much money they had earned. And here's the interesting part. Some of the time, our participants earned *more* money because their partner had lied to them. That is, some lies were prosocial.

We ran several different variations of this study, and we kept finding the same pattern of results. When people told prosocial lies they were judged to be *more* moral than those who told the truth. And people trusted these prosocial liars more, too.

As we think about using deception, we should keep two things in mind: expectations and intentions. In many competitive situations, we *expect* our foes to deceive us. For example, in poker or in a negotiation, we'd be shocked if our counterparts *didn't* bluff.

In contrast, in many cooperative situations we expect graciousness. So when our neighbors invite us to dinner and ask how we liked the food, they may not be seeking an honest review. As Alison Fragale of the University of North Carolina found, sometimes deception is even seen as a sign of respect; when a colleague misses our party, they might (respectfully) cite an illness rather than their preference to catch up on a TV series.

Sometimes deception is even good for our health. Consider a doctor who overstates the likelihood that an experimental drug will work. This may be deceptive, but often it is done with benevolent intentions. Lisa Iezzoni of Harvard Medical School found that over 55 percent of doctors tell their patients that their prognosis is better than it really is. By misleading patients, many doctors hope to activate the self-healing potential of the placebo effect and the power of optimism.

In other words, people care about honesty (and they should), but sometimes it pays to care more about other things, like kindness and concern.

Though we are taught that lying is unethical and harmful, the truth is that many lies actually bind us together and promote trust. So is it ethical to tell prosocial lies? Our answer is yes.

And we'd even take this claim a step further. Rather than admonishing our children to never lie, we should teach them the guiding principle of benevolence, and that they should make careful—and deliberate—choices when they face a conflict between telling the truth and being kind.

Of course, sometimes telling the truth and potentially hurting someone else's feelings is actually prosocial because it helps the person in the long run. When we lie and tell someone they performed better than they really did, we deny them the opportunity to learn from their mistakes. Without honest feedback, we can get stuck in mediocrity. After a middling performance, there is a trade-off between helping someone feel good and helping them learn from their mistakes. As a result, we need to consider two key questions when we decide whether to be brutally honest or tell a prosocial lie. First, how important is it to boost a person's self-esteem? Will candid feedback sting so badly that it demoralizes them? Second, how useful is the feedback for their long-term success? For tasks that really matter for future success, honesty may be the best route to take. But when a task really doesn't make much difference—like your grandmother's meatloaf—prosocial lies can be just the right thing to say. Many of us, including teachers, parents, coaches, or managers, navigate this balance all the time.

So sometimes deception builds cooperation. Other times, deception can exploit and undermine us. What should we look for to guard against being fooled and exploited?

Going Up 96 Percent of the Time, Captain Mbote, and $57 Million in Cash

Bernie Madoff perpetuated the largest Ponzi scheme in the history of the United States, producing billions of dollars in fraudulent funds. Somehow, the SEC missed Bernie Madoff's red flags. But they were there. Securities industry executive Harry Markopolos saw them. To Harry, the flags were abundant and crystal clear. He even pointed them out to the SEC, but nobody listened to him. They should have.

Here is what Harry saw. First, Madoff's returns were too high and too positive. Anyone who's invested in the stock market knows that stocks go up . . . and down. But Bernie reported returns that nearly always went up: He reported negative returns in only 4 percent of the months!

Second, Madoff's activities were unusually secretive. For example, he refused any outside audits; no one was allowed to do any due diligence. And he wouldn't let third-party hedge funds that invested with him advertise their connection. Because he wouldn't allow due diligence, he was shut out of short-term credit markets and had to borrow money at a very high rate, another red flag.

Third, Madoff claimed to be "timing" the market, hopping in and out of stocks. Nobody invests that way. He also claimed that he hedged his stock purchases with OEX index options. But Harry knew that this couldn't be true because the number of OEX options Bernie would need simply didn't exist.

None of this made sense. The red flags were waving everywhere but the SEC missed them. It's possible that the layers of bureaucracy within the SEC made it hard for the organization to spot these signs. Are individuals better than organizations at spotting clues? How might an ordained minister and psychotherapist do if a parade of red flags were waved right in front of them? As we will learn, not too well.

Consider John Worley. His first mistake was opening the e-mail addressed to the generic "CEO/Owner." His second mistake was replying to it, even after reading the words "I decided to seek your assistance in transferring some money out of South Africa into your country, for onward dispatch and investment." The e-mail was signed by Captain Joshua Mbote, who explained that he had $57 million in cash and needed a partner with a foreign bank account.

Would *you* trust Captain Mbote? Our quick reaction is "No way!" Yet scams just like this one reel in millions of dollars from people just like us, and just like John Worley.

The e-mails John received waved almost every red flag you could imagine. The e-mails lacked personalization. John was asked to provide bank account information, wire money, and fly to Africa at the request of complete strangers. In return, he was promised a fantastic sum of money—$16 million.

In thinking about John Worley, we want to understand *why* John was so trusting in the face of clues that should have sounded the alarm and caused him to run, not just walk, for the nearest exit.

Curiously, John did exhibit skepticism at various points of this scam. But his concerns were easily allayed by the scammers. For example, when John asked Mbote how he had found him, Mbote explained that the South African Department of Home Affairs had supplied his name. Most of us would be thinking, *the South African Department of what??* But this answer satisfied John.

Worse, when John received a check from a "fellow investor" for $47,500, and found it odd that it was drawn from an account belonging to something he'd never heard of, called the Syms Corporation, John was skeptical enough to call the bank before he deposited it. It was a good idea, because the check was a fraud. So he confronted "Mbote" and told him he was through.

Soon after this declaration that he was finished, however, he began to receive e-mails signed by a different person: "Mohammed Abacha," the alleged son of a former Nigerian dictator who had money hidden in Ghana. Mohammed Abacha explained that Joshua Mbote had been operating on his behalf, but had bungled things badly. He apologized for how things had been handled, and he assured John that now he, Mohammed, was taking over and that the situation could be righted. And Mohammed put John in touch with Maryam Abacha, the purported widow of a general who needed help transferring a similarly fantastic sum of money.

It was in this e-mail exchange that John noticed Maryam's name was spelled differently across e-mails. In one it was Maryam, in another Maram, and still another Mariam. John wrote, "I would think that everyone would know how to spell their own real name. Obviously, someone does not."

But even this was not enough to scare him off. The scam artists managed to calm his fears and win over his trust. They even subjected *him* to a credit check. With misplaced confidence, John dove deeper into the scam; he set up an offshore account and he went on to deposit two checks, one for $95,000 from the Robert Plant Corporation and one for $400,000 from a Michigan marketing company. At first, the checks cleared. The money appeared in John's account, and he promptly wired the money to a Swiss account following Maryam's directions.

The checks, however, had been fraudulent, and John's world came crashing down.

John was arrested and brought to trial for bank fraud, money laundering, and possession of counterfeit checks. He was found guilty on all counts, and sentenced to two years in prison and ordered to pay restitution for $600,000.

Why was John so willing to believe their flimsy explanations, especially after they had mixed up their stories, misspelled their own name, and sent him a fraudulent check?

We may think that we are masters at spotting the clues of deception. In actuality, however, we are terrible lie detectors.

Deception is often successful for two reasons. First, we are inherently trusting creatures. Unless we have evidence to the contrary, we typically accept that people are telling the truth and trust what they tell us. This is particularly true of people we know—our family members, our friends, and our coworkers.

We call this the "truth bias." The truth bias tilts the odds in the liars' favor.

When we want to believe, our minds help us overlook even the most glaring of reasons not to. This was true for John Worley, and it is just as true for anyone who's ever been deceived by a con artist; think about the thousands of investors who gave their life savings to Bernie Madoff.

There is a second reason why lies often succeed. We are *overconfident* in our ability to detect lies. This is especially true for romantic partners. We think that we know our partners so well that we would automatically detect the first sign of deception. When a husband claims, "I'd know in an instant if she ever lied to me!" he is mistaken more than he might care to imagine.

Before we place our trust in others, we need to first consider what we want to believe. Then, we need to think carefully about what we do *not* want to believe. Though it can be uncomfortable, the best way to avoid being exploited is to actively look for those very clues we hope *not* to find. Because, if we are being deceived, we're better off knowing about it sooner rather than later, before we get taken for a ride.

It is hard to detect deception. But the clues, the red flags, are often right there in front of us. Yet, we often miss them entirely. Fortunately, science has taught us a lot about the clues that liars leave behind.

Putting It All Together: Spotting Red Flags

Before we can detect the signs that someone is being deceptive, the very first thing we need to do is establish a baseline. In finance, if we know how frequently the market goes up and down, we can recognize that positive returns 96 percent of the time are "unusual." Similarly, for our friends and foes, it is only after we know how they behave normally that we can spot changes that indicate that they might be lying. After all, what constitutes "normal" behavior differs across individuals. Some people avoid eye contact routinely. Some people always use the phrase "To be honest." Others act inappropriately in situations on a regular basis. So while each of these behaviors can indeed be a sign of deception (as we'll explain), they aren't very diagnostic if they are "normal" behaviors for that person.

Establishing a baseline is exactly how a polygraph test starts. As many of you know, the polygraph only measures arousal. Because some people show more arousal on average than others, it would be terribly unreliable without a baseline reading to account for a person's normal level of arousal. So a polygraph administrator needs to compare your arousal levels when you answer simple questions (e.g., what is your name?) with your arousal level in the face of tough questions.

In fact, if you know what to look for, baseline measures can even help you spot the bluff of a professional poker player. As Michael Slepian of Columbia University found, even professional poker players raise red flags. While poker players are experts at masking their facial expression, they still leak physical cues that reveal whether or not they have a good hand. How? By the way they extend their arms to move their chips! A steady move in is a sign of real confidence. But when players bluff their arms zigzag and don't follow a direct path. This shows us that even the best liars among us leak cues. Establishing that baseline helps you figure out what to look for.

Once you have a baseline, you then need to pay attention to what people are saying.

How do you begin? By asking the right questions. In work led by Julia Minson of Harvard, we studied what types of questions work best for detecting deception.

Let's say you are looking at a used car. You could ask general questions that elicit broad and open-ended answers, such as "What can you tell me about the car?" General questions are good for starting a conversation, but they are not very good at uncovering the truth. In answering a general question, it is simply too easy to omit key information.

You might ask questions that have positive assumptions, such as "The car doesn't have any transmission problems, does it?" These are better at detecting deception because they force the person to address a key issue by coming clean or affirming false information.

But the best questions to ask are open-ended ones that involve *negative* assumptions: "What problems does the car have?" This phrasing forces the responder either to reveal information or actively come up with a deceptive answer.

Another way to make deception easier to detect is to increase what we call cognitive load. When someone is lying, they have to think harder. As Mark Twain put it, "If you tell the truth, you don't have to remember anything." In other words, when we lie, we need to fabricate a story *and* keep track of the truth. The need to process and remember more information when we lie places us under greater cognitive load.

So how does this help us detect deception? It turns out that when we think harder, it changes how we communicate. We are more likely to use pause fillers (um's and ah's) as we collect our thoughts, and it takes us longer to answer questions. We gesticulate less, and when we do move our hands or nod our head it might look mechanical or delayed. Under cognitive load we also make mistakes. We might emphasize the wrong words, such as saying "yes," but shaking our head "no." We might even catch and correct ourselves midway through as in "yeah—I mean no." Detectives and investigators routinely exploit cognitive load to catch liars. They know that if they can add to the mental strain a liar is under, a mistake becomes almost inevitable.

How do you increase cognitive load? Some investigators ask questions out of chronological order or ask for seemingly irrelevant details about the story, e.g., "What was the weather like then?" Or they might play talk radio or have the TV on in the background to serve as a distraction. Then, they sit back and watch for mistakes.

Once you have established a baseline and have started to ask pressing questions under cognitive load, you're ready to start looking more closely at how they are *acting*. Here we identify four red flags and describe how to spot them.

Red Flag #1: Inappropriate Behavior

Laci Peterson was last seen alive Christmas Eve in 2002. She was seven and a half months pregnant.

When her husband, Scott Peterson, returned from a fishing trip one evening, her car was in the driveway and her purse, keys, and phone were in the house, yet Laci herself was nowhere to be found. So he called Laci's mother and asked if Laci was there. When Laci's mother replied that she wasn't, Scott calmly said, "Laci's missing."

Tragically, three and a half months later, Laci's body and the fetus washed ashore in San Francisco Bay. Laci had been murdered, and her body had been dumped in the bay.

To investigators, there were several clues from Scott's behavior following her disappearance that made them highly suspicious. The first was the fact that Scott's behavior was highly inappropriate for a distraught husband. Stop for a moment and try to imagine how you might behave if your pregnant wife had just gone missing.

Would you be calm during the search, chatting away on your cell phone? Would you go out and play golf? Would you add not just one, but two pornographic channels to your cable account just days after your wife's disappearance? Would you sell her car? Scott did all of these things.

Remember our discussion of baselines—we need to know what is normal for a particular person. Take the routine task of baking. A college student (who will remain unnamed) was home on a break from college. He asked his father to borrow some butter because he was going to his friend's house to make brownies. This might seem like a fairly innocent request, but his father immediately became suspicious and directly asked his son if he was going to make pot brownies . . . and he was! How did his dad know? Because his son had *never* made brownies before! The son's behavior deviated from the baseline and therefore was uncommon and unusual for him.

So, the first clue for detecting deception is whether the behavior is unusual, uncommon, or inappropriate. Scott's behavior clearly was.

Red Flag #2: Running for the Exit

During a family press conference, a reporter asked Scott if he was a suspect in the case. In response, he stormed out of the press conference.

When we lie, we often feel anxiety at the prospect of getting caught. When we feel anxiety, we seek to relieve it by exiting the situation, as Scott Peterson did. This is exactly why liars frequently look at the door, check their watch, and express eagerness to get out of the interview. Some lean toward the exit or engage in "eye blocking," closing their eyes imagining being somewhere else.

So if you ask someone a tough question and their eyes start darting to the nearest way out, there is a chance that they could be lying.

Red Flag #3: Overcompensating

As President Clinton faced allegations of having a sexual relationship with one of his interns, he famously stated on camera, "I'm going to say this again. I did not have sexual relations with that woman, Miss Lewinsky. I never told anybody to lie, not a single time—never. These allegations are false. And I need to go back to work for the American people."

In this statement, you probably noticed his eagerness to get "back to work" (Red Flag #2). But there is a second clue in this statement: the over-the-top repetition, "I never told anybody to lie, not a single time—never. These allegations are false." And by overdoing it, we see Red Flag #3.

Motivated by a desire to appear credible, liars tend to go overboard. They might overuse phrases such as "To be honest." They might refer to their religious upbringing, or continuously reference their credentials or friends to bolster their status and credibility.

For example, there have even been cases of criminals who tip off authorities by overcompensating and appearing *too* relaxed during questioning, even resorting to medication to gain this effect. Yet by trying to create the impression that everything is normal, they often go too far and give themselves away.

Similarly, by working hard to create the right impression, cheaters often overcompensate as they try to craft the "perfect" lie. Consider this example from a few years ago. Dirk Smeesters was a rising star in academia at the prestigious Erasmus University in the Netherlands. He was publishing articles at breakneck speed. He was promoted quickly and he received accolades for his research.

So it was hardly a surprise that one of his papers caught the attention of one of our colleagues, Uri Simonsohn. As scientists, we are routinely asked to share the results of our studies. So when Uri asked Smeesters for his data, Smeesters passed them right along. As Uri puzzled through the numbers, he knew something wasn't right.

In one of Smeesters's studies, he had asked people how much they were willing to pay for T-shirts with different designs on them. It turns out that many scholars have conducted studies like this one. Uri looked at the distribution of responses when people were asked how much they would pay for a T-shirt and found that about 80 percent of these other studies were in *multiples of five*. Yet, if the data were *randomly* generated, only about 20 percent of the data would be in multiples of five. What Uri noticed was that this is exactly how Smeesters's data looked. Smeesters had made up his data but he tried to make it look "normal" by making it appear random. He had overcompensated.

Of course, the broad investigation into Smeesters's work hinged on much more than this, but these data were a red flag for Uri. In an effort to appear credible, he had purposefully avoided round numbers and tried to make the results look as though they were generated by real participants. Ironically, this effort made his data less likely to look like they came from real participants.

Red Flag #4: Mismatch Between Words and Body Language

As we look for flags, we also need to pay attention to the match between what people are saying and *how* they are saying it. At Jerry's trial, the jury found Seemona credible because of the match between what she said and her physical impression. As the jury forewoman, Caryn Eyring-Swick, explained, this was one of the reasons why the jury believed Seemona: "She didn't fall apart or crumble on the stand. You could see her jaw tighten. We knew that Ramrattan had done something that would affect his victims forever."

In contrast, consider the former Olympic hero Marion Jones. She won five medals at the 2000 Summer Olympics in Sydney, Australia, but was later accused of having used performance-enhancing drugs. When she called a press conference to refute the charges, she *said* she was furious. But her demeanor and vocal tone only suggested sadness. What she said did not match how she said it.

So we should look carefully when people make claims about how they are feeling. If they say they are happy, do they really look happy or do they look upset? If they say that they are enthusiastic, do they really look bored?

Finally, rather than asking yourself if someone is lying, our advice is to ask yourself the following question: Are you completely comfortable with their answer? If you have a nagging suspicion that something isn't quite right, probe further. Sometimes, outside of our conscious awareness, we have seen a red flag.

Finding the Right Balance: Trust but Verify

So we've seen that if we trust too much, our foes can exploit us. But if we trust too little, we will fail to make friends and reap cooperative rewards. To find the right balance between cooperation and competition, we need to make ourselves vulnerable, but at the same time guard against exploitation.

Ronald Reagan famously quoted the Russian saying "Trust but verify." He recognized that we need to trust people, but that we must also have some process to protect ourselves from being deceived.

Let's consider this challenge within the context of online dating. As we saw earlier, many of the claims people make online are false. If we trust the information we receive too much, we will believe that people are taller, thinner, and younger than they really are. However, if we trust too little, we might never go out on a date.

We need to strike a balance to resolve this tension. We need to rely on what we read (with a grain of salt), but we also need to collect additional information. Sometimes this involves checking out someone's social media profiles; other times it involves reaching out to a mutual acquaintance, or—in some cultures—hiring a private investigator to research a potential romantic partner.

Another way we find our balance is by following protocol. Though sometimes they can be aggravating, policies, procedures, and protocols are *designed* to raise our guard and save us from exploitation.

And what happens when we fail to follow protocol? Tragedy can strike.

After the 9/11 attacks, the CIA faced intense pressure to produce actionable intelligence on al-Qaeda. And by 2009, they had begun to gain solid, human intelligence which ultimately enabled the United States to target al-Qaeda in Pakistan. Speaking to this issue, Richard Barrett, head of the UN's al-Qaeda and Taliban monitoring group, said, "Human sources have begun to produce results."

One of their sources was a doctor named Humam Khalil Abu-Mulal al-Balawi. Al-Balawi had posted extremist views on the web, and the Jordanian intelligence agency had told al-Balawi that they would end his medical career and put him in jail for his posts unless he agreed to cooperate with the agency.

And so the Jordanians sent al-Balawi to Pakistan, where he infiltrated al-Qaeda. According to a U.S. intelligence official, "First, the guy had extremist credentials, including proven access to senior figures. Second, you had a sound liaison service that believed they'd turned him and that had been working with him since. And third, the asset supplied intelligence that was independently verified."

When al-Balawi promised to provide information that would lead to Ayman al-Zawahiri, the deputy leader of al-Qaeda, CIA officials were excited.

They arranged a face-to-face meeting with al-Balawi, and on December 30, 2009, an Afghan driver drove al-Balawi to the CIA's forward base near Khost, Afghanistan, Camp Chapman.

According to CIA protocol, he and his car should have been searched. But al-Balawi wasn't searched as he entered the base. Perhaps the CIA operatives were confident in al-Balawi, perhaps they didn't want to offend him, or perhaps it was some combination. Whatever it was, the effect was devastating. As al-Balawi stepped out of the car he detonated his explosive vest, killing seven CIA officers, a Jordanian officer, and the driver. What had just minutes earlier seemed like a promising lead turned into one of the worst single-day losses for the CIA.

In hindsight, clues had been missed. Some CIA and Jordanian intelligence officers had serious concerns about his intentions. In fact, one Jordanian official had even passed along a concern to the CIA that al-Balawi might be trying to "lure Americans into a trap."

Why were the CIA agents too trusting? Several psychological forces conspired against them. First, they were under intense pressure to produce results. Second, like so many other victims of deception, the CIA *wanted to believe* that al-Balawi had actionable information.

Finally, al-Balawi had credentials: The Jordanian service vouched for him and al-Balawi had given them enough information in the past to appear credible. The CIA trusted the credentials and put too much stock in the information they could observe.

But the key lesson we want to draw is this: To guard against exploitation, we need not only to *establish* protocols, but to follow them—even when they are inconvenient.

And finally, we must remember that deception is everywhere. From online dating profiles to criminal investigations, deception is a part of our social world. We need to appreciate and prepare for it in order to compete and cooperate more effectively.

When deception is discovered, trust is broken and relationships are shattered. When this happens, what can we do to restore trust and put the pieces of the relationship back together? We turn to that question next.

Putting the Pieces Back Together

An ER nurse was the first to notice that 18-month-old Kaelyn Sosa's chest was not moving.

Kaelyn had been cut off from oxygen while undergoing an MRI. Prior to the MRI, Kaelyn had been sedated, and a flexible tube had been inserted into her trachea to connect her to a ventilator. Somehow her breathing tube had become dislodged.

The nurse immediately raised the alarm, but help arrived slowly, too slowly it turned out. The only resuscitation equipment the nurse could find was adult-sized, and as the nurses and doctors scrambled to locate child-sized tubes and masks, Kaelyn lost precious minutes. During these minutes, Kaelyn was starved for oxygen and as a result suffered severe brain injury, particularly to the basal ganglia region, which controls movement. She was left unable to speak or walk.

Only a few hours before, the Sosa family had been preparing to celebrate New Year's Eve when Kaelyn took a fall and bumped her head while playing with her brothers. Kaelyn's mother, Sandy, rushed her daughter to Miami's Baptist Children's Hospital emergency center to have her checked over. Worried that Kaelyn might have suffered from a seizure, the medical team at the hospital ran a CT scan, followed by the fateful MRI.

For most grief-stricken parents, this kind of medical error

would motivate fury, outrage, and legal action. The hospital staff
had clearly made a huge mistake, and this mistake had caused
devastating, long-term damage. In the United States, patients
and their families file approximately 10,000 medical malpractice lawsuits every year. The Sosas could easily have been one of
them.

This competitive path, however, is not the one the Sosas took.
Though they knew that a large malpractice award was possible,
even likely, they never sued the hospital. In fact, the Sosas not
only brought Kaelyn back to Baptist Hospital for future treatment, they eventually even became *advocates* for the hospital;
Sandy became a community liaison for Baptist's Quality and Patient Safety Steering Council, and both of Kaelyn's parents participated in the production of a 15-minute educational video for
Baptist Hospital employees.

The Sosa family could have been Baptist Hospital's greatest
foe. Instead, the hospital transformed them into a remarkable
ally. How did Baptist Hospital accomplish this seemingly impossible feat? With a simple, yet highly effective act: They apologized.

Earlier in this book, we challenged the conventional wisdom
that trust is slow to build. We described how trust can be built
quickly, and we also explained how trust can be exploited. Here,
we shift perspective and take up the challenge of how to restore
trust when it is violated. We will learn the mechanics of rebuilding relationships and how we can turn even the most adversarial
of relationships into cooperative ones. Though few of us will ever
do something as consequential as disconnect a breathing tube,
all of us, at some point, will fall short of the expectations that
others have for us—as spouses, friends, and colleagues. To be
successful in our personal and professional life, we need tools to
repair these relationships. As we'll discuss, a sincere apology like
the one Baptist Hospital made to the Sosas can be a powerful
way to do so.

In the pages that follow, we identify key lessons about repairing relationships, learned from people who have done an amazing job restoring their own, as well as from those who have failed miserably. We explore when apologies work—and when they don't—and why so many of us have such a hard time with these simple words: "I'm sorry."

Why Arthur Andersen and Eliot Spitzer Never Recovered but Martha Stewart Came Roaring Back

To Arthur Andersen, his reputation was paramount. Since the founding of his accounting firm in 1916, he did everything he could to build a reputation for honesty and integrity. As legend has it, early in his career, when a railroad executive purportedly insisted that Andersen certify a flawed accounting report or lose a major client, Andersen replied that there was "not enough money in the city of Chicago" to tempt him to certify a false report. Famously, Andersen's motto was "Think straight, talk straight."

By the end of the twentieth century, Arthur Andersen had grown to become one of the dominant accounting firms in the United States. Unfortunately, as Arthur Andersen grew, the culture changed. Though Arthur Andersen himself had resisted the temptation to certify flawed statements, decades later partners at his firm did certify flawed statements. In 2002, in one of the biggest corporate bankruptcy cases in the history of the United States, Arthur Andersen surrendered its license to practice after being found guilty of shredding documents related to its accounting practices at Enron.

In 2005 the Supreme Court reversed Andersen's conviction, enabling Arthur Andersen to resume operations. However, by that time people had lost trust in the firm. Even though it was legally allowed to resume operations, Arthur Andersen collapsed.

Eliot Spitzer is another man who invested heavily in his reputation early in his career. As an attorney general, he vigorously
prosecuted a wide range of cases, from white-collar crimes to
prostitution rings. Indeed, his sterling reputation for being
tough on crime helped him become the 54th governor of the
state of New York. Just one year later, his world came crashing
down. Investigators discovered a money trail revealing that in
spite of his vigorous prosecution of prostitution, Spitzer had pa-
tronized the Emperors Club VIP prostitution service—to the
tune of at least $15,000!

By participating in the very criminal activities he had worked
so hard to prosecute, Eliot Spitzer shattered his reputation for integrity. He was exposed for being both unethical and hypocriti-
cal. He had violated the trust that the people of New York had
placed in him, and within a week of the news breaking, Spitzer
resigned from office.

Five years after leaving the governor's office, Spitzer tried to
rebuild his political career by running for the relatively obscure
office of comptroller of New York City. In an effort to win back
the trust of his constituents, Spitzer employed the same technique that Baptist Children's Hospital had employed; he apologized: "I'm hopeful there will be forgiveness, I am asking for it."
Spitzer never made it past the first round of the electoral process, losing to a relatively unknown candidate in the Democratic
primary.

Like Arthur Andersen, Eliot Spitzer was unable to rebuild the
trust he had violated even after extensive efforts to atone for
his transgressions. Why? Because he hadn't just committed an
ethical violation, he'd committed a very particular type of trust
violation: a *core* violation.

To understand trust, we need to distinguish between two types
of violations: core violations and noncore violations. Core violations are breaches of trust within the most relevant, reputational
domain. Noncore violations are breaches of trust in peripheral

domains. Core violations can be devastating to reputations. But noncore violations cause surprisingly little long-term harm. This was certainly true for Martha Stewart.

In the 1990s, Martha Stewart became a household name, building a media empire that included several bestselling books, a highly rated television show, a ubiquitous magazine, *Martha Stewart Living*, and a popular website.

Martha later became infamous for something very different: a stock trade she made on December 27, 2001. That day, Stewart sold all of her 3,928 shares of ImClone Systems stock. Of course, lots of people sell stocks every day. But this sale was different. The day after the sale, ImClone reported that the FDA had refused to review their cancer drug, Erbitux, and their stock tumbled as a result. By selling her stock a day earlier, Martha saved tens of thousands of dollars. The coincidental timing of the sale caught the eyes of investigators from the Securities and Exchange Commission. Suspecting that she had received an inside tip, investigators pointedly asked her why she decided to sell her shares. Through the course of the investigation, she insisted that she had simply been lucky, that she had not learned about the FDA review ahead of time. This denial would cost her five months in prison. In a very public trial, a jury concluded that she had lied to investigators, and Martha went to prison for perjury.

At the time of her conviction, pundits wondered what would become of Martha Stewart once she was released from prison. After all, her media and marketing empire revolved around her public image. Almost every facet of her business was branded with her name: Martha Stewart. After a very public conviction and prison sentence, could Martha Stewart, at age 63, revive her media empire?

To many people's surprise, Martha Stewart came roaring back. Less than six months after her release from prison, *The Martha Stewart Show* debuted to high ratings, and she was soon even starring in a second show, *The Apprentice: Martha Stewart.* Over the next several years, Stewart launched almost a dozen bestselling books, plastered her face on a wide range of products sold at Kmart and Macy's, and even launched a line of houses branded "Martha+KB Home" in "Martha Stewart communities." Anyone who wondered what would become of Martha Stewart had their answer. She was back in business!

After committing a violation, why did Martha succeed in winning back the public's trust when Arthur Andersen and Eliot Spitzer failed? It has to do with the nature of the violation.

People look to Martha Stewart for fashion tips, recipes, and home decorating advice. In short, people trust Martha Stewart for her style and her taste. The insider trading allegations and her misleading statements to federal investigators are serious violations, but they are *unrelated* to why people turn to and trust her.

In contrast, Arthur Andersen was trusted to certify financial records and Spitzer was trusted to support the rule of law. Arthur Andersen and Eliot Spitzer violated the very principles they were expected to uphold. Their transgressions were core violations.

Let's consider a second example of a noncore violation. Like Eliot Spitzer, David Letterman had a roaming eye. But the nature of David's trust violation is more similar to Martha's. David Letterman had affairs with women whom he worked with. In 2009, things came to a head when a CBS News producer handed David's driver an envelope marked "Privileged and Confidential." In that envelope was a screenplay containing sordid tales of David's relationships with staffers and a demand for a $2 million payment to keep his affairs secret. It seems that in developing the material he later used to blackmail David, the producer had even gotten hold of the diary of one of David's girlfriends.

How did David Letterman react to the blackmail attempt? He got out ahead of the story. He admitted to having relationships with women who worked in his office, and he used his core talent—comedy—to defuse the situation. In one segment of his

Late Show, he joked that so many women were mad at him that, "on the drive to work today, even the navigation lady wouldn't talk to me." As the scandal broke, David's ratings surged. Turned out, viewers were not the slightest bit turned off by Letterman's philandering behavior. Why? Because people turn to David Letterman for his wit and humor, not for tips on marital fidelity. Like Martha, David Letterman committed a violation of trust, but his violation was not a core violation.

So we see that relationships can be easily repaired after a non-core violation. Often, merely expressing remorse will do. But for core violations, restoring trust is much, much harder. Yet it can be done. And in some cases, if handled correctly, such violations even create an opportunity to *build* trust.

It's the Apology, Stupid

The Ritz-Carlton Hotel is renowned for its service. It's the type of place where, if you request something like a wake-up call, you can assume that the phone will ring at the appointed hour. But during Stacey Hylen's stay at the Ritz-Carlton in Tucson, the wake-up she requested never came. When she did wake up and realized how late she was, Stacey was furious! She called the front desk to complain . . . and then a funny thing happened. Her fury soon dissipated.

How did the agent at the front desk manage that? Upon learning about the mistake, the agent immediately apologized. She then offered to send breakfast to Stacey's room. Stacey had other plans and declined the breakfast. When she returned to her room later, however, she found fresh strawberries, candy, dried fruit, and a handwritten note of apology. As a result of these few small gestures, instead of turning to the Internet to lambaste the Ritz-Carlton, she became an advocate for the hotel and raved about their "5 Star Customer Service."

Consider another example of how a good apology can earn a company high marks . . . and even enhance their brand in the process. In 1989, Toyota launched the Lexus brand to serve a growing demand for high-end luxury cars. Yet, just months after the launch of this new brand in the American market, a problem arose. Lexus needed to recall the first model it had released and make repairs. This certainly was a core violation, a mistake that hit at the very heart of the relationship between the brand and its consumers—one built on the expectations of safety and reliability—and it could have had devastating consequences for Lexus.

But what Lexus did next transformed this violation into a marketing coup. They responded to the crisis aggressively. Rather than simply sending out consumer notices and making a public announcement, Lexus called every single owner—yes, individually, on the phone. Then they tried to make the repair as easy as possible; they even flew mechanics to customers if a dealership wasn't nearby. After making each repair, Lexus detailed every car and gave it a full tank of gas. Within three weeks, Lexus emerged from the crisis with an enhanced brand—Lexus was no longer just about quality, they now were also known for their customer service. As one magazine put it, Lexus's response was the "Perfect Recall."

Clearly, whether it's a missed wake-up call, a faulty car, or even a dislocated breathing tube, violating a customer's trust places the relationship at risk. In the unstable aftermath, former friends can easily become foes. But quick repair efforts can tip the balance back to friendship. Often it is the recovery effort, rather than the violation itself, that matters most. And sometimes an effective apology can actually *improve* your image and your relationships.

If these examples don't convince you, consider a study of German eBay users led by Johannes Abeler of the University of Nottingham. The authors contacted 632 eBay customers who had given feedback that was neutral or negative and asked them to remove their feedback. Along with this request, the scholars gave these customers either money or a verbal apology. Some got 2.50 euros, others got 5 euros, but some only got words: "We are sorry to discover that you were not satisfied with our service . . . and want to apologize for this."

Of the customers offered 2.50 euros, 19.3 percent removed their negative evaluations. Of those offered 5 euros, 22.9 percent removed their negative evaluations. But after an apology—without any money—*44.8 percent* of customers removed their negative ratings.

The simple words "I'm sorry" are surprisingly powerful. But how we say them and what we do as we say them can make a world of difference.

Why a Faulty Phone Antenna Elicited More Outrage than a Plane Crash

On December 8, 2005, Southwest Airlines Flight 1248 departed Baltimore and headed to Chicago Midway International Airport. Winter weather can be tough in Chicago, and on that day the pilots encountered heavy wind and blinding snow as they prepared to land.

The landing did not go well. The plane was unable to slow down and it tore past the runway. It rammed through a fence that separated the airport from the outside world. It continued to lurch into a road, plowing into cars along the way. By the time the plane had stopped, a six-year-old boy had been killed and 13 people had been injured. This was Southwest's first fatal accident in their 35-year history, and it goes without saying that it was a core violation.

Within hours, chief executive officer Gary Kelly expressed condolences:

This is a sad day for us here. There are no words to ade-
quately convey our grief and sorrow over this tragedy. It was
with great sadness that we learned of the death of a child
who was in one of the vehicles hit by the aircraft. The entire
Southwest family is grieving this loss and our thoughts and
prayers go out to the child's family.

Southwest will do everything in our power to provide information and comfort to those who have been affected . . .

And he did. Gary immediately flew with his top executives to
Chicago. He held an additional press conference in Chicago. He
expressed sympathy for each person who had been harmed and
he pledged to help those injured. He also pledged to implement
any recommended action from the subsequent investigation.

To understand the success of this apology all we need to do
is look at how the *Chicago Tribune* characterized Gary's apology:
"swift" and "caring." The impact on the airline was undetectable.
In 2006, demand for Southwest Airlines flights rose by almost 8
percent, and the airline was more profitable than ever.

To understand everything Gary did right, we contrast his actions with an apology that went badly wrong.

Apologies are hard. And even a widely acknowledged genius
can struggle to deliver an effective one. Had Steve Jobs, the CEO
of Apple, paid attention to Gary's apology or studied the results
from the German eBay study, he might have delivered a very different press conference than the one he held on July 16, 2010, to
deal with "antennagate."

As CEO of Apple, Steve Jobs launched a series of transforma-
tive products including the iMac, the iPod, iTunes, the iPhone,
and the iPad, earning Apple—and Steve Jobs—a cult-like following and a reputation for creating products that are innovative,
reliable, and fun. The value of Apple's stock rose dramatically
as a result.

Against this backdrop, the launch of the iPhone 4 was an

uncharacteristic stumble. Consistent with prior versions of the iPhone, this version had launched successfully: The iPhone 4 sold three million units in the first three weeks.

As sales continued to grow, however, early reviews of the iPhone 4 began to reveal a problem with the phone's reception. Merely touching the iPhone 4 in the wrong place, it turned out, disrupted the signal. It wasn't long before the blogosphere lit up with a firestorm of criticism.

Apple initially discounted these complaints. But then *Consumer Reports*, the publication from the independent consumer protection agency Consumers Union, delivered a damning verdict: They identified the defect as both real and something under Apple's control. Apple could no longer ignore their reception problem.

Like Ritz-Carlton and Lexus, Steve Jobs had an opportunity to set things right. After all, a sincere apology had worked for Gary Kelly after his airline had killed a young boy and for Baptist Hospital after causing brain damage to a small child. Surely an apology could mollify customer concerns about phone reception. So on July 16, 2010, Apple held a press conference to address the iPhone 4 defect: the perfect opportunity for Jobs and Apple to regain the trust and admiration of their customers and shareholders.

But a sincere apology proved too much for the mercurial Jobs. Even as he faced the press and offered to help Apple customers contend with their problem, he did so grudgingly, haughtily, and without a modicum of contrition. He even used the words "I have no apology."

Jobs offered customers a free cell phone case, but little in the way of an apology—just like the German eBay customers who were offered a small amount of compensation, but no apology. In fact, Jobs actually managed to express disrespect for Apple customers, Apple shareholders, and the media covering the story, by making light of the situation and flaunting Apple's reputation for creating great products. During the press conference, Jobs played the satirical "The iPhone Antenna Song" music video created by Jonathan Mann, which includes the lyrics: "If you don't want an iPhone 4 don't buy it. If you bought one and you don't like it, bring it back . . . but you know you won't."

Jobs later claimed to be "deeply sorry," but added, "To those investors who bought the stock and are down by five dollars, I have no apology." And then he went on to blame the media for their coverage and for "blow[ing the problem] out of proportion."

Rather than viewing the press conference as an opportunity to build cooperation, Jobs adopted a competitive stance. Apple has since continued to develop terrific technological products, but this episode represented a major stumble for an otherwise storied company.

The Apology Formula: The Key Ingredients of Successful Apologies

When we look at the stark contrast between Kelly's apology for the Southwest crash and Jobs's response to the antenna episode, it's easy to see the difference between an effective apology and an unsuccessful one. But what exactly makes an apology effective? Here are the key ingredients.

Speed: One of the most important aspects of Kelly's apology on behalf of Southwest Airlines—and what set his apology apart from every prior apology from a major airline—is how quickly he apologized. In this case, speed signaled his concern. Speed was also one of the most salient aspects of the apology Baptist Children's Hospital gave the Sosas. Rather than delay an official comment or offer vague claims about what had happened, Baptist Hospital *immediately* informed the Sosas of everything they knew about the mistakes they had made.

When you screw up, time is of the essence.

Candor: An effective apology is transparent; in other words, the perpetrator must be open and candid in disclosing what went wrong.

As the Sosas explained, Baptist's full disclosure of their mistakes was a critical step in regaining their trust. As Kaelyn's mother later explained, Baptist's candid disclosure "helped her to move past the initial shock."

Vulnerability: Earlier in the book, we emphasized the role of vulnerability in building trust. When it comes to *re*building trust, vulnerability is again a critical ingredient. Recall how Baptist Children's Hospital revealed their mistakes to the Sosas. Ironically, part of what helped Baptist avoid a lawsuit was their decision to candidly disclose their errors—which also made them vulnerable to a lawsuit.

We can even see the effect of vulnerability in rebuilding trust among primates. After fighting, some monkeys and apes will "apologize" by putting one of their fingers in the victim's mouth. This is a risky move. With powerfully set jaws, a disgruntled monkey could easily bite off the finger. This vulnerable move, however, serves a crucial purpose: It sends a powerful signal that they trust their former adversary.

Focus on the victim: Effective apologies demonstrate concern for the victim. As obvious as this statement sounds, all too often apologizers remain self-focused.

Consider the following story. One afternoon, Stephen King did what he usually did after a morning of writing: He headed out for a walk. He was strolling along the shoulder of an empty country road in Maine when he met Bryan Smith. Bryan was driving his minivan at about 45 miles per hour, but was paying closer attention to his Rottweiler rummaging through his cooler in the back than he was to the road ahead. In fact, he was so oblivious to where he was going that when he hit King, he thought he had collided with a small deer. When Bryan saw the writer's glasses that had somehow flown into his front seat, he began to realize that the situation was more serious.

It turns out that King hit the windshield so hard that he flipped over the van. Part of his scalp was torn away, he had a collapsed lung, and had broken his ribs, knee, and hip, and shattered one of his legs. King would go on to require five operations and experienced years of incredible pain.

As King recalled, while waiting with Bryan for help to arrive, Bryan turned to him and commiserated, "Ain't the two of us just had the shittiest luck." Of course, the accident was not great for Bryan, but by classifying his situation as unlucky as King's, Bryan reflected an incredible amount of self-focus. Similarly, consider the self-focused apology Tony Howard, the CEO of BP, delivered after the Deepwater Horizon oil rig explosion. When the rig exploded in 2010 it killed 11 workers and produced the largest marine oil spill of all time. A month after the explosion, Howard delivered this apology: "We're sorry for the massive disruption it's caused their lives. There's no one who wants this over more than I do. I'd like my life back." The point is, while the importance of being focused on the person to whom you are apologizing seems obvious, in the moment it is often surprisingly difficult.

Promise to change: Effective apologies also articulate a plan of action. Southwest's Kelly promised to implement any recommended action from the subsequent investigation. And following the botched MRI, Baptist Hospital instituted new procedures. For example, MRIs are now only conducted on a scheduled basis with an anesthesiologist or nurse anesthetist present. Pediatric crash carts equipped with child-sized resuscitation equipment are now readily accessible. In addition, the hospital has installed Code Purple buttons to summon help specifically for pediatric emergencies.

In our own research, we have found that a promise to change is one of the most important components of an apology. In one study, we had participants make a series of repeated monetary decisions with a partner (really a confederate of the experiment) who behaved in an initially untrustworthy way. Following the transgression, the confederate behaved in one of four ways: a) they communicated no message; b) they offered a simple apology; c) they promised to change (without an apology); or d) they offered a simple apology accompanied by a promise to change. Though the simple apology helped, it was the promise to change that had the most impact on how much trust their partner placed in them in subsequent rounds of the experiment.

The famed sociologist Erving Goffman argued that a successful apology splits the apologizer into essentially two different people: One is the individual responsible for the transgression, and the other is the individual who deserves a second chance. Following a successful apology, the second individual should be perceived to be fundamentally different from the first. When this happens, relationships can be repaired.

The promise to change is what helps split the person in two: the "old me" who committed the violation and the "new me" who is a completely different person. We see this in the Baptist Children's Hospital example. Upon seeing the changes they implemented, Kaelyn's mother remarked, "It was a whole new procedure," and her father claimed that the hospital's dedication to changing their procedures helped him forgive the hospital.

Penance: Although apologies and promises to change are surprisingly powerful, offers of penance can also make a profound difference. What do we mean by penance? Anything that involves making amends to the victim.

In many traditional cultures, gift giving is an essential part of the relationship repair process. Even if the gift is of negligible monetary value (though the costlier, the better) it is a symbolic gesture that signals contrition. From a fruit basket to free medical care for life, it pays to make amends.

But as we saw from the results of the German eBay study, it

isn't just any material offering that will do; to be successful, the penance has to send the right *signal*.

Signals are nonverbal messages that communicate information that is very difficult, or even impossible, to prove. To send a signal, we need to engage in an effortful action. When you go for an interview, you could tell the interviewer that you are really interested in working at their company. But to *signal* your interest, you would need to prepare for the interview by doing background research. Similarly, you might tell someone that you are committed to your relationship with them. But to *signal* your commitment you might pick them up from the airport or buy them a meaningful gift. It is always helpful to say the right words, but sometimes signals speak louder.

Colin Camerer at Caltech characterizes signals along two dimensions: *clarity* and *power*. Clear signals communicate a message unambiguously. Powerful signals communicate a message in a credible way.

To be powerful, a signal needs to be costly—in time, money, or some other resource. A really powerful signal is so costly that only someone truly committed could afford to make that type of investment. For example, suppose Charlie Sheen wants to signal his commitment to a new relationship. So, he goes out and buys his date a dozen red roses. In a culture that associates red roses with romance, this is a *clear signal*. Sending a dozen red roses, however, is *not* a powerful signal. Why? Charlie Sheen can easily afford to buy thousands of women a dozen red roses.

So what can someone do to send a powerful signal of their commitment to a romantic partner? We actually have a social norm to solve exactly this problem: a diamond ring. The reason a diamond ring has become the standard symbol of a lifetime commitment (in addition to aggressive marketing by the diamond industry) is the fact that it is *so* costly that no one would make the investment unless they were truly committed. If you are deeply committed, you can afford an expensive ring. If you are not deeply committed, however, a diamond ring is prohibitively expensive.

And the cost of the ring is an essential characteristic of the signal. In fact, we even have a culturally entrenched guide for how much people should spend: It is a function of one's income (three months' salary in the United States). Powerful signals need to be costly to prove that you are truly committed.

In addition to the other key actions Baptist Hospital took, Baptist Hospital offered to provide free medical care for all of Kaelyn's future needs. Kaelyn would need years of care, and this offer not only addressed a key concern for Kaelyn's family, but it was costly for the hospital, and hence a powerful signal of their remorse.

Taken together, these examples highlight the following critical insight: Trust can easily be broken. So the question isn't whether or not we'll ever commit a transgression, but when. And when we do miss the mark, we need to be prepared to respond quickly, candidly, and powerfully.

Finding the Right Balance: Be Prepared to Say You're Sorry

We have shown that apologies are critical mechanisms for repairing trust and restoring relationships. So why don't people apologize more often? Elton John was onto something when he sang "Sorry Seems to Be the Hardest Word."

One obvious barrier to apologizing is a fear of liability. But perhaps a less obvious barrier is a fear of losing status and power. By apologizing, we not only make ourselves vulnerable, which is uncomfortable and risky, but we also put ourselves in a one-down position. When we worry about our standing and our status, we are reluctant to apologize.

In fact, as Tyler Okimoto of the University of Queensland has found, people who refuse to apologize feel a greater sense of power than those who apologize. Why? By admitting we are at fault, we grant others power over us, while diminishing our own power in the process. This is related to the third reason we refuse to apologize: a reluctance to acknowledge that we have committed a violation. When we apologize, we send the message that we recognize that we were wrong. And this can be hard to admit.

Even though these admissions can be hard to make, when they are quick and candid they can help repair the relationship and get us back on a cooperative path. So we need to set up systems that help us apologize even when our first instinct is to protect ourselves and justify our actions, just as Steve Jobs did in antennagate.

Part of what made the Ritz-Carlton, Southwest Airlines, and Baptist Hospital apologies so successful is that they were *prepared* to apologize. In fact, they had even set up institutional processes to help them apologize quickly and candidly with an action plan to change.

The Ritz-Carlton, for example, empowers its employees to address potential problems by allowing them to spend up to $2,000 each day to improve and repair relationships with their customers. The message they communicate with this policy is twofold: First, we care deeply about our customer relationships, and second, each employee is empowered to repair relationships when trust is broken.

Some organizations prepare their employees by creating rules to force candid disclosure when something has gone wrong. Throughout this chapter, we have given Baptist Hospital credit for their repair efforts, but the credit should really be shared with the Baptist Health system in South Florida. Shortly before Kaelyn's accident, the Baptist Health system had instituted a policy of full disclosure following a medical error. Although Baptist had made serious mistakes that contributed to Kaelyn's brain damage, they followed the disclosure policy to the letter.

Similarly, in 2006 the University of Illinois medical center adopted a policy of full disclosure for every medical error. They even set up a special service to help staff disclose errors and apologize to families. In contrast to the four years before adopting the policy, in the four years after adopting this policy, the number of lawsuits against the University of Illinois medical center dropped by 40 percent.

Organizations may be able to set up rules and hire people to apologize. But for us as individuals, we need to create our own rules and overcome our own hurdles. When we fall short, it is easy to blame others, blame the situation, or play down the harm we might have caused. But as we've seen, excuses and denials only make repairing relationships harder. For us, as individuals, we need to create a tripwire—a rule that guides our own behavior. Here is what we propose: As soon as you start to feel defensive or begin to rationalize some action that might have caused harm, take a moment of reflection. Take a step back and consider what an apology might accomplish. Even when we *are* justified in our actions and even when we acted with the best of intentions, there are times when an apology is the right course of action. By appreciating the powerful effects that the right kind of apologies can have, we can take steps to put the pieces of our relationships back together and regain our cooperative balance.

To overcome the psychological obstacles to apologizing and help get us back on the cooperative path, we need to feel secure with ourselves and we need to understand how others around us see the world. To help us do this, we need to master the art of perspective-taking, and we turn to this challenge next.

Seeing It Their Way to Get Your Way

Humans are different from every other species on the planet. But what is it that makes us so unique? To answer this question we need a mirror and three mountains.

When you look into a mirror, what do you see? The answer—if you're human—is obvious: a reflection of yourself. This is a pretty simple idea, but it is this recognition that separates us from most other species. When we (humans) look in the mirror, we know that we are looking at ourselves, and not at some other person. But if you put a hyena in front of a mirror, the hyena would not recognize the reflection as an image of itself. Rather, it would perceive the image to be another hyena. The hyena would bare its fangs to mark its territory—and then feel threatened when the "other" hyena did the exact same thing. This might provoke a gesture of aggression, which would immediately be reciprocated. Things might escalate to the point where the hyena outside the mirror attacked the hyena inside the mirror. Don't try this at home: you'd be out a mirror, and you'd have a very confused hyena on your hands.

This mirror test measures an evolutionary milestone: the ability to recognize the self and to distinguish the self from others. Interestingly, humans are not born with self-recognition. We need to develop it. If you have a young child at home, you can test their level of self-awareness with a simple test. Just take a washable marker and surreptitiously mark their forehead. Then, place them in front of a mirror. Very young children will coo, hit the mirror, and toddle away. However, by 18 months of age, toddlers will do something else: try to wipe the marker off their forehead! By two years of age almost all human toddlers have achieved this developmental milestone: the ability to recognize that they are seeing a reflection of themselves, not another person, in the mirror.

The mere ability to pass the mirror test, however, isn't enough to distinguish us from other animals. Dolphins, for example, have passed the mirror test and demonstrated self-recognition. So we need another test—one involving three mountains—to help us truly understand what makes humans human.

In the Three Mountains test, you place a child on one side of a model of three mountains that gradually increase in size from left to right, and you place a doll on the other side. First, you ask the child to draw what the mountains look like from their perspective. Then, you ask the child to draw what the mountains look like from the *doll's perspective*.

Most four-year-olds will get the task wrong—when drawing what the mountains looks like from the doll's perspective, they will (incorrectly) draw a mountain range exactly as they see it, increasing in size from left to right. It is only around the age of five that kids start to realize that the scene should be flipped to capture the doll's vantage point. Eventually, children come to understand that they need to draw the mountain range from how things look from the *doll's* perspective.

To see the world from another's perspective is a magnificent ability. It's a skill that can help us learn from each other, create new ideas, and solve disputes; it is social glue that binds us together. Sometimes, however, perspective-taking can fan the flames of conflict; it can be like pouring gasoline on a fire of animosity. One of our key challenges is figuring out when perspective-taking helps us and when it hurts. And when it helps, we need to figure out how to put this uniquely human ability to use.

We will show how to use perspective-taking to help you in a host of situations, from securing a promotion, to starting a successful business, to avoiding being called a racist. And we will help you become a better perspective-taker, so you can use this powerful ability more effectively to become both a better friend and a more formidable foe.

Getting Inside Their Head
to Get a Better Deal

Imagine that you were the bank teller in the following real, high-stakes situation. A man walks into your bank. He has no visible weapon, but says he has a bomb in his backpack and he wants $2,000. What would you do?

Most people offer the following answer: Give him the money! This is the cooperative (and arguably much safer) approach. Others offer a different answer: Sound an alarm and try to tackle him to the ground. This is the competitive (and risky) approach.

On the surface these would seem to be the only two options. Yet in 2010, one bank manager who found herself in this situation tried a third approach. She asked the man, "Why do you need the $2,000?" The bomber, Mark Smith, explained that he needed the money to help his friend pay rent. The bank manager then suggested that he apply for a loan to help his friend. She went to get the paperwork and while doing so also surreptitiously called the police. As Lt. Darren Thompson explained, "[she] kept the man calm and distracted him with some paperwork until we arrived." By asking "why?" she gained insight into Mark's perspective, and this insight helped her identify a creative solution.

The point is that simply seeking another's perspective by asking "why" can help defuse even the most volatile of situations. Indeed, we found this to be true in studies we conducted with Will Maddux of INSEAD. In one study, we simulated a negotiation over the purchase of a restaurant. Some of the buyers spent time considering the seller's perspective before the negotiation. Specifically, we asked them to "try to understand what they are thinking; what their interests and purposes are in selling their restaurant." We found that buyers who were led to take the seller's perspective were more likely to construct a creative deal. Simply urging negotiators to think about the other side's interests prompted them to ask more critical "why" and "what" questions, which led to innovative solutions that met both parties' needs.

To succeed in a negotiation, it helps to understand where the other party is coming from. Interestingly, as it turns out, empathy—actually *feeling* the other person's emotions—is less effective in a negotiation than is perspective-taking. Why? Because empathy tips the balance too far in the direction of accommodation and acquiescence. When people feel too much empathy, they make deep concessions and cooperate even when they're likely to be exploited.

To be successful, we need to appreciate the needs of the others . . . and at the same time we need to advance our own interests and concerns. Indeed, our research has found that perspective-takers both expand the pie *and* secure additional resources for themselves. That is, perspective-takers get a better deal—and they manage to do this without making their counterpart worse off! Empathizers, it turns out, often just lose.

Consider the power of perspective-taking in the presidential campaign of Theodore Roosevelt. In 1912, as Election Day approached and the campaign was coming to a close, Roosevelt decided to make one last campaign push with a train trip across the country. At each stop, Roosevelt's campaign planned to pass out pamphlets with a photograph of Roosevelt looking rugged and in charge. His campaign found the perfect photo and they printed nearly three million pamphlets. But just before they embarked on their trip, a campaign worker noticed that the photograph on the pamphlet had a copyright: Moffett Studios, Chicago. The campaign had failed to secure the copyright and faced a potential copyright fee of $1 per pamphlet. In 2015, this would equal more than $73 million. What would you do in this situation?

The two obvious solutions were to pay up or tear up the pamphlets. But Roosevelt's campaign chose neither of these options. Instead, his campaign manager considered Moffett's perspective. By doing so, he recognized two critical things. First, he recognized that Moffett did not know that the Roosevelt campaign had already printed the pamphlets. Second, he recognized that Moffett might benefit from this great publicity. Armed with these insights, the Roosevelt campaign cabled Moffett and simply stated, "We are planning to distribute millions of pamphlets with Roosevelt's picture on the cover. It will be great publicity for the studio whose photograph we use. How much will you pay us to use yours?" Moffett responded, "We have never done this before. But under the circumstances, we'd be pleased to offer you $250." And the deal was done. Perspective-taking transformed a potentially devastating liability into a small profit.

One way to achieve perspective-taking is by consciously choosing to actively get inside the head of another person. But sometimes, perspective-taking is simply triggered by a few subtle movements by the person on the other side of the table.

The Art of the Mimic

You have probably seen couples who look eerily alike. It sounds a lot like an old wives' tale, but in fact, research has shown that couples *do* look more alike than two randomly chosen people. Now this could occur because two people select a partner with similar physical characteristics. That's actually why dogs often look like their owners. People choose, often unconsciously, dogs that reflect their own features; for example, one study found that women with long hair covering their ears prefer dogs with longer, lopped ears such as a spaniel or beagle, whereas women with visible ears prefer dogs with visibly perked-up ears such as a Siberian husky or basenji.

But human couples actually *grow* to look more alike over time. Robert Zajonc of Stanford University took photographs of couples when they were first married and again after they had been married for 25 years. After showing the two sets of photos to objective third-party observers, he found that the couples were judged to look more similar 25 years after being married than when they were first married.

What's going on here?

Couples grow more physically similar over time because of something called facial and bodily mimicry. Years of subconsciously mimicking the expressions of our spouses actually produce changes in the movement of facial muscles that can permanently alter the physical features of our face.

But why do husbands and wives mimic each other's facial expressions in the first place? Because mimicry facilitates perspective-taking: It helps us truly understand what another person is experiencing. And as a result, married couples with a greater capacity to mimic each other's facial expressions form stronger bonds. It is why couples that become physically similar over time report more joy in their marriage.

Mimicry also explains why Botox can make us beautiful but ultimately lonely. One way that we understand what another person is experiencing is by subtly and unconsciously mimicking their expressions. David Neal of USC devised a clever experiment to demonstrate this by having some participants receive

Botox injections while others received Restylane injections. Both are designed to reduce wrinkles. But there's a key difference between the two: Botox paralyzes expressive muscles, whereas Restylane is simply a dermal filler that does not alter muscle functions. Because Botox injections impair facial mimicry, they actually reduce the ability to accurately detect others' emotions.

Not only does mimicry lead to more effective perspective-taking; perspective-taking also increases mimicry. Tanya Chartrand of Duke University found that skilled perspective-takers are particularly artful at mirroring others. She measured perspective-taking ability by asking people how much they tried to get inside the head of others in general. Then she had two people work on a task together. She found that people high in perspective-taking were more likely to match the posture of their partners and more likely to engage in the same behavioral movements. So if one person rubbed their face or tapped their foot, those who were high in perspective-taking tended to engage in those same behaviors themselves.

People like being mimicked . . . as long as it is subtle of course. When Tanya Chartrand had a research assistant mirror the behavioral mannerisms of participants as they worked on a task together, she found that when participants had their mannerisms subtly mirrored—for example, if the participant crossed their legs, so did the assistant—they liked the assistant more and felt that their interaction went more smoothly. And Jeffrey Sanchez-Burks of the University of Michigan found that when people were mimicked during a work-related interview, they became less anxious and their performance improved.

Because mimickers seem cooperative, they engender greater trust and cooperation, and this in turn enables them to secure more resources. Consider a negotiation. In research we conducted with Will Maddux of INSEAD, we found that when one negotiator physically mimicked the other, they secured more profitable deals.

So how can we put mimicry into practice? This is how we instructed our students in the negotiation study we just described.

> We want you to mimic the mannerisms of your negotiation
> partner. For example, when the other person rubs his/her
> face, you should too. If he/she leans back or leans forward
> in the chair, you should too. However, *it is very important that*
> *you mimic subtly enough that the other person does not notice what*
> *you are doing.* Also, do not direct too much of your attention
> to the mimicking so you don't lose focus on the outcome of
> the negotiation.

And it's not just body mimicry that yields these benefits; we also benefit from mimicking others with our words. This certainly works for waitresses; in one study, waitresses instructed to verbally mimic their customers received 100 percent more in tips! In another study, Roderick Swaab of INSEAD told some negotiators to mimic their opponent during an e-mail negotiation: "When the other person uses emoticons in their message like :-) you should too. If he/she uses certain jargon, metaphors, grammar, specific words, or abbreviations such as 'y'know [you know],' you should do the same." In both Thailand and the United States, mimickers secured more profitable agreements in their negotiations.

Even on the presidential stage mimicry can come in handy. Along with Daniel Romero of the University of Michigan, we analyzed the transcripts of all U.S. presidential debates between 1976 and 2012 and found that the presidential candidates who matched their opponent's linguistic style increased their standing in the polls. Mimicry helped them seem smooth and in touch.

By appreciating the link between perspective-taking and trust, we can understand why mimicry helps us both cooperate and compete more effectively. It helps us understand another person's perspective, create trust, and produce smooth interactions. Mimicry can lead to a competitive advantage while making us appear more cooperative as well.

Perspective-taking not only makes us a better mimic, it can also help us become a more successful entrepreneur.

Leaping Without Looking

Should I start a new business? Is now the time to open up that restaurant or launch that new software company I have always dreamed of?

When we make these life-altering decisions, we can't do it in a vacuum; we need to consider the competitive landscape. Part of this involves assessing our own capabilities. Most of us do a great job of asking questions about ourselves: What are *my* skills, what are *my* strengths, what are *my* weaknesses?

Someone starting a restaurant, for example, might focus on their culinary talents and their unique specialties. "Everyone loves my chicken alfredo!" However, when we focus only on ourselves, it's easy to make the leap from "I make good chicken alfredo" to "I can make chicken alfredo that people will pay for" to "I can definitely run a restaurant."

But questions about our own talents are only one small part of the equation. Unfortunately, the second two pieces of the puzzle often receive too little attention from budding entrepreneurs. When Don Moore of UC, Berkeley, analyzed the reasons entrepreneurs gave for starting a new business, he found that most were focused on factors that had to do with themselves or their ventures, like their personal capabilities or the high quality of their product. But what they rarely mentioned were external factors like supply (their competitors) and demand (the base of customers in the market).

In other words, these entrepreneurs failed to take the perspectives of both their customers and their competitors. This lack of perspective-taking helps to explain why so many businesses fail; in one analysis, *80 percent* of entrepreneurs failed within the first 18 months of starting a new business!

Only when we look at the situation from our customer's point of view can we start asking the right questions. How many people actually like and would *buy* chicken alfredo in general? And why would customers choose *our* chicken alfredo over a competitor's?

This perspective-taking problem is so common that it has its own name: competition neglect.

How important is competition neglect? Well, if you understand it deeply enough, it could help you become an Olympic contender. It did for Eddie the Eagle (formerly known as Michael Edwards). When we think of Olympians, we often think of sculpted athletes who have committed to grueling training regimens from young ages. But this was not Eddie. He wore thick glasses, was a bit chubby, and had little athletic training. Still, in 1988, Eddie captivated worldwide audiences when he became the first athlete ever to receive a specific, individual mention during the closing speech of the Games. When the Olympic president mentioned Eddie in his remarks, "at this Olympic Games some competitors have won gold and some have broken records, and one has even flown like an eagle," thousands in the crowd started to chant his name.

How did Eddie earn a spot in the 1988 Winter Olympics and capture the attention of the world?

He considered *relative* demand and entered a weak market. Eddie knew that competition for spots on the swimming, gymnastics, or figure skating teams would be brutal. So he skipped those sports. Instead, Eddie tried out for the British ski jumping team.

Prior to 1998, Britain had never had an Olympic ski jumping team. In fact, there wasn't even a ski jumping facility in the entire country. When Eddie tried out for the team, he had zero competitors!

As you might imagine, Eddie didn't win gold, silver, or bronze. But thanks to a clever understanding of relative demand, Eddie became an Olympian and competed on the grandest of stages.

Now let's think about how a seller might profit from understanding relative demand. Consider a question every auction seller faces: When should you end your auction? You might think it makes sense to end your auction when demand is at its highest peak. Data show that demand on eBay is highest between 5:00 p.m. and 9:00 p.m. PST. So most sellers end their auction during this "happy hour," when absolute demand is highest.

But these sellers are making a mistake. Uri Simonsohn of the Wharton School found that profits were *lower* when demand was highest. How can this be? The problem is that every seller crowds into this time period, and as a result, competition is fierce.

You don't want to end your auction when demand is highest— in absolute terms. You want to end your auction when *relative* demand is greatest. And when is that? On eBay it turns out to be 2:00 a.m.! Although there are far fewer buyers online at 2:00 a.m. than there are at 8:00 p.m., there are also far, far fewer auctions that end at this time. As a result, every auction that ends at 2:00 a.m. captures greater attention than auctions that end at 8:00 p.m.

We can see that understanding relative demand and asking questions that reveal the perspective of our competitors can help us decide which competitions to enter. In the next section, we'll talk about how asking the right questions can help us more broadly—to resolve disputes, move up the corporate ladder, and even climb out of debt.

How Asking for Advice Can Free You from Debt

Surgery is never fun. But imagine waking up a few days after surgery to find that, on top of everything else, you have been hit with an $18,000 bill.

That is what happened to one of our colleague's former students. The day before a major surgery, Karen's surgeon called and asked if she would agree to have her surgery at a different surgical center. Karen decided to cooperate: "Sure, why not, if it helps you out." A few days after the surgery, as the painkillers began to wear off, she learned that she had been billed $18,000. Although the doctor's portion of the bill had been covered under her insurance, the surgery center fees had not.

After receiving a bill like this, what would you do?

Many of us would have taken the competitive approach and flown into a rage at this outrageous bill. But Karen tried out a different strategy: Instead of blaming the surgeon's office, she called the office and asked to speak with a nurse. But instead of yelling or arguing, Karen simply asked the nurse for advice.

And a remarkable thing happened. The nurse not only helped Karen navigate the red tape of the surgical center, but even intervened and secured a complete waiver of the entire bill! In the end, Karen didn't owe a penny. Asking for advice turned the nurse from a potential foe into not just a friend but an advocate.

Asking for advice doesn't just turn adversaries into advocates. It can also help you supercharge your advocates and lead them to help you climb up the corporate ladder.

To get ahead professionally, we need to broadcast our accomplishments and talents. But there is a problem: Self-promotion doesn't always work very well; self-promoters just aren't very likable. Thus we face a self-promotion conundrum: We need to advertise our accomplishments, but when we do it we are not well liked.

How can we solve this problem?

Consider Peter, a young associate in a law firm with aspirations of partnership (the context of this example has been changed to preserve anonymity). He was invited to give a talk by an important legal society based on a law review article he had written. Naturally, Peter was flattered. But he knew that in order to prepare the best talk possible, he needed some additional support.

So Peter approached a senior partner, Jennifer, who had previously presented to this society. And he simply asked her for advice: "I was just asked to give a talk at the Law Society and I would love to get your advice on the best way to frame my arguments for this audience. I know you have spoken to this society before and I am sure you have some great insights on what would work best."

The simple act of asking his higher-status colleague for advice yielded a number of benefits. First, she was flattered by the request and impressed by Peter's humility; she took it as an implicit endorsement of her opinions and expertise. As a result, she liked Peter more. Second, it inspired her to spread the news of Peter's prestigious invitation to all of the other partners. For the next week, other partners would stop by Peter's office to say "way to go" and "congrats." They were all thrilled that one of their own rising stars had been selected by this illustrious society. Third, it made Jennifer more than happy to work closely with Peter to make his talk a spectacular success.

Seeking advice and another's perspective can lead to long-term benefits because it invokes commitment. Jennifer's advice represented an investment in Peter. As a result of this investment, Jennifer became more committed to his future success. This is similar to numerous studies that show that asking for a small investment at one point can help you secure a larger investment later on. Asking for a little bit of advice now will make people feel committed to your success and they'll be more likely to offer you more advice and more help later.

Asking for advice is a particularly effective mechanism to get other people to take *your* perspective as well. As our research with Katie Liljenquist of Brigham Young University's Marriott School has shown, when we ask others for advice, they put themselves in our shoes and look at the world from our vantage point. Thus, just like Jennifer, they are more willing to help us.

Although we have shown that asking for others' counsel provides strategic benefits, people are often reticent to seek it. In a project led by Alison Brooks at Harvard, we found that people fear that by asking for advice, they will appear less competent. But this is a perspective-taking failure: When we ask for advice, as long as the request is not completely obvious, we appear to be *more* competent. After all, we have just flattered someone by seeking *their* advice.

We always get asked this question: What should you do when you ask someone for advice but don't end up taking that advice? Won't the person be offended? Not if you frame it correctly. You simply need to explain that although you didn't take their advice, it was their insight that helped you think about your situation in a different light, and that their unique perspective turned out to be essential for your success. This strategy also leads to a broader insight: Follow up with *every one* of your advice givers and let them know how much their insights have helped.

Because asking for advice signals respect, it is a strategy that works equally well up and down the hierarchy. It clearly works up the hierarchy because it shows deference and respect. But asking advice of someone *below* you on the hierarchical ladder—like when the boss asks a subordinate for their opinion—can have a powerful effect as well. The person below you in the hierarchy will be delighted to be acknowledged for their opinions and thrilled to have their expertise acknowledged. And often, as we discussed earlier in our exploration of hierarchy, someone on a different rung of the corporate ladder can offer a fresh perspective on a problem or situation.

Asking those with less power for help is an effective way to empower others and make them feel valued. To understand how important this is, let's turn our attention to what happens when the powerful *don't* consider the perspective of the less powerful.

Amplified Sounds and Soothing Jangled Nerves

On February 17, 2014, a plane traveling from Denver to Montana suddenly and without warning dropped nearly 1,000 feet in 12 seconds. That is the equivalent of jumping off the Chrysler Building in New York. A woman flew up from her seat so forcefully that she cracked the ceiling with her head. A mother's infant flew back two rows, thankfully uninjured. A flight attendant was knocked unconscious and remained so when the plane landed.

Despite the severity of the turbulence and the free fall, nobody in the cockpit ever addressed the passengers. Not a word . . . only silence. This is how one passenger described how terrifying this silence was and why he desperately wanted communication, any communication, from those in charge:

> The lack of information from the cockpit, and the increasing realization of how severe the incident with the turbulence had been, coupled with the progressively shaky landing, caused my fear to spike. My mind began to try to fill the information void, and I searched for an explanation for what might be wrong. I imagined that perhaps the pilot had been injured during the turbulence and that the less experienced assistant was handling the landing. I wondered if the wings, or perhaps the engines, had been damaged by the violent shaking of the plane . . . I raced to understand what was going on . . . The point is, without any communication from the cockpit I felt unsafe, and [I] was left to search for possible answers to fears that would have and should have been allayed by the pilots.

That is what happens when leaders don't communicate—our fears run rampant and we fill our heads with worst-case scenarios.

There are three mistakes that leaders and the powerful make when they communicate. Each of these can easily be corrected through perspective-taking.

The first mistake is too little communication. We just saw this error with the pilots. Had the pilots considered the perspective of their scared and worried passengers, they would have realized that even a short message would have been dramatically reassuring.

The second mistake is not appreciating that the words of the powerful, even the most innocuous phrases, are infused with portentous meaning. It is easy to forget how seemingly cryptic statements can be particularly unsettling for those in a subordinate position. To the less powerful, seemingly straightforward requests can produce unchecked worry.

Take the simple request of a boss asking to meet with a subordinate later in the day. Back in the early 2000s, Adam was an assistant professor at Northwestern University—that meant that he had power and authority over grad students but was subordinate to the chair of the department. One morning he walked by a grad student, Gail, and said, "I need to talk with you about something this afternoon. Can you come by at 3:00 p.m.?" Later that afternoon, Gail approached Adam's office with great trepidation. He asked Gail something so trivial and so minor that he can't remember what it was. She then said, "Never do that to me again!" "Do what??" "Scare the hell out of me by saying you needed to talk to me this afternoon. I spent the whole day obsessing about whether I was in trouble." Now we might chalk this up to Gail being particularly neurotic, but the very next day, Adam got an e-mail from the chair of his department asking him to come by and see her later in the day. Adam was racked with worry and consumed with fear he had done something wrong . . . until he met with her and learned that the topic was trivial.

There is any easy solution to this problem: Communicate your motives so as not to activate unnecessary worry in those who have less power. Whenever you need to talk to someone with less power than yourself, explain the topic along with the request so they don't worry. Or, if it is too complicated to explain, at least put their fears to rest: "I need to see you later today, but don't worry, it is nothing bad."

The third error is that leaders forget the powerful boom of their voice and words. As we rise in power, even our smallest gestures can have big consequences. Some call this the "Executive Amplification effect": The softest gestures of executives get amplified and become loud, blaring, all-caps messages. A quick thank-you becomes GRATITUDE. Constructive feedback becomes CRITICISM.

By taking a moment to think about how your words might affect your subordinates, you will communicate more often and more effectively. And in the process, their worry and fear will float away like gossamer.

We have discussed how perspective-taking can help people connect to others and give others a stake in our own success. Forging these connections is particularly difficult, however, when interacting with people from different races and backgrounds. Perspective-taking can help here, too.

How to Avoid Being a Racist

Nobody wants to be called a racist. It's distressing, and for those with public personalities, it can kill their career. The irony is that sometimes, the more unprejudiced we *try* to appear, the more we sound like a racist.

Consider the mortifying experience of entertainment reporter Sam Rubin in an interview with Samuel L. Jackson about his upcoming film *RoboCop*. As the interview started, Rubin asked Samuel Jackson about his Super Bowl commercial.

SAM RUBIN: Working for Marvel, the Super Bowl commercial, did you get a lot of reaction to that Super Bowl commercial?

SAMUEL L. JACKSON: What Super Bowl commercial?

SAM RUBIN: Oh, you know what? I've been—my mistake. I, you know what—

SAMUEL L. JACKSON: I'M NOT LAURENCE FISHBURNE.

SAM RUBIN: That's my fault. I know that. That was my fault. Uh, my mistake. You know what—

SAMUEL L. JACKSON: WE DON'T ALL LOOK ALIKE. We may all be black and famous, but we don't all look alike.

Ironically enough, Samuel L. Jackson *was* in a Super Bowl commercial—for the movie *The Avengers*. But that wasn't the point. As Rubin said later, "I immediately felt so dumb, I didn't bring that up." Jackson had essentially accused Rubin of being a racist, and Rubin felt so mortified that he became paralyzed and was unable to defend himself.

Sam Rubin's fear of being seen as racist was well placed. He knew what had happened to southern TV chef Paula Deen when accusations that she was a racist surfaced. When Deen formally admitted in the course of a lawsuit that she had used racial epithets, her admission cost her multiple endorsements and her popular show on the Food Network. The original lawsuit was dismissed, but not before Deen was humiliated and her career had been derailed. A year later, Deen said, "I feel like 'embattled' or 'disgraced' will always follow my name."

Even those of us without a nationally broadcast television show will expend great effort to avoid being labeled a racist. Michael Norton of Harvard University has shown the lengths that people will go to to avoid using race when they describe another person. To study this, he created an experiment called the Political Correctness Game. You can play it yourself here: http://blogs.hbr .org/2013/07/the-two-minute-game-that-reveals-how-people -perceive-you/.

Mike's game was a variant of the childhood game Guess Who. Here's how it worked. One of the two players would pick a card from a deck, turn it over, and see a photograph of a face. Then, the partner had to figure out which face, out of an array of faces, their partner had picked. The partner could ask questions to narrow down the options, but they all had to be yes or no questions. Half the photographs were of white individuals and half were of black individuals. Even though race was an easy and obvious descriptor that would have efficiently helped participants to identify the target person, few participants asked whether the person was white or black, and this was especially true if their game partner was black. Indeed, almost half of the participants refused to ever mention race in any of their questions.

This strategy of avoiding any mention of race not only hurts your performance in the Political Correctness Game, it defeats its intended purpose, as Evan Apfelbaum of MIT's Sloan School of Management has found. The more someone tries to be color-blind and ignore race, the *more* they come across as racist.

And it's not just trying to avoid *saying* certain words that makes things worse. Actively trying to banish negative thoughts from our minds—a simple and intuitively appealing strategy known as suppression—is also counterproductive.

To understand this, try the following task: Do not think about a white bear.

Okay, what happened? If you're like most people, the second you are told *not* to think about a white bear, all you can do is think about a white bear. After all, in order *not* to think about a white bear you have to think about a white bear, at least somewhere in your mind. And you have to be on the lookout for any reference to white bears; thus, you become hypersensitive to white-bear references. And not only that but suppressing thoughts about white bears is exhausting.

As you might imagine, the same principle applies when we try not to think about race. When we try to suppress any thoughts about race, we actually think more about race. So suppression only increases attention to stereotypes.

Our research shows that perspective-taking offers a way out of this conundrum. Consider a simple experiment we did with Gordon Moskowitz of Lehigh University. We showed undergraduates a photograph and asked them to write about a day in the life of the person in the photograph. In one version of the experiment the photograph was of a black man. Some of the participants were asked to suppress any stereotypes they might have of that person. Others were told to take the perspective of the person and go through the day as if they *were* that person, looking at the world through his eyes. Participants then wrote their essays. Later, participants engaged in a task that was designed to surreptitiously measure racial bias. The perspective-takers exhibited less racial bias than did those who had been asked to suppress thoughts of race.

Suppressors also make *others* feel uncomfortable. In contrast, perspective-takers put others, even interracial others, at ease. In a study we did with Andrew Todd of the University of Iowa, we used the same paradigm as above, but instead of measuring racial bias with a computer, participants were interviewed by a black woman who asked them questions about their experiences on campus. Black interviewers rated their interactions with perspective-takers as more comfortable and more enjoyable than their interactions with control participants. And our videotapes confirmed why: Perspective-takers smiled more, made more eye contact, and leaned forward more. While perspective-takers sat closer and with more immediacy, suppressors sat further and further away.

These effects are not just limited to the lab; they also occur in the doctor's office and the workplace. Going to a doctor is anxiety producing. This is especially true when the doctor is white and the patient is black. But what if we turned doctors into better perspective-takers?

In research we conducted with Jim Blatt of George Washington University, we did just that. For some medical students we asked them to "put themselves in the shoes" of their upcoming patients. To get them in a perspective-taking frame of mind, we also asked them to recall a recent interaction and to put themselves in the shoes of the other individual and reflect on what that person was thinking or feeling.

Here is what we found: Patient satisfaction was higher following interactions with clinicians who had been given our simple perspective-taking prompt. And importantly, this effect occurred for both white and black patients.

So, instead of trying to pretend that racial differences don't exist, we should try to learn about others' experiences. Perspective-taking is a much better strategy for connecting to diverse others, reducing anxiety during interracial interactions, and preventing stereotypes from dominating our thoughts. Suppression makes us look like a racist. Perspective-taking makes us appear engaged and present.

Finding the Right Balance: How to Make Sure Glue Doesn't Become Gasoline

What is the key to a happy marriage? It may not surprise you at this point to learn that perspective-taking is a key predictor of a strong marriage.

But it might surprise you to learn that perspective-taking can also increase the propensity for divorce! How can the same ability lead to such divergent outcomes?

Perspective-taking is often the glue that binds spouses together. Perspective-taking enables us to connect with our spouse by anticipating the other's wants and needs—sometimes even before they do. But when spouses begin to compete, perspective-taking can do far more harm than good. Why? When we put ourselves in the shoes of a foe, we consider how they can harm us and imagine all the devious chicanery they might be plotting against us, and we pivot into a mode of paranoid self-protection.

Consider two spouses locked in a serious argument, or even a divorce battle. Taking the perspective of an estranged spouse leads you to imagine the duplicitous, scheming, and underhanded activities they may be plotting against you. So you preemptively beat them to the punch by engaging in these very activities yourself.

In hypercompetitive contexts like divorce, imagining what the other person is thinking can act like gasoline poured onto a roaring fire of suspicion. In these cases, perspective-taking perverts the Golden Rule from "Do unto others as you would have them do unto you" to "Do unto others as you *think* they will do unto you."

Our research has shown that even when two people don't know each other very well, perspective-taking can bring these individuals closer together by facilitating communication, increasing cooperation, and reducing prejudice. But for perfect strangers, just as in couples, when competitive feelings escalate, adding perspective-taking to the mix only intensifies the competition. When resources are scarce, perspective-taking promotes selfish behavior. And when we perceive someone to have transgressed against us, we can be driven to greater retaliation.

Consider an experiment we ran with Jason Pierce of Universidad Adolfo Ibañez. We asked MBA students to think about a negotiation in which their counterpart was either a fierce rival or a collaborative partner. We had half of the participants take the perspective of their rival; the other half were given no additional instructions. We then asked them about the lengths they would go to to come out ahead in an upcoming negotiation. When people actively tried to get inside the head of their heated rival, it *increased* their own use of unethical negotiation strategies. It accelerated and inflamed their competitive impulses and incited these negotiators to protect themselves from the potential deviousness of their competitor. They fought *anticipated* fire with greater fire.

Earlier, we said that perspective-taking was more effective than empathy in producing efficient and beneficial negotiation outcomes. However, perspective-taking without *any* empathy is dangerous. Take bullies: They are great at appreciating someone's vulnerabilities . . . and taking advantage of them.

These effects of perspective-taking also apply to the thorny question of whether we should meet our foes face-to-face or not. It's generally believed that face-to-face meetings are the key to establishing rapport and incipient feelings of trust. As we wrote earlier in our discussion of trust, face-to-face meetings can be the glue that binds people together. But in overly competitive situations, face-to-face meetings can cause conflict to erupt into full-scale animosity.

President Jimmy Carter came to appreciate this dynamic back in 1978. When trying to broker a peace treaty between Egypt and Israel, Carter brought President Anwar El Sadat of Egypt and Prime Minister Menachem Begin of Israel to Camp David. After days of face-to-face negotiations, President Carter was confronted with increasing suspicion. His hope of a landmark peace treaty was on the verge of collapse as he found himself caught between two feuding adversaries. "It was mean," he told his wife. "They were brutal with each other, personal."

President Carter then made a dramatic decision: He temporarily cut off face-to-face contact with these adversaries and met with each leader individually. He shuttled back and forth, receiving offers and counteroffers, while preventing direct interaction between the two leaders. The physical distance calmed their competitive impulses. The result was a groundbreaking peace treaty, one that would earn Carter the Nobel Peace Prize. Ironically, what allowed them to come together in their famous handshake photo was actually being physically apart during the negotiation.

We have shown that face-to-face communication can lubricate the wheels of cooperation, but other times, it can fan the flames of competition. So how do we know when to meet face-to-face or to keep our distance?

Along with Roderick Swaab of INSEAD we conducted a large-scale quantitative analysis of over 100 negotiation and group decision-making studies to answer that very question. We found that the key factor that determines whether it is better to be face-to-face or far apart is where people are on the friend-foe continuum. When people are unsure of whether to compete or cooperate, meeting face-to-face creates rapport that guides the interaction into cooperative territory. Closer contact helps smooth the cogs of social interaction and enables trust to develop.

But if two individuals already feel great animosity toward each other, the ability to see and hear each other inflames competitive feelings. In this case, the ability to see your partner decreases the likelihood of reaching a settlement.

The dilemma of whether to meet face-to-face is just one of many questions we need to answer when placed in the one situation that requires the utmost balance between competition and cooperation: a negotiation. Next, we discuss when it's best to compete and when it's best to cooperate to get the most out of any negotiation.

When to Start Your Engines

Nobody expected Alvin Greene to win. After all, no African American had ever won a Senate Democratic or Republican primary in South Carolina. Yet in 2010, Alvin Greene made history when he not only beat his opponent in the Democratic primary, but routed him with a shocking 18 percent point margin.

What made his victory all the more surprising was the fact that Alvin was essentially a ghost candidate. He had not evidenced any signs of having even waged a campaign. Alvin had no advertising, no staff, and no money. In fact, at the time of the election, he was reportedly living with his father and had no cell phone or computer.

Yet Alvin had one major political advantage over his more experienced and accomplished opponent, Vic Rawl: the first letter of his last name. The order on the ballot was determined alphabetically by last name, and strange as it might seem, this may have made all the difference. As we'll explore in the pages ahead, research shows that political fortunes can rise and fall simply by where you are placed on a ballot.

In fact, research shows that subtle factors like going first or last can affect how you fare in a variety of competitive realms.

So in this chapter we explore the mechanics of when and how to begin a competition. We explain when, as in Alvin Greene's case, it's good to be first. But we will also see that sometimes—from figure skating to job interviews—it can be better to be last. And we also tackle the related and vexing question of whether or not—and how—you should make the first offer in a negotiation. We will help you develop a framework for understanding the different types of competition. And we will offer concrete tools that will allow you to navigate any competitive situation more effectively.

From Political Ballots to Parole Hearings: When It's Good to Be First

Let's examine why Alvin Greene's placement atop the ballot order made such a difference in his political fortunes. To understand the role of the name order effect on election results, Jon Krosnick of Stanford University analyzed a naturally occurring field experiment in Ohio. Why Ohio? Because, in the Buckeye State, the placement of names on ballots is randomly rotated, precinct by precinct. With these data, Jon could compare how many votes candidates received as a function of their rank on the ballot. Here is what he found: The first candidate listed almost always had an advantage.

As you might expect, the ballot order effect is strongest among unfamiliar candidates like Alvin—if we have no other information to go on, we're more likely to make our decision based on ballot order. But what about in a presidential election, where candidates spend millions of dollars mailing materials, running advertisements, making public appearances, and carefully crafting platform-thematic messages. Shouldn't the familiarity of presidential candidates overwhelm any ballot order effects?

Not entirely. Consider the 2000 presidential election. When

Jon Krosnick looked at the order effect in three states that rotated candidate names (California, North Dakota, and Ohio),
being listed first always led to an advantage. Though only two
candidates, George W. Bush and Al Gore, captured more than
96 percent of the vote, there were actually seven candidates on
the ballot. In California, Bush received 9.4 percent *more* votes
when he was listed first versus last. And in North Dakota and
Ohio, Bush received about 1 percent more votes when he was first
versus last. That may not seem like much, but it corresponded to
thousands of votes.

As you might recall, in 2000, the outcome of the presidential
election in the United States came down to just a few hundred
votes cast in one state, Florida, where Bush received 2,912,790
votes to Gore's 2,912,253 votes. In other words, Bush beat Gore
by 537 votes, less than $\frac{1}{100}$th of a percent of the votes cast.

What was the ballot order in Florida? Bush was listed first on
every ballot. (You might be wondering how a candidate's position on the ballot is determined in Florida. In Florida, the governor gets to decide the order; in this case, the governor was
Jeb Bush, George W. Bush's brother.) Based on this research,
had the ballot order been rotated in Florida, the outcome of the
presidential election would likely have been quite different.

Is voting behavior really that capricious? And why, exactly,
would ballot order matter? Because although we typically make
choices that reflect our preferences, when we are "on the fence"
we look for any shortcut or signal, however arbitrary, to help us
make our decision. In these cases, we are sensitive to any indi-
cation that one candidate is better than another. We use ballot
order because we interpret, often subconsciously, the first name
on a list as an implicit recommendation. This thought process
isn't quite as crazy as it sounds. In many cases, the first name on
a list is the one we should pay more attention to. For example,
when we see a movie poster, the first actor listed is usually the
one with the starring role in the movie.

In the world of politics, it is good to be first. But it's not just presidential candidates who benefit from going first. Prisoners do, too.

Shai Danziger of Tel Aviv University followed eight Israeli judges for 10 months as they presided over 1,000 parole applications made by prisoners. When prisoners apply for parole, their application reviews are randomly assigned to time slots during the day. And when Shai looked at the relationship between the assigned time slot and the likelihood of being released, he found that the probability of being granted parole was far higher at the beginning of the day than at the end. If you were the first prisoner reviewed on a particular day, your odds of getting released were 65 percent. However, if a prisoner was unlucky enough to be reviewed at the end of day, their probability plummeted to nearly zero!

What was also interesting is that the probability of parole decreased over the course of the morning but rose again right after lunch, once hungry judges were recharged. How can we make sense of this pattern?

It turns out that the natural default response is for judges to deny the parole request. It makes sense: If the question is whether to release a potentially dangerous criminal onto the streets, when in doubt, saying no is the way to go. At the beginning of the day or after lunch, when judges are rested and energetic, they can engage in effortful thinking and focus on the merits of the case. However, as judges get tired and their blood sugar drops, they lack the energy for careful processing and they become more likely to revert to the default: "no" on parole. A tired and hungry judge is not a lenient one.

On ballots and in parole hearings, it is good to go first. But sometimes, in competitive situations, it's better to be last.

From Professors to *American Idol* Contestants: When It's Better to Be Last

Singers and ice skaters can appreciate the benefits of going last. So can academics.

In 1997, Adam was on the job market as a fifth-year graduate student at Princeton University. In December of that year, he got exciting news that the business school at the University of Chicago was inviting him for an interview. The head of the search committee at Chicago asked him to be the first candidate interviewed (they were interviewing six candidates over a four-week period). He asked his professors at Princeton if he should go first or schedule his interview for one of the later dates. To Adam, they all said the same thing: They would want to go first. Going first signals prominence, they said. Adam agreed to be the first candidate interviewed at Chicago. He did not get the job.

Later, after the sting of the rejection had worn off, he sifted through all the job interviews he had observed at Princeton while he was a student. In his five years there, the last candidate had gotten the job every time!

This effect isn't limited to Princeton or to academia. Study after study has found that in serial competitions—situations in which each candidate performs one after the other—it pays to go last. For example, when Wändi Bruine de Bruin of Leeds University analyzed data from nearly 50 years (1957–2003) of the Eurovision Song Contest, she found that contestants who went later in the competition got higher scores.

This same effect has been documented on *American Idol*. Lionel Page of the University of Westminster devised a clever analysis that used data from the popular TV show to calculate the benefit of going last. In each episode of *American Idol*, contestants perform a song and at the end of each week, one of them is voted off the show until a final contestant wins the competition. So what effect did performing last have? Of the first 111 *Ameri-*

can Idol episodes, the singer who performed last advanced to the next round a whopping 91 percent of the time.

You might think this effect only occurs for trivial television shows and would vanish in rigorously evaluated professional competitions. Well, when Wändi addressed this question by analyzing data from the European and World Figure Skating Championships from 1994 to 2000, she found the exact same effect: Going later was better than going earlier. Skaters who were randomly assigned to perform later received better scores in the first round. And these skaters also got an extra boost in the second round; in many cases, skaters with higher scores in the first round skated later in the second round, too.

Here's a powerful example of the effects of going later: In the 2010 Winter Olympics, there were two leading competitors in the male figure skating competition: Evgeni Plushenko and Evan Lysacek. But one of the two was heavily favored to win: Plushenko. In fact, in betting markets, the payout for a bet on the underdog Lysacek was *18 times greater* than the payout for Plushenko. Everyone thought Plushenko would win. But across the two events, Lysacek skated 13 positions later than Plushenko. Lysacek finished with 257.67 points to Plushenko's 256.36, a difference of just over one point. (The third place finisher was more than 10 points behind Lysacek.) Of course, there are many factors that influence the scores skaters earn, but the order effect could well have tipped the balance.

So why is this happening? For one thing, when judges evaluate everyone at the end of the competition, the memory of earlier candidates fades. Recognizing this, movie producers who hope to win an Academy Award release their movies late in the year. Indeed, the vast majority of Best Picture winners come from movies released between October and December.

Yet what is interesting about this effect is that it occurs regardless of whether all candidates are judged only at the end of competition (as in *American Idol*) *or* if they are judged after each candidate performs (as in figure skating).

How do we make sense of the later-is-better effect in figure skating, where each skater is evaluated after each performance as they skate? Here, a number of effects contribute to the "later-is-better" pattern. First, judges like to give themselves room to reward later candidates. In other words, a judge may want to give a perfect 10 to someone early, but worry that someone else who performs later might do even better. As a result, judges are stingy with very high ratings in early rounds, essentially saving them for later contestants. Second, judges hold very high standards at the beginning. They start with an idealized image of how well skaters can perform, and the benchmark for early skaters is extremely high. And third, going later may help the performers themselves; having seen others give stellar performances may motivate later contestants to put extra effort into their performance or take a risk that pays off.

Whenever multiple candidates compete in order—again, we call this a *serial* competition—going later is better. This has been documented across competitions of all types, no matter how evaluators judge performance. The judgments might involve ranking the candidates (i.e., deciding who is first, second, third, etc. as in the Queen Elisabeth Classical Music Competition), or the judgments might consist of selecting one candidate (like voting on *American Idol*), or the judgments might involve rating each candidate (selecting a number from a scale, as in the World Aquatics Championships, high school gymnastic meets, etc.). It doesn't matter, later candidates do better.

Finding the Right Balance: When to Go First,
When to Go Last, and How to Make This All Fair

So what are the rules that we can use to know when to go first versus last in a competitive situation?

There is a simple solution that depends entirely on two factors.

The first factor is the nature of the competition: Are we being selected from a *list* (like voting)? Or are we being evaluated *one at a time* (like an interview process)? Or is it a *yes/no* decision (like whether or not to release someone on parole)?

If a candidate is being picked from a list, we assume that the first option is somehow better or more credible than the others. The person listed first on a ballot gets an implicit recommendation. Thus, going first is better.

When competitors perform sequentially, however, it's better to be last. Here, the combination of recency (the last contestants are the most salient and vivid) and high standards early on helps later contestants receive more positive evaluations.

For binary decisions, like a yes/no decision, it all depends on what the default is. When the decision-maker is fatigued, they tend to go with the default decision, like keeping a potential parolee in prison. So if the default option works against you—like it did for the Israeli prisoners—you want to be first. But if the default is in your favor, it can pay to be last.

Job interviews can be a bit more complicated. They typically resemble a serial competition, so later is better. Yet in some settings, the judgments are binary; managers make a series of yes/no decisions because there are many positions to fill. In this case, fatigue can become an issue—if the default is to say no, you want to be early (or just after lunch). However, if the default is yes, then you want to be late in the day (or just before lunch).

The second critical factor is how many candidates there are. Dana Carney of the University of California, Berkeley, has shown that when there are only two options, the first option usually wins. For example, when encountering salespeople, customers and clients disproportionately choose to work with the first person they meet. Or when evaluating two similar products (in the case of her experiment, Bubble Yum versus Bubblicious gum), people chose the first option nearly two-thirds of the time. So when there are only two options, first is best.

But what happens as the number of options increases? When does it become better to go last?

Antonia Mantonakis of Brock University tested this idea by varying the number of wines that people tasted. Consistent with Dana's work, when there were only two wines, the first wine was selected almost 70 percent of the time. Even with three wines, there was a clear advantage for the wine that was tasted first. However, as the number of wines grew beyond four, an advantage for the *last wine* emerged. Analyses of martial arts competitions also reveal a later-is-better effect when there were five or more competitors.

By understanding these order effects—how they operate—we can learn to pick a position that will lend us a greater advantage and yield better outcomes in competitive situations.

Here is a quick cheat sheet to gain a competitive advantage:

- If names are listed sequentially, like on a ballot, be listed first.
- If it is a serial competition with more than a few candidates, go later and preferably last.
- If it is a yes/no decision, know the default. If the default is unfavorable to you, go first. If the default is favorable, go last (or right before lunch).

These are the keys to gaining a competitive advantage. But, as friends, we also need to consider ways to make selection processes fair to promote legitimacy and cooperation.

To promote fairness, we endorse randomized, rotational systems. For example, on political ballots the best way to account for order effects is to ensure that every name appears in each ballot position equally at the precinct level. A randomized, rotational system supports democracy and mutes the effects of political machinations and inequity. Surprisingly, only 12 of the 50 states (24 percent) in the United States currently use a rotational system. Some states use an alphabetical order, others use a lottery, and some, like Florida, allow the sitting governor to decide.

In sequential competition in which there is only one round, randomization is the best solution. Randomization does not eliminate order effects, as those who go later will still have an advantage, but it does allow each candidate to have an equal probability of benefiting from the later position.

In sequential competition with multiple rounds, however, we can promote even greater fairness by randomly determining starting order in the first round and reversing the order in the second round. In contrast, many competitions often compound the benefits of going at the end in the first round, by determining second-round position by the first-round score.

Here is a quick cheat sheet to create a fair system that breeds cooperation:

- For ballots, use randomized, rotational systems.
- For serial competitions with one round, randomly determine starting order.
- For serial competitions with two rounds, randomly determine starting order in the first round and reverse the order in the second round.

Up to now our discussion of whether to go first or last has been in the context of influencing the judgment of external judges or audiences. The question of whether to move first or last is particularly important in the domain of negotiations, where our counterpart is sitting across the table from us. What should we do in a negotiation? We turn to this question next.

Should You Make the First Offer?

In 1996, when Michael Jordan negotiated his contract with the Chicago Bulls, he opened by requesting an ambitious $52 million, more than double what any professional U.S. athlete had ever been paid. After a back-and-forth exchange of offers, the parties settled for $30 million. Jordan's salary of $33.14 million for the 1997–98 season, a 10 percent increase from the previous year, remains the single highest annual salary in the history of the National Basketball Association. By making the first offer, Jordan positioned himself to earn the highest salary that any NBA player has ever earned.

The Michael Jordan example addresses one of the most vexing questions that plague negotiators: whether or not we should make the first offer. This question is beset by uncertainty. Will I make an offer that undercuts my position and sell myself short? Or will I make an offer so outrageous that the other side walks away from the bargaining table in a huff?

To answer the question of whether or not to go first, we turn to data—a lot of it. Over the past decade, we and others from around the world have conducted dozens of studies that investigate the question of whether or not to go first. The vast majority of these studies find that it *is* better to go first in most negotiations!

But in looking closely at this data we've also learned that the benefits of going first hinge on two principles. The first principle is information. If we lack information then going first makes us vulnerable to exploitation. The second principle is a concept first introduced by Daniel Kahneman called anchoring.

An anchor is a numeric value that influences subsequent

evaluations. It is called an anchor because it quite literally pulls judgments in its direction. When a seller lists a price for their home, for example, the list price anchors subsequent bids. As the buyer prepares their offer, it is almost impossible not to be pulled in the direction of the list price. Just as an anchor keeps a boat close, numerical anchors keep subsequent judgments closer than they might otherwise be.

Anchors exert outsized influence for two reasons. First, we underestimate the force that anchors can exert. Take the sticker price for a used car. Let's say the list price is $30,000. We know that the car is worth less than the asking price and so we adjust away from that price. We think, hmm, the car has to be worth less than $30,000. So we start with $30,000 and move down from there. Perhaps we ultimately agree on a price of $28,500. We might feel pretty good about ourselves, right? After all, we paid much less than the sticker price. But in reality, we may have moved too little as we adjusted away from that sticker price. Even though we knew $30,000 wasn't right, we often fail to appreciate how far away we need to adjust.

Second, every item that we negotiate over, whether it is a car, a job, or a firm, has both positive and negative features; some qualities suggest a higher price and other qualities suggest a lower price. When the seller of a used car makes the first offer, this higher anchor directs our attention toward positive features of the used car such as low mileage or the leather interior; however, when the *buyer* makes the first offer, this lower anchor directs attention to the poor features that suggest low quality, such as dents and the rattle in the dashboard, thus reinforcing the effects of the lower or higher anchor.

When we make the first offer, we anchor the negotiation in our favor. With Thomas Mussweiler of the University of Cologne, we have empirically established that it is often better to go first in a project. We ran a very simple experiment. We randomly assigned which negotiator—buyer or seller—would make the first offer in a negotiation over the sale of a pharmaceutical plant. If the two negotiators could not reach a deal, the buyer would need to build a new plant for the cost of $25 million, and sellers would strip their plant and sell the equipment separately for $17 million. Given these alternatives, we expected the final price to be in the range of $17 million–$25 million, giving the negotiation a bargaining zone of $8 million.

If it is better to go first, the final price should be higher when the seller makes the first offer than when the buyer does so. And that is exactly what we found across our experiments. On average, when the seller made the first offer, the final price was $24 million, but when the buyer made the first offer, the final price was only $20 million.

The first-mover advantage is not an American phenomenon. We have found these effects all over the world. In studies we conducted in both France and Thailand, the negotiator who made the first offer got a better deal.

Making the first offer can also curtail power differences in a negotiation. In a variation of the study we just described, we gave either buyers or sellers more power by making their alternatives even more attractive. When they had power *and* they made the first offer, they did particularly well. When they had power and their counterparts made the first offer, however, the advantage of having power was canceled out by the disadvantage of going second. Going first, in other words, can be an equalizer of power differences.

But in some situations, it's *not* in your interest to go first. Why? As one book boldly titled *Never Make the First Offer* argues, receiving a first offer gives you insight into the other side's bargaining position. By waiting and listening, you protect yourself from error and gain valuable intelligence.

To determine when it makes sense to wait and let the other side make the first offer, we need to take stock of how much information we *don't* have. There are two types of missing information that can get us into trouble. First, we might have no idea how much our counterparts are willing to accept (or pay). Second, when negotiations involve many issues, some of them may be a common-interest issue where we both want the exact same outcome (e.g., we both want an early closing date). When we make a first offer without those pieces of information, we can tip our hand and reveal information that makes us vulnerable.

Let's consider this first problem—when we don't have a good sense of what our counterparts will accept. In situations like this, it may be better to wait to receive the first offer.

In fact, the invention of the lightbulb and the phonograph may have depended on going second. Thomas Edison had a new invention that he thought would improve the telegraph machine. So he took his new ideas to the Western Union telegraph company. When Western Union asked him to name his price, his initial instinct was to shoot for the moon and ask for $2,000. But for some reason he stopped himself and said instead, "How about you make me an offer?" Western Union opened with $40,000! That is at least 20 times what he was going to ask (and is the equivalent of $833,333 in today's dollars). He used this unexpected windfall to build a laboratory, "The Invention Factory," where he created the phonograph and the electric lightbulb.

Some of you may be fans of the History Channel show *Pawn Stars*, a reality show that depicts customers selling items at a pawn shop. You may have noticed that in this show, the pawnbroker often asks the seller to make the first offer. Bryan McCannon of St. Bonaventure University analyzed data from this show and found that in this case, for the pawnbroker buyer there was an advantage to going second. Why? Because most sellers who come on this show haven't the first idea about what their item is worth: because they were unaware of the true value of their item their offers were far too low.

We confirmed this result in a project we conducted with Elizabeth Wiley of Columbia University using a negotiation simulation involving the sale of a used 1970 Ford Thunderbird. The car wasn't in good condition, and the sellers only wanted a minimum of $300 for it. However, the buyer wanted the car for its parts; for the buyer, the car was worth at least $2,000. When sellers made the first offer, they undervalued the car. And when the buyer went first, they overvalued how much the car was worth to the sellers.

So, when we have no idea how much our counterparts will value the item up for negotiation (as we found with the *Pawn Stars* and Ford Thunderbird negotiations), going first can get us into trouble.

Now let's consider the second problem. Going first can also get us into trouble when we have common interests. Here's how. Imagine, after weeks of searching, you find the home of your dreams. You make an offer and ask for the early closing date that you really want. By revealing your preference for an early closing date, you create an opportunity for a strategic foe. Even if the seller also prefers an early closing date, they might ask for a *concession* to accommodate your request for the early closing date. So even though the seller actually wanted an early closing date, they pretend this date will hurt them and ask for $10,000 more for the house to "accommodate" your need for an earlier closing date.

Whenever a negotiation involves multiple issues, be on the lookout for common-interest issues. A savvy counterpart can use the information revealed in our offer to demand concessions on other issues.

Research we conducted with David Loschelder of Saarland University reveals how this works.

In one study, we used the same negotiation we described earlier over the sale of a pharmaceutical plant but we added a new issue to the negotiation. When the parties had opposing preferences for this issue (one side wanted more and the other side wanted less), we found a large first-offer advantage: Negotiators who made the first offer captured the lion's share of the pie, approximately 60 percent of it. However, when the additional issues were common-interest issues, and both parties wanted the same outcome, making the first offer was a disadvantage. Here, negotiators who made the first offer got less than 40 percent of the pie. In other words, when a negotiation has a common-interest issue, there can be a disadvantage to making the first offer.

Finding the Right Balance: How to Resolve the First-Offer Dilemma by Making Your First Offer Later

So we see that every negotiator faces the first-offer dilemma. Going first can give you an advantage by anchoring the negotiation in your favor. But if you lack information, it can leave you vulnerable to exploitation. Receiving the first offer, on the other hand, can leave you susceptible to being anchored but it can also give you an advantage by providing you with important information.

The million-dollar question is: How can we get the anchoring advantage of making the first offer without revealing information that the other side can use to strategically gain an advantage over us?

No solution is perfect, but here's our advice: Make your first offer *later in the negotiation process*, after you have had time to talk with your counterpart and gain information.

Think back to the used-car negotiation. The buyer valued the car a lot for its valuable parts but the seller valued it very little. By making an early offer, the buyer or seller can't help but reveal how much they value the car. This makes them vulnerable.

But let's imagine an alternative to making the first offer right away. Instead of jumping right in with a first offer, what if you asked your counterpart some questions? For example, as the seller you might ask, "What do you plan on doing with the car?" By asking questions, we can gain valuable information that helps us understand how the other side values the car. Armed with this knowledge, we can then anchor the negotiation in our favor by making the first offer.

In an experiment we conducted with Marwan Sinaceur of INSEAD, we varied not only who made the first offer but *when* the first offer was made. Some negotiators were told to make their first offer very early on in the negotiation, in the first minute or so. Other negotiators were told to make their first offer only after discussing the negotiation with the other side for at least 15 minutes.

And indeed, we found that a late first offer afforded a competitive advantage without making the negotiator vulnerable. Negotiators who made late offers were able to anchor the negotiation in their favor without suffering from an informational disadvantage.

Here is the key idea: *A well-informed negotiator does better by going first.* But when the other side has much more information than you do about the negotiated item, it can be better to go second. So always take the time to gain more information—information about the item, about the industry, about your opponent's preferences—both through due diligence before the negotiation and by asking probing questions during the negotiation.

There is another benefit to waiting to begin the negotiation with an immediate offer: Having discussions before an offer is made produces more creative deals that can satisfy the interests of both sides. A late offer, in other words, produces both a competitive advantage and a cooperative solution.

Here is a quick cheat sheet to decide when to make the first offer:

- Ask questions to get information before you make the first offer. You want to find out:
  - Why are they negotiating? You want to figure out why they want to buy or sell the item.

  o How much do they value the negotiated item? You want to
    figure out if they know more than you do *or* if they know
    less than you do.

  o Are there any issues where you might have common prefer-
    ences? You want to ask questions first, before you reveal in-
    formation that might reveal a common-interest issue, which
    they could use to extract concessions from you on other
    issues.

- When you have full information and know how the other side
  values the item, you should make the first offer.

- When you are unsure of the true value of an item, you should
  wait to make the first offer.

Of course, the decision of *when* to make an offer is only part
of the story. When we make an offer, we also have to decide *what
kind of* offer to make. Should we start high or low? How ambitious
should we be? We turn to these questions next.

How to Put Your Offer
on the Table

Morton Franklin's financial future looked bleak.[1] For the past
three years he had been the only business in a one-block radius.
Unlike his previous neighbors, Morton had refused to sell his
property to a developer, even when he was offered $1 million,
nearly double the investment he had made six years earlier. And
now, after a multiyear legal battle, the court had ruled that the
state could seize his property.

Why had Morton turned down such a clearly attractive offer?
The developer wanted to build a new office complex and Morton
believed the new development would destroy his neighborhood.

---

1. Name has been changed.

By refusing to sell, he thought, he could prevent the new development from happening. But he was wrong.

To make matters worse, the court ruled that the developer only had to pay Morton the current appraised value, an amount equal to half of what the other businesses received to relocate. And the court also gave Morton an eviction notice: He had to move his business in short order.

As he thought about his plight, however, Morton realized that he still had leverage: He could fight the date of his eviction. Sure, he would probably lose, but he realized, through a little perspective-taking, that this option was problematic for the developer. Morton knew that a new development team was looking to buy his property, and that by delaying his eviction, he might disrupt the sale of the property.

So Morton developed a plan. He would propose a simple deal: He would agree to vacate the property immediately . . . for a price. And on deciding what that price should be, Morton asked himself a simple question: What was it worth to the developer for him to leave now?

Morton decided to make the first offer and to start high, very high—his opening offer was for over $4 million, more than *nine times* what the court said he was due.

Sounds ridiculous, right? Yet incredibly, the parties eventually settled for around $3 million. Morton had started very high, and as a result, he walked away with six times the amount he was officially entitled to under the court ruling.

Unlike Morton, most of us are apprehensive about making an extremely ambitious initial offer, whether it's a salary negotiation, the sale of a car or home, a settlement agreement, or even in a friendly arrangement with a friend or neighbor. If we are too ambitious, we fear we will offend our counterpart and lose credibility as we backpedal. Or worse, what if we so offend our counterpart that the other side storms away from the bargaining table? These are valid fears, of course, but our research shows they are often exaggerated. In fact, most people make first offers that are too wimpy!

What do we mean by an ambitious first offer? An ambitious first offer is one that is extreme and optimistic. An ambitious first offer is one that would produce your ideal outcome; it would make you jump for joy if the other side agreed to it. But it should be grounded in reality. Your first offer should be just *this* side of crazy, as opposed to *that* side of crazy.

To determine where exactly the line falls between this side and that side of crazy, we propose the straight-face test: Can you make the offer with a straight face? A related test is this: Can you provide a rationale for your offer? It doesn't have to be the most complete or compelling rationale, but you should be able to provide one. So, if you can make the offer with a straight face and you can justify it, then go for it—reach for the stars.

We should point out that the unfair double bind that women face, which we discussed earlier in the book, affects how ambitious one's offer can be. Hannah Riley Bowles of Harvard University found that women can face a social penalty for making aggressive offers. Gender unfortunately affects which side of crazy an offer falls on.

To understand why it pays to make an ambitious first offer, it is important to think back to our conversation on anchoring. As we just learned, first offers anchor the negotiation. And more extreme first offers produce a more extreme anchoring effect and give you a better outcome.

Let's return to our example of searching for a new home. You've found something you like and you prepare to make your offer. As you consider the price you'll propose, how influenced are you by whether the list price is high or low? Greg Northcraft of the University of Illinois investigated this very question. He showed professional real estate agents a home and gave them lots of background information (10 pages' worth, actually), and then he asked them to estimate the true value of the house. Everyone saw the same house and read the same 10 pages. The only piece of information that Greg varied was the property's list price. Some agents saw a high list price (i.e., an aggressive anchor) of $149,900 and others saw a low list price of $119,900. Although these trained real estate professionals all saw the same house, if they had seen documents with the higher list price, they thought it was worth on average $14k more!

This effect has been found to persist with used-car sales as well. In one experiment, Thomas Mussweiler took his 10-year-old car, a 1987 Opel Kadett E, to a number of different German mechanics to find out whether it was worth getting a dent fixed or not, given the age of the car. He then asked the mechanics what they thought the car was really worth. Before they could answer, Thomas casually mentioned what he thought it was worth. To some, he said 2,800 German marks ($1,556 at the time), to others, 5,000 marks ($2,778). Just like the real estate agents, the mechanics' estimates were heavily influenced by Thomas's anchor. Despite their vast expertise and knowledge about cars, the mechanics estimated the car to be worth a full 1,000 marks more when they were given the high versus low value!

What's interesting to note about both of these examples is that the experts knew the house or car wasn't worth the high anchor, and they adjusted down from it. The problem was that they didn't adjust *enough*. Even experts are tugged in the direction of an anchor.

Making an ambitious first offer is also advantageous because of the social norms that govern the negotiation process. When we engage in a negotiation, we *expect* to exchange offers, make roughly matching concessions, and "split the difference." In fact, many negotiators routinely use those very words, "Let's split the difference." The midpoint of the opening offers from each side seems fair. What this means is that after we make an offer, we can only go in one direction, down from our first offer. To make a later offer that is more extreme than your first offer violates social norms. The negotiation script means you can't ask for more than your first offer; that is, you can't add new demands later in the negotiation. And if you do, your counterpart will see you as a competitive foe to be vanquished.

Given the power of anchors and the social norms that govern negotiations, one of our central mantras when we teach negotiations is this: *If you don't ask, you can't get what you want.*

Consider a real-life negotiation involving our colleague Thomas Mussweiler. One Thanksgiving, Thomas was waiting for a plane that was severely overbooked, and the airline was looking for volunteers to get bumped off the flight and take one the next day for a $500 voucher. He went up to the gate official who had just given another traveler a single voucher and nothing else, and asked a simple question: "Will you put me in first class if I get bumped?" She said yes. Then he asked a follow-up question: "Will you pay for a hotel room for me tonight?" Again the answer was yes. "Okay, will you pay for my dinner tonight at the hotel?" "Yes" came the reply. And finally, "When we reach my final destination, will you pay for a cab to take me back to my home?" "Hmmm, okay." [2]

Thomas asked for and got lots of perks. Others did not ask for anything and got nothing in return. Sometimes it really is as simple as that.

Making an ambitious first offer not only gives you a competitive advantage, it also makes you appear more cooperative because it gives you room to make concessions and still reach a better deal. By contrast, when your opening offer is close to your bottom line, you have little room to maneuver. If your counter-

---

2. Incidentally, this event also contained a humorous example of cross-cultural miscommunication. When the first-class flight attendant asked Thomas, who is German, if he wanted the eggs with kielbasa or the Special K breakfast, he chose the "special" breakfast because, well, he thought it was special. He was severely disappointed when it was just cereal!

part demands a concession, you can only make a very small one.

Giving ourselves room to make concessions is a key to turning a competitive negotiation into a cooperative one. One reason is simply that ambitious first offers alter your counterpart's expectations: If you start aggressively, they expect a tough negotiation, and can be pleasantly surprised when you seem conciliatory as you make some concessions. Second, the number and amount of concessions help the other side save face. When people tell tales of their negotiation prowess, they often describe how much they moved the other side off of their first offer. People want to think of themselves as effective negotiators, good at securing concessions. By making ambitious first offers with room for concessions, you can let the other side feel good about themselves and give them tales to tell of their negotiation prowess.

In other words, ambitious first offers let you competitively anchor the negotiation while giving you room to make concessions. By being competitive with an ambitious first offer you actually appear more cooperative!

President Barack Obama learned this principle the hard way. In 2011, the United States faced an economic crisis with a looming deadline for the debt ceiling, the limit on the amount of debt that the Treasury can issue. In the past, Congress would pass a bill to raise the debt ceiling without any stipulations. But this time, the Republican opposition wanted to extract concessions before they approved legislation that would allow the United States to continue to borrow money to pay its bills on time.

The Republicans made an aggressive, ambitious first offer in 2011. They proposed a plan entitled "Cut, Cap, and Balance" that would cut spending significantly, cap future expenditures, and amend the Constitution to require a balanced budget—all measures the Democrats vehemently opposed.

President Obama's first offer, however, was too accommodating. In response to the unprecedented move by the Republicans, Obama offered a compromise, including a blend of the spending cuts that Republicans wanted, along with tax increases on the wealthiest Americans that the Democrats wanted. But rather than accept this first offer, the Republicans demanded the president move off of his position and make even more compromises. And he did. Obama's next proposal no longer called for tax increases but simply tax reform, and he even offered cuts to the sacred Democratic programs of Social Security and Medicare.

Eventually, the United States avoided default when a deal was passed that included almost $1 trillion in spending cuts as well as a promise to cut spending by more than $1 trillion in the future—all measures favored by the Republicans. And Obama only got a modest rise in the debt ceiling; one that ensured that another showdown over the debt limit would arise in the near future. As one person lamented, he came across as "a pushover who will cede more and more ground the harder and longer they push." It all started with a weak first offer.

But President Obama learned from these mistakes when he faced a similar debt-limit battle just two years later in 2013. This time he declared, "I will not negotiate over whether or not America keeps its word and meets its obligations. I will not negotiate over the full faith and credit of the United States." It took a government shutdown, but the two sides finally reached a deal in which the president made almost no concessions. As one commentator noted, "They've learned the lesson. They've adjusted their tactics and taken a much harder line this time around."

This example teaches us three key lessons. First, we need to guard against the psychological anchoring effect of the ambitious first offers that our counterparts make. How can you do this? Here's our advice: Write down your first offer before you hear the other side's offer.

Second, don't make your first offer close to your compromise solution. The other party will never accept it as the ideal solution and will demand you make further compromises to reach a deal.

You want to make an ambitious first offer since the other side will almost always ask for concessions regardless of your offer.

And third, just keep in mind that there can be risks in making a very ambitious first offer. For Republicans, their extreme initial offer worked the first time—they gained steep concessions. But the second time, it cost them a government shutdown, for which the Republicans received a disproportionate share of the blame.

Precision Matters

Some anchors are heavier than others. Here is a way to make your first offer as heavy and impactful as possible.

Imagine you are selling your car and you make the first offer to a potential buyer. How precise should you make your first offer? Two different groups of scientists, one group in Europe and the other in the United States, tackled this question independently and came to the exact same conclusion.

In one study, Malia Mason of Columbia University created three different first offers in a negotiation over jewelry. She found that people secured better deals when their first offer was more precise, at either $19.85 or $21.15, than when it was a round first offer of $20. Malia found that precise first offers are "heavier" anchors because they are seen as more informed compared to round offers. Indeed, other researchers have found that when people generate answers to trivia questions that are more precise, they are seen as more confident in their answers: e.g., How long is the Niger River in miles? Precise answer: 2,611 miles versus round answer: 2,600 miles. The more precise number conveys confidence and is taken more seriously.

A similar study was conducted in a shop that specialized in the restoration and sale of antique furniture. David Loschelder of Saarland University studied people who were browsing in an antique shop. He asked the shop owner to conduct an experiment for him. The shop owner asked customers to analyze a *secretaire* (which was worth approximately €700 in its unrestored condition) and offer what they would be willing to pay for it. It was listed with one of four prices: a nonaggressive round price of €900, an aggressive round price of €1,200, a nonaggressive precise price of €885, or an aggressive precise price of €1,185. David found that people were willing to pay the most when the first offer was both aggressive and precise, the €1,185 value. This was the only condition in which people were willing to pay more than €1,000. Ambitious offers that are precise are the heaviest anchors of them all.

Of course, a first offer can be too precise. Excited by this new research, Adam once gave a friend of his advice on how to list his house: Be as precise as possible. So this friend listed his condo in a high-rise building in Chicago with great precision, down to the $50 point. No one made an offer.

Inspired by this failure, we have conducted studies with Alice Lee of Columbia University and found that precise offers can create barriers to entry by scaring away potential buyers. Why? Precise offers signal confidence but they can also signal inflexibility. When you make a precise first offer you convey the message that you are confident in the amount you expect to receive and are not very flexible. This appearance of inflexibility can drive potential buyers away. Luckily, there are strategies we can use to prevent this from happening.

Finding the Right Balance: How to Make an Ambitious First Offer but Come Across as Cooperative

We have seen how ambitious first offers can help us gain a competitive advantage. But they can also be *too* ambitious and drive our counterparts away from the bargaining table.

We need to find a way to produce the right balance between being ambitious and appearing cooperative. There are two strategies that work, and they both involve the idea of dropping *multiple* anchors.

In keeping with the metaphor, Daniel Ames of Columbia University, a boater himself, notes that when the seas become particularly rough and unstable, boaters drop a second anchor, called a tandem anchor, to provide greater resistance to the turbulent seas. Applying this logic to negotiations, Daniel has explored the effect of presenting a second anchor. What he did was turn offers from a single value into a *range* of values.

Daniel has found that ranges can produce more attractive settlements, but *only* when they are ambitious. What you want to do is take your ideal number and produce a range whereby the lower bound is your ideal outcome. An ambitious range offer allows you to get a better deal but still seem reasonable; you can strike a balance between being competitive and cooperative.

Offering a range works especially well when there is only one issue on the table. But what should you do when you are dealing with multiple issues to capture both competitive *and* cooperative benefits?

You should make more than one offer. In a project led by Geoffrey Leonardelli of the University of Toronto, we have explored the benefits of giving the other side a *choice* among offers. By offering multiple options, negotiators combine aggressiveness with flexibility, competition with cooperation.

Imagine you are offering a job in your company to a new recruit, and your first offer includes a salary and a location: Let's say a salary of $86k in the Tucson office. With multiple offers, you could offer a choice among two or more packages. So your first offer is either a) $86k in the Tucson office or b) $87k in the Savannah office.

The key feature of making multiple offers is that each package has *the same overall value* to you, so you are happy with either outcome. But to the person on the other side of the negotiating table, one might be vastly more valuable. By letting *them* choose, you secure better economic *and* interpersonal outcomes. Why?

Recipients see the presentation of multiple packages as a signal of cooperation. People are less resistant and more accepting of the first offer because choice is involved. Psychologically, multiple offers are the opposite of an ultimatum.

We have empirically established that making multiple offers leads to better outcomes for oneself. However, *it does not lead to a worse outcome for the other side.* By making multiple offers, you walk away with a better deal for yourself but leave the other side just as well off as if you had made only one package offer. You expand the pie, but you also get most of that expanded part.

Multiple offers can also help you overcome the potential costs of being too ambitious when you lack power. When a low-power negotiator, someone without good alternatives, makes an aggressive first offer, their high-power counterparts often simply walk away from the table as Martin Schweinsberg of INSEAD has shown. But multiple offers allow low-power negotiators to obtain control over the process and accrue reasonable outcomes without this risk. They let low-power negotiators lean into the negotiation without getting pushed back.

Here we have emphasized when and how to start your engines as you enter into a competition or negotiation. We next turn to the importance of balancing cooperation and competition as you cross the finish line.

How to Cross the Finish Line

They thought he had a bomb.

When the Miami SWAT team arrived, they were confronted by an unusual scene. At the top of a 400-foot radio tower was a 36-year-old man tossing leaflets to people below. The leaflets simply read, LISTEN TO PARIS.

Carlos Paris Alvarez had scaled the barbed wire fence and climbed hundreds of feet, carrying three suitcases with him. After securing the scene, the SWAT team had a decision to make. Should they act competitively and scale the tower and use tear gas to compel Paris to come down? Or, should they adopt a more cooperative approach and try to talk Paris down?

The SWAT team chose the latter and turned to their crisis negotiator, Angel Calzadilla. As Angel surveyed the bizarre scene, he encountered his first obstacle: How do you communicate with someone at the top of a radio tower—more than a football field away—who has no cell phone?

It wasn't an elegant solution, but Angel had one. He boarded a helicopter with a giant pad of paper and a marker. Up in the helicopter, Angel would write words on large sheets of paper, press the paper against the helicopter window, and see if Paris nodded or shook his head.

As you might imagine, communication was slow. And Paris was in no hurry. In his three suitcases, which the SWAT team worried contained a bomb, Paris had packed a change of clothes and enough food to last him a week.

After seven hours, Angel finally convinced Paris to climb down by promising him that if he climbed down *now*, Angel would let him talk to the reporters who had gathered below. If Paris waited, however, the reporters might leave to deal with other stories, and Paris would miss his chance to spread his message.

This argument convinced Paris to climb down. As he descended, the SWAT team looked on. After seven long hours of waiting, they wanted nothing more than to throw Paris into their police van and haul him away. Now that they had Paris just where they wanted him, the SWAT team was primed to pivot to competition.

But Angel didn't pivot. Instead, he insisted on maintaining his cooperative course and had the SWAT team stand down as he followed through on his promise. He asked the camera crews to do him a favor; even if they weren't interested in hearing what Paris had to say, would they at least turn on the camera lights and let him speak for a couple of minutes?

The media obliged, and what they heard was more interesting than they had expected. Paris believed he was a messenger from God, and that God wanted him to accomplish four goals for the planet: less asphalt, more horses, and more bicycles. The final demand was an end to Russian pornography. Not all pornography, just Russian pornography. This demand was particularly important to him. (This, by the way, is a true story.)

And then there was something Paris wanted for himself. Bob Dole had just won the Republican nomination for president of the United States, and Paris wanted to be Bob Dole's running mate for vice president of the United States.

After making his demands to the media, Paris was taken away and committed to a mental institution. But because Paris hadn't had an actual bomb, he was judged to be a low threat to the community and was soon released.

But the story doesn't end there.

Several months later, on Easter Sunday, Angel got a page from the police department. There was a crisis, and he was needed. The initial details were sparse. A man had climbed up a pylon and wanted to communicate a message. And strangely, this man wanted to talk to Angel in particular.

As Angel sifted through the initial pieces of information, he began to think. Could it be? No, he thought to himself, it couldn't. But it was. There at the top of the pylon was Carlos Paris Alvarez.

This time, however, there was no protracted negotiation. Angel had developed a foundation of trust with Paris by following through on his earlier promise to allow Paris to hold his press conference. As a result, this second negotiation ran smoothly and Angel and Paris reached a quick resolution.

Now, in Angel's line of work you generally *do not expect repeat business*, so it can be incredibly tempting to cut corners and break a commitment. And in this case, Angel had every reason to believe that his encounter with Paris was a one-time deal. Still, he followed through on his promise. As Angel learned firsthand, even the most unlikely of single-shot transactions can turn into repeat business, and how we resolve one encounter can profoundly influence our next one.

There are many things we can learn from Angel's experience, but here we highlight one key lesson: Endings matter. As we wrap things up, we might mistakenly assume that our hard work is done. It is not. To cooperate and compete effectively in the future, we need to take great care in how we make our last move.

Endings Matter More Than You Think

Before we tackle specific strategies for managing the end of an interaction, it's useful to understand *why* endings matter so

much. It turns out that how we end an interaction disproportionately influences how others judge the entire episode.

As we all know, our memories are far from perfect. One way
in which our memories mislead us, however, has particular relevance for how we close. It turns out that when we recall past
events, we are particularly influenced by how things end.

Research led by Nobel Prize winner Daniel Kahneman demonstrated this with an unusual experiment. His research team
recruited participants to come to a lab, roll up their sleeves, and
immerse one hand in very cold water: 57°F (14°C) to be exact—
for 60 seconds. After that, they took a short break and then sub-
merged their other hand in 57°F water for 90 seconds. However,
during the final 30 seconds the water warmed to 59°F (15°C),
a temperature that was still unpleasant, but just a little less unpleasant than the 57°F water (the researchers varied the order
of the two trials, and half the time people got the 90-second
treatment first). The experimenter asked the participants which
of the two trials they wanted to repeat and which had been more
comfortable.

Surprisingly, not only did participants rate the longer trial (90
seconds) as *more* comfortable than the shorter trial (60 seconds),
but even more shockingly, 69 percent wanted to repeat the longer trial! The longer trial was objectively worse—they had en-
dured pain for a longer period—but because it had ended a little
better, the participants *remembered* it as more pleasant.

This finding was so surprising that Donald Redelmeier led
a team in a follow-up experiment where pain really matters—
colonoscopies. In fact, colonoscopies are so painful that doctors
often give patients the drug Midazolam to erase their memory
of the experience. In the colonoscopy study, Donald randomly
assigned patients to one of two conditions. In one condition, patients had their normal colonoscopy. When the colonoscopy was
done, Donald removed the colonoscope quickly. The experience
was short, but the intensity of the pain at the end of the experi-

ence was great. In the other condition, after patients completed their normal colonoscopy, Donald removed the colonoscope slowly. This added to the experience and increased the duration of the pain, but it decreased the intensity of the pain at the very end.

What did he find? Just like the study with cold water, patients who had experienced the longer (and objectively worse) colonoscopy—but had less intense pain at the end—remembered the entire experience as less painful and were more likely to *return for a follow-up colonoscopy*!

These studies hold an important lesson: How an experience ends profoundly influences how we remember it. Whether it is a family vacation, a corporate retreat, or a negotiation, it is important to end on a good note.

For Angel, ensuring that his first encounter with Paris ended with a happy Paris made his second negotiation with him go far smoother. And this isn't just true for crisis negotiations. When we agree on a starting salary, reach a deal with a client, or arrange for a neighbor's child to mow our lawn, there is a good chance that we will need to work with our counterpart in the future. If the other party feels that they got a bad deal, they may be reticent to work with us again. But if we end on a cooperative note instead, they will be more likely to transact with us—and maybe even give us a better deal—the next time around.

A friendly ending can also give us great opportunities in the future. Just as a satisfied customer returns, a satisfied negotiation partner also returns. In addition, a satisfied counterpart can spread the word, bolstering our reputation and building a network of people eager to work with us. By reaching an agreement on terms that leave our counterpart happy, we increase our chances of having successful outcomes not just with him or her but with others in the future.

Moreover, our counterpart's satisfaction today makes it far easier to gain concessions tomorrow. *"Remember how I gave you that great deal last time? Well, I'm going to need a little help from you this time.*" And the converse is certainly true. If our counterpart felt that they got a bad deal the last time, they will be looking to make up for it the next time. A feeling of lingering injustice, in other words, can transform a friend into a foe.

Be Careful When You Smile

So what can we do to make sure that our counterparts walk away happy? One strategy relates to an idea we developed at the very outset of this book: social comparisons. Remember, social comparisons help us make sense of where we stand in the world—whether it's in regard to our salary, our weight, or our relationships. And equally important, social comparisons can affect how satisfied we are with our outcomes.

When we reach an agreement, *we* become our counterpart's first source of social information. And what is the first clue they will look for to find out whether or not they got a good deal? *Our* expression. If we hang our heads a little, we might send the message that this was a tough agreement for us—and that the other side ended up with the better bargain. If we break into a broad smile, we send a very different message; we are very happy with this agreement . . . and our counterpart might worry that they got taken to the cleaners. In fact, Leigh Thompson of Northwestern University has shown that expressing too much joy as a contract is being signed can signal to the other side that they got a bad deal. You can express satisfaction that a deal has been reached, but be sure not to look so happy that the other side believes that you took them for a ride.

Experienced politicians recognize this principle. Consider the Cold War between the United States and the Soviet Union. Over decades, the two foes spent trillions of dollars competing with each other for dominance around the globe and in space.

One of the most intense flashpoints of the conflict was the division of Germany: East versus West. As the Soviet Union began to lose influence over Eastern Europe, there was one particularly dramatic moment that drew the Cold War to a close: the fall of the Berlin Wall. With hammers and even bare hands, euphoric Germans smashed the wall to pieces.

For Americans, after decades of conflict with few clear victories, here at last was something to cheer. So how did the American president, George H. W. Bush, react to this news? So unremarkably—a flat "I'm very pleased"—that he had to defend his reaction later by explaining, "I'm not an emotional kind of guy." But there may have been much more to it than that. As his secretary of state, James Baker, recalled, "Bush refused to gloat." Bush knew that he still needed to work with Soviet leaders, and that gloating would have made future deals far more difficult.

And there is something else we need to do to ensure that we don't upset our counterpart as we reach a deal: take our time. To understand this point, consider a common experience many of us have had in our foreign travels. You visit a local market filled with stalls selling similar merchandise. You stop in one, and a decorative vase catches your eye. You pick up the vase to take a closer look, and the merchant invites you to make an offer. You think back to other vases you have seen and make your opening offer, "I'll pay you $40 for this vase." The shopkeeper immediately accepts your offer and begins to wrap the vase.

How would you feel in this situation?

Now, imagine that instead, the shopkeeper shakes his head, and demands $60. You hold your ground, and after a protracted and difficult negotiation the shopkeeper finally agrees to a price of $50. Now, how would you feel?

Of course, you *should* feel better in the first case. You saved $10 and 20 minutes of your time. But according to our research with Victoria Medvec of Northwestern University, when someone immediately accepts our first offer, we are instantly racked by remorse: "I offered too much!" Even though you may be getting a good deal, this quick acceptance leaves you dissatisfied.

When we consider the other side's perspective, we realize that we should never immediately accept someone's first offer. By asking the other side to raise their price and make concessions, we can get a better deal *and* leave them feeling more satisfied.

Commencement

As we draw this book to a close, we have learned that even as we seal a deal, we still need to navigate the tension between cooperation and competition. And we need to focus on the future.

The term "commencement" helps us understand this idea. Typically, when we hear the word commencement we think of an event that signifies an ending, like a graduation ceremony from high school or college. But the word "commence" means to start. So a commencement is really about a new beginning. Just as graduates set out for fresh opportunities, how we end one interaction or close a deal sets the stage for everything that comes next.

And remember that what comes next will not take the shape of cooperation *or* competition, but rather a shifting dynamic between the two. As we compete for scarce resources in our unstable social world, it's not enough to be prepared to cooperate *or* compete. We must be prepared to do both.

Acknowledgments

It took many people to help us cross the finish line. The first person we are indebted to is Jim Levine, our agent. Without his encouragement, wisdom, and gentle nudges, we would never have completed this book. The second person responsible for helping us craft a readable manuscript is Talia Krohn. For anyone who struggled with our writing, you should have seen it before Talia's edits! Talia has not only a keen eye, but also an open mind, and we appreciated her willingness to discuss nearly every aspect of this book with us.

We endeavored to fill our book with compelling examples, and Sean Fath, Tim Flank, and Anastasia Usova were responsible for many of these. We also thank Sean and Anastasia for making sure every study and every story was properly referenced. We are grateful for their efforts.

There are so many people that offered edits and thoughts on chapters. They saved us from many embarrassing errors and always steered us toward a tighter and more coherent shore: Eric Anicich, Adam Grant, Erika Hall, Sheena Iyengar, Alice Lee, Joe Magee, Sheryl Sandberg, Claude Schoenberg, Sargent Shriver, Roderick Swaab, Andy Todd, Jenn Whitson, and Cindy Wang.

We are grateful to Joshua Keay for inspiring the design of the book cover. He brilliantly converted the very essence of this book into a stunning visual design; his red ampersand against the black-and-white contrast even led us to tweak the name of the book!

FROM ADAM:

This book would not have existed without my brother, Michael, and my partner, Jennifer Olayon. Michael pushed and cajoled and challenged me at a time when I really needed it. He is a brilliant creative artist and documentary filmmaker and he brought his cinematic wisdom to help edit the book throughout the first draft. Jenn provided the love and support that I needed to climb this literary mountain without withering along the way. She offered key insights from her work programming diversity conferences and always pushed us to ensure that inclusive perspectives were represented in the book. She provided unimagined levels of emotional sustenance. This achievement is as much hers as it is my own.

There are many mentors, colleagues, and students that I want to thank for having shaped my thinking and for motivating me to write this book. My supportive mentors: Jeanne Brett, Galen Bodenhausen, Joel Cooper, Deb Gruenfeld, Richard Hackman, Daniel Kahneman, Marcia Johnson, Erin Lehman, Vicki Medvec, Dale Miller, Keith Murnighan, Gordon Moskowitz, Jeff Stone, and Leigh Thompson. My inspiring colleagues: Hajo Adam, Cameron Anderson, Evan Apfelbaum, Daniel Ames, Alia Crum, Tina Diekmann, Nate Fast, Nir Halevy, Hal Hershfield, Jacob Hirsh, Ena Inesi, Sheena Iyengar, Sonia Kang, Aaron Kay, Gavin Kilduff, Brayden King, Laura Kray, Sei Jin Ko, Joris Lammers, Geoffrey Leonardelli, Joe Magee, Benoit Monin, Will Maddux, Malia Mason, Michael Morris, Keith Murnighan, Thomas Mussweiler, Loran Nordgren, Willie Ocasio, Gerardo Okhuysen, Kathy Phillips, Richard Ronay, Derek Rucker, Garriy Shteynberg, Pam Smith, Harris Sondak, Roderick Swaab, Ithai Stern, Brian Uzzi, Adam Waytz, and Judith White. My stimulating students that I have been lucky to work with: Eric Anicich, Jiyin

Cao, Ashli Carter, Eileen Chou, David Dubois, Brian Gunia, Erika Hall, Dennis Hsu, Li Huang, Sunny Kim, Gillian Ku, Alice Lee, Katie Liljenquist, Jackson Lu, Brian Lucas, Ashley Martin, Rachel Ruttan, Niro Sivanathan, Andy Todd, Jennifer Whitson, Cynthia Wang, Andy Yap, and Chenbo Zhong.

I also want to offer my gratitude to Maurice. When we started on this journey, I thought I was a good writer. Maurice was and is better. But rather than see Maurice as a writing foe, I saw him as a role model and strove to achieve his level of ease and precision. He was the perfect companion on our writing adventure.

FROM MAURICE:

My thinking for this book has been shaped by many people. I want to thank my mentors, my colleagues, and my friends. These include Krishnan Anand, Dan Ariely, Max Bazerman, Brad Bitterly, Alison Brooks, Daylian Cain, Colin Camerer, Jennifer Dunn, Francesca Gino, Michael Haselhuhn, Chip Heath, Jack Hershey, Jessica Kennedy, Bruce Kothmann, Howard Kunreuther, Emma Levine, Roy Lewicki, Robert Lount, Cade Massey, Peter McGraw, Katherine Milkman, Julia Minson, Simone Moran, Keith Murnighan, Michael Norton, Lisa Ordonez, Graham Overton, Devin Pope, Todd Rodgers, Naomi Rothman, Nicole Ruedy, Joe Simmons, Uri Simonsohn, Kristin Smith-Crowe, Steve Ulene, Danielle Warren, Sam Wojnilower, and Jeremy Yip.

And I want to thank my daughters, Avital, Danielle, Lindsey, and Tessa, and the center of my world, my wife, Michelle. They allowed me to retreat to my laptop on vacations, on the weekends, and late into the night. They have taught me what friendship means and what balance is, and they inspired me to get this done!

Finally, I thank Adam. When I ran into Adam years ago at a conference, I told him I was going to write a book. I began to describe the book, and he told me not to write that book, but instead that we should write a book together. He added that the

book we coauthored would be better. And so we began our journey as friends and foes, and I have learned tremendously from
Adam along the way. This book is nothing like the one I might
have written years ago. It is, as Adam knew it would be, much
better.

References

Introduction

Foster, C. "Breastfeeding and Fertility." *New Beginnings* 23, no. 5 (September–October 2006): 196–200.

Siegel, Ronald K. "Hostage Hallucinations: Visual Imagery Induced by Isolation and Life-Threatening Stress." *The Journal of Nervous and Mental Disease* 172, no. 5 (1984): 264–272.

Rubenstein, D. I. "The Ecology of Female Social Behavior in Horses, Zebras, and Asses." *Animal Societies: Individuals, Interactions, and Organization* (1994): 13–28.

Sherman, P. W. "Nepotism and the Evolution of Alarm Calls." *Science* 197, no. 4310 (1977): 1246–1253.

Sims, Calvin. "Guerrillas in Peru Threaten to Kill Hostages." *New York Times*, December 19, 1996, accessed December 12, 2014.

"Worker Dies at Long Island Wal-Mart After Being Trampled in Black Friday Stampede." *New York Daily News*, November 28, 2008. Retrieved online version.

Chapter 1

Barnett, Ruth. "Labour Leadership: Ed Miliband Beats Brother." Sky News Online, September 25, 2010, http://news.sky.com/story/807839/labour-leadership-ed-miliband-beats-brother.

Castle, Stephen. "Brother (and Rival) of British Party Leader Quits Politics." *New York Times*, March 27, 2013.

Lyall, Sarah. "An Englishman in New York." *New York Times*, December 8, 2013.

Christakis, Nicholas A., and James H. Fowler. "The Spread of Obesity in a Large Social Network over 32 Years." *New England Journal of Medicine* 357, no. 4 (2007): 370–379.

"Eating for Two: Fathers Put on Baby Weight Too, as Average Man Is Prone to Put on a Stone." *Daily Mail Online*, May 22, 2009. http://www.dailymail.co.uk/femail/article-1185627/Eating-Why-fathers-baby-weight-pregnancy.html.

Klein, Hilary. "Couvade Syndrome: Male Counterpart to Pregnancy." *The International Journal of Psychiatry in Medicine* 21, no. 1 (1991): 57–69.

Sanburn, Josh. "Top 10 Tennis Rivalries." *Time*, September 8, 2010.

Neely, Kaylyn. "Greatest Lakers Rivalry: Larry Bird vs. Magic Johnson." *Rant Sports*, September 17, 2012.

Kilduff, Gavin J., Hillary Anger Elfenbein, and Barry M. Staw. "The Psychology of Rivalry: A Relationally Dependent Analysis of Competition." *Academy of Management Journal*, 53, no. 5 (2010): 943–969.

"For the Press." *Happy Brain Science*, http://www.happybrainscience.com/.

Brosnan, Sarah F., and Frans B. M. De Waal. "Monkeys Reject Unequal Pay." *Nature* 425, no. 6955 (2003): 297–299.

"American Airlines Unions Approve Concessions Deal." *USA Today*, April 15, 2003.

Wong, Edward. "American's Executive Packages Draw Fire." *New York Times*, April 18, 2003.

Wong, Edward. "Under Fire for Perks, Chief Quits American Airlines." *New York Times*, April 25, 2003.

Allen, Arthur. "The Mysteries of Twins." *Washington Post*, January 11, 2008.

Segal, Nancy L. *Born Together—Reared Apart: The Landmark Minnesota Twin Study*. Cambridge, Massachusetts: Harvard University Press, 2012.

Schweitzer, Maurice E. Interview with Sam Wojnilower, June 14, 2013.

Neumark, David, and Andrew Postlewaite. "Relative Income Concerns and the Rise in Married Women's Employment." *Journal of Public Economics* 70, no. 1 (1998): 157–183.

Tait, Rosemary, and Roxane Cohen Silver. "Coming to Terms with Major Negative Life Events." *Unintended Thought* (1989): 351–382.

Medvec, Victoria Husted, Scott F. Madey, and Thomas Gilovich. "When Less Is More: Counterfactual Thinking and Satisfaction Among Olympic Medalists." *Journal of Personality and Social Psychology* 69, no. 4 (1995): 603.

Matsumoto, David, and Bob Willingham. "The Thrill of Victory and the Agony of Defeat: Spontaneous Expressions of Medal Winners of the 2004 Athens Olympic Games." *Journal of Personality and Social Psychology* 91, no. 3 (2006): 568.

Goodman, Peter S. "U.S. Job Seekers Exceed Openings by Record Ratio." *New York Times*, September 27, 2009.

Bianchi, Emily C. "The Bright Side of Bad Times: The Affective Advantages of Entering the Workforce in a Recession." *Administrative Science Quarterly* 58, no. 4 (2013): 587–623.

Davies, James C. "Toward a Theory of Revolution." *American Sociological Review* (1962): 5–19.

Takahashi, Hidehiko, Motoichiro Kato, Masato Matsuura, Dean Mobbs, Tetsuya Suhara, and Yoshiro Okubo. "When Your Gain Is My Pain and Your Pain Is My Gain: Neural Correlates of Envy and Schadenfreude." *Science* 323, no. 5916 (2009): 937–939.

Leach, Colin Wayne, Russell Spears, Nyla R. Branscombe, and Bertjan Doosje. "Malicious Pleasure: Schadenfreude at the Suffering of Another Group." *Journal of Personality and Social Psychology* 84, no. 5 (2003): 932.

Berger, Jonah, and Devin Pope. "Can Losing Lead to Winning?" *Management Science* 57, no. 5 (2011): 817–827.

Statement by the President upon Signing the National Defense Education Act. The American Presidency Project. Dwight D. Eisenhower: September 2, 1958. Retrieved online version.

Rogers, Simon. "NASA Budgets: US Spending on Space Travel Since 1958 UPDATED." *The Guardian*, February 6, 2010.

Kilduff, Gavin J. "Driven to Win: Rivalry, Motivation, and Performance." *Social Psychological and Personality Science* 5, no. 8 (2014): 944–952.

"Tonya, Nancy Reflect on the Whack Heard 'Round the World." *USA Today*, January 3, 2014.

"15 Golden Moments from ESPN's Tonya Harding–Nancy Kerrigan Doc." *Rolling Stone*, January 17, 2014.

Kilduff, Gavin, Adam Galinsky, Edoardo Gallo, and J. Reade. "Whatever It Takes: Rivalry and Unethical Behavior." International Association for Conflict Management, IACM 25th Annual Conference, 2012, 12–14.

Gregory, Martyn. *Dirty Tricks: British Airways' Secret War Against Virgin Atlantic*. New York: Random House, 2010.

Edelman, Benjamin, and Ian Larkin. *Demographics, Career Concerns or Social Comparison: Who Games SSRN Download Counts?* Harvard Business School, 2009.

Dellasega, Cheryl. *Mean Girls Grown Up: Adult Women Who Are Still Queen Bees, Middle Bees, and Afraid-to-Bees*. Hoboken, N.J.: John Wiley & Sons, 2005.

Dunn, Jennifer, Nicole E. Ruedy, and Maurice E. Schweitzer. "It Hurts Both Ways: How Social Comparisons Harm Affective and Cognitive Trust." *Organizational Behavior and Human Decision Processes* 117, no. 1 (2012): 2–14.

Wood, Joanne V., Shelley E. Taylor, and Rosemary R. Lichtman. "Social Comparison in Adjustment to Breast Cancer." *Journal of Personality and Social Psychology* 49, no. 5 (1985): 1169.

Galinsky, Adam D., Thomas Mussweiler, and Victoria Husted Medvec. "Disconnecting Outcomes and Evaluations: The Role of Negotiator Focus." *Journal of Personality and Social Psychology* 83.5, (2002): 1131.

Chapter 2

"HP's Mark Hurd Made $42.5 Million in Fiscal 2008." *Mercury News*, January 20, 2009, http://www.siliconbeat.com/2009/01/20/2522/.

Hardy, Quentin. "Letter Surfaces That Led to Fall of Hewlett's Chief." *New York Times*, December 30, 2011.

Hesseldahl, Arik. " 'Uncomfortable Dance': Here's the Sexual Harassment Letter That Got Mark Hurd Fired." *All Things D*, December 29, 2011.

Jackson, Eric. "Mark Hurd's Excesses Were in Plain Sight." *The Street*, August 7, 2010.

"Mark Hurd's Sex Scandal Letter Emerges." *CNN Money*, December 30, 2011.

Pimentel, Benjamin. "The Rise and Fall of Mark Hurd." *Market Watch*, August 6, 2010.

Russell, Bertrand. *Power: A New Social Analysis*. Routledge, 2004, 4.

Magee, Joe C., and Adam D. Galinsky. "8 Social Hierarchy: The Self-Reinforcing Nature of Power and Status." *The Academy of Management Annals* 2, no. 1 (2008): 351–398.

Galinsky, Adam D., Deborah H. Gruenfeld, and Joe C. Magee. "From Power to Action." *Journal of Personality and Social Psychology* 85, no. 3 (2003): 453.

Carney, Dana R., Amy J. C. Cuddy, and Andy J. Yap. "Power Posing: Brief Nonverbal Displays Affect Neuroendocrine Levels and Risk Tolerance." *Psychological Science* 21, no. 10 (2010): 1363–1368.

Hsu, Dennis Y., Li Huang, Loran F. Nordgren, Derek D. Rucker, and Adam D. Galinsky. "The Music of Power: Perceptual and Behavioral Consequences of Powerful Music." *Social Psychological and Personality Science* 6, no. 1 (2015): 75–83.

Helin, Kurt. "LeBron's Pregame Music: Wu-Tang, Jay-Z and Some DMX." NBC Sports, March 30, 2012.

Galinsky, Adam D., Deborah H. Gruenfeld, and Joe C. Magee. "From Power to Action." *Journal of Personality and Social Psychology* 85, no. 3 (2003): 453.

Ko, Sei Jin, Melody S. Sadler, and Adam D. Galinsky. "The Sound of Power: Conveying and Detecting Hierarchical Rank Through Voice." *Psychological Science* (2014): 0956797614553009.

Boksem, Maarten A. S., Ruud Smolders, and David De Cremer. "Social Power and Approach-Related Neural Activity." *Social Cognitive and Affective Neuroscience* 7, no. 5 (2012): 516–520.

Keltner, Dacher, Deborah H. Gruenfeld, and Cameron Anderson. "Power, Approach, and Inhibition." *Psychological Review* 110, no. 2 (2003): 265.

Carney, Dana R., Andy J. Yap, B. J. Lucas, P. H. Mehta, J. McGee, and C. Wilmuth. "Power Buffers Stress." Working paper (2015).

Jordan, Jennifer, Niro Sivanathan, and Adam D. Galinsky. "Something to Lose and Nothing to Gain: The Role of Stress in the Interactive Effect of Power and Stability on Risk Taking." *Administrative Science Quarterly* 56, no. 4 (2011): 530–558.

Lammers, Joris, David Dubois, Derek D. Rucker, and Adam D. Galinsky. "Power Gets the Job: Priming Power Improves Interview Outcomes." *Journal of Experimental Social Psychology* 49, no. 4 (2013): 776–779.

Kilduff, Gavin J., and Adam D. Galinsky. "From the Ephemeral to the Enduring: How Approach-Oriented Mindsets Lead to Greater Status." *Journal of Personality and Social Psychology* 105, no. 5 (2013): 816.

"Ethan Couch Sentenced to Probation in Crash That Killed 4 After Defense Argued He Had 'Affluenza.'" *The Huffington Post*, December 12, 2012.

Voorhees, Josh. "A Wealthy Teen's Defense for a Deadly Drunken-Driving Crash: 'Affluenza.'" *Slate*, December 12, 2013.

Anderson, Cameron, and Adam D. Galinsky. "Power, Optimism, and Risk-Taking." *European Journal of Social Psychology* 36, no. 4 (2006): 511–536.

Lammers, Joris, Diederik A. Stapel, and Adam D. Galinsky. "Power Increases Hypocrisy: Moralizing in Reasoning, Immorality in Behavior." *Psychological Science* 21, no. 5 (2010): 737–744.

Galinsky, Adam D., Joe C. Magee, M. Ena Inesi, and Deborah H. Gruenfeld. "Power and Perspectives Not Taken." *Psychological Science* 17, no. 12 (2006): 1068–1074.

Muscatell, Keely A., Sylvia A. Morelli, Emily B. Falk, Baldwin M. Way, Jennifer H. Pfeifer, Adam D. Galinsky, Matthew D. Lieberman, Mirella Dapretto, and Naomi I. Eisenberger. "Social Status Modulates Neural Activity in the Mentalizing Network." *Neuroimage* 60, no. 3 (2012): 1771–1777.

Hogeveen, Jeremy, Michael Inzlicht, and Sukhvinder S. Obhi. "Power Changes How the Brain Responds to Others." *Journal of Experimental Psychology: General* 143, no. 2 (2014): 755.

Whitson, Jennifer A., Katie A. Liljenquist, Adam D. Galinsky, Joe C. Magee, Deborah H. Gruenfeld, and Brian Cadena. "The Blind Leading: Power Reduces Awareness of Constraints." *Journal of Experimental Social Psychology* 49, no. 3 (2013): 579–582.

Campbell, Dorothy. "Binocular Vision." *The British Journal of Ophthalmology* 31, no. 6 (1947): 321.

Land, M. F. "The Eyes of Hyperiid Amphipods: Relations of Optical Structure to Depth." *Journal of Comparative Physiology A* 164, no. 6 (1989): 751–762.

Rucker, Derek D., David Dubois, and Adam D. Galinsky. "Generous Paupers and Stingy Princes: Power Drives Consumer Spending on Self Versus Others." *Journal of Consumer Research* 37, no. 6 (2011): 1015–1029.

Piff, Paul K., Michael W. Kraus, Stéphane Côté, Bonnie Hayden Cheng, and Dacher Keltner. "Having Less, Giving More: The Influence of Social Class on Prosocial Behavior." *Journal of Personality and Social Psychology* 99, no. 5 (2010): 771.

Cohan, William D. *House of Cards: A Tale of Hubris and Wretched Excess on Wall Street.* New York: Random House, 2010.

Brion, Sebastien, and Cameron Anderson. "The Loss of Power: How Illusions of Alliance Contribute to Powerholders' Downfall." *Organizational Behavior and Human Decision Processes* 121, no. 1 (2013): 129–139.

"Alexander Haig, Former Secretary of State, Dies." *Journal Now*, February 20, 2010.

"How Haig Is Recasting His Image." *New York Times*, May 31, 1981.

"The Day Reagan Was Shot." CBSNews.com, April 23, 2001.

Lammers, Joris, Diederik A. Stapel, and Adam D. Galinsky. "Power Increases Hypocrisy: Moralizing in Reasoning, Immorality in Behavior." *Psychological Science* 21, no. 5 (2010): 737–744.

Cogswell, David. "Spitzer Sues Agency for 'Sex Tours'." *Travel Weekly*, August 22, 2003. http://www.travelweekly.com/Travel-News/Travel-Agent-Issues/Spitzer-sues-agency-for-sex-tours-.

Hawn, Carleen. "Eliot Spitzer: Leadership Has No Sacred Cows." *Gigaom*, March 11, 2008.

Richburg, Keith R., "Spitzer Linked to Prostitution Ring by Wiretap." *Washington Post*, March 11, 2008.

"Rod Blagojevich Guilty on Just One Count of 24 in Corruption Trial." *The Guardian*, August 17, 2010.

"Iraq Prison Abuse Scandal Fast Facts." *CNN Library*, November 7, 2014.

Fast, Nathanael J., Nir Halevy, and Adam D. Galinsky. "The Destructive Nature of Power Without Status." *Journal of Experimental Social Psychology* 48, no. 1 (2012): 391–394.

Galinsky, Adam D., Joe C. Magee, Diana Rus, Naomi B. Rothman, and Andrew R. Todd. "Acceleration with Steering: The Synergistic Benefits of Combining Power and Perspective-Taking." *Social Psychological and Personality Science* (2014): 1948550613519685.

Tost, Leigh Plunkett, Francesca Gino, and Richard P. Larrick. "Power, Competitiveness and Advice Taking: Why the Powerful Don't Listen." *Organizational Behavior and Human Decision Processes* 117, no. 1 (2012): 53–65.

Pitesa, Marko, and Stefan Thau. "Masters of the Universe: How Power and Accountability Influence Self-Serving Decisions Under Moral Hazard." *Journal of Applied Psychology* 98, no. 3 (2013): 550.

Vonk, Roos. "The Slime Effect: Suspicion and Dislike of Likeable Behavior Toward Superiors." *Journal of Personality and Social Psychology* 74, no. 4 (1998): 849.

Chapter 3

Schmich, Mary. "What One Word Describes the Rev. Michael Pfleger?" *Chicago Tribune*, April 29, 2011.

"Reverend Pfleger's Biography." The Faith Community of St. Sabina. http://www.saintsabina.org/about-us/our-pastors/senior-pastor-rev-michael-pfleger/rev-pfleger-s-biography.html, accessed December 6, 2014.

Lutz, B. J. "Pfleger Suspended from St. Sabina." NBC Chicago, April 28, 2011.

"Pfleger Says Return to Pulpit Is 'The Greatest Gift of All.'" CBS Chicago, May 22, 2011.

Hastings, Michael. "The Runaway General." *Rolling Stone*, June 22, 2010.

Lubold, Gordon, and Carol E. Lee. "President Obama: Stanley McChrystal Showed 'Poor Judgment.'" *Politico*, June 22, 2010.

Tautz, Jürgen, and David C. Sandeman. *The Buzz About Bees: Biology of a Superorganism.* Berlin: Springer, 2008.

Wilson, Edward O. *Success and Dominance in Ecosystems: The Case of the Social Insects.* Oldendorf, Germany: Ecology Institute, 1990.

Garvin, David A. "How Google Sold Its Engineers on Management." *Harvard Business Review* 91, no. 12 (2013): 74–82.

Willer, R. "Groups Reward Individual Sacrifice: The Status Solution to the Collective Action Problem." *American Sociological Review* 74, no. 1 (2009): 23–43.

Friesen, Justin P., Aaron C. Kay, Richard P. Eibach, and Adam D. Galinsky. "Seeking Structure in Social Organization: Compensatory Control and the Psychological Advantages of Hierarchy." *Journal of Personality and Social Psychology* 106, no. 4 (2014): 590–609.

Sales, Stephen M. "Economic Threat as a Determinant of Conversion Rates in Authoritarian and Nonauthoritarian Churches." *Journal of Personality and Social Psychology* 23, no. 3 (1972): 420–428.

Kay, Aaron C., Jennifer A. Whitson, Danielle Gaucher, and Adam D. Galinsky. "Compensatory Control Achieving Order Through the Mind, Our Institutions and the Heavens." *Current Directions in Psychological Science* 18, no. 5 (2009): 264–268.

Gelfand, Michele J., Jana L. Raver, Lisa Nishii, Lisa M. Leslie, Janetta Lun, Beng Chong Lim, Lili Duan, et al. "Differences Between Tight and Loose Cultures: A 33-Nation Study." *Science* 332, no. 6033 (2011): 1100–1104.

Kwaadsteniet, Erik W. de, and Eric van Dijk. "Social Status as a Cue for Tacit Coordination." *Journal of Experimental Social Psychology* 46, no. 3 (2010): 515–524.

Anicich, Eric A., Frederic Godart, Roderick Swaab, and Adam D. Galinsky. "Co-Leadership Kills Ideas and People." Unpublished, 2014.

"LeBron and Wade: Can It Work?" ESPN, October 29, 2010.

Reid, Eric. "On Stage Interview with Wade, Bosh and James." NBA: The Miami Heat, July 9, 2010.

Melanson, Phil. "Miami Heat Troubles." *Outside the Box*, November 29, 2010.

Simmons, Bill. "LeBron Makes LeLeap." *Grantland*, June 25, 2012.

Swaab, Roderick, M. Schaerer, E. Anicich, R. Ronay, and A. D. Galinsky. "The Too-Much-Talent Effect: Team Interdependence Determines When More Talent Is Too Much or Not Enough." *Psychological Science* 25, no. 8 (2014): 1581–1591.

"Questions for Jerry Colangelo." *Wall Street Journal*, August 22, 2008.

Deeter, Baily. "Why Andre Iguodala Will Be the Key to Team USA's Olympic Success." *Bleacher Report*, July 13, 2012.

Groysberg, Boris. *Chasing Stars: The Myth of Talent and the Portability of Performance*. Princeton, N.J.: Princeton University Press, 2012.

Groysberg, Boris, Jeffrey T. Polzer, and Hillary Anger Elfenbein. "Too Many Cooks Spoil the Broth: How High-Status Individuals Decrease Group Effectiveness." *Organization Science* 22, no. 3 (2011): 722–737.

Bendersky, Corinne, and Nicholas A. Hays. "Status Conflict in Groups." *Organization Science* 23, no. 2 (2012): 323–340.

Muir, William M. "Group Selection for Adaptation to Multiple-Hen Cages: Selection Program and Direct Responses." *Poultry Science* 75, no. 4 (1996): 447–458.

Ronay, Richard, Katharine Greenaway, Eric M. Anicich, and Adam D. Galinsky. "The Path to Glory Is Paved with Hierarchy: When Hierarchical Differentiation Increases Group Effectiveness." *Psychological Science* 23, no. 6 (2012): 669–677.

Lutchmaya, Svetlana, Simon Baron-Cohen, Peter Raggatt, Rebecca Knickmeyer, and John T. Manning. "2nd to 4th Digit Ratios, Fetal Testosterone and Estradiol." *Early Human Development* 77, no. 1 (2004): 23–28.

Bergman, T. J., J. C. Beehner, D. L. Cheney, R. M. Seyfarth, and P. L. Whitten. "Interactions in Male Baboons: The Importance of Both Males' Testosterone." *Behavioral Ecology and Sociobiology* 59, no. 4 (2006): 480–489.

Simmons, Bill. "A-Rod Is a Clubhouse Guy? In a Manner of Speaking, Yes?" ESPN, July 10, 2012.

"Ideas, Not Hierarchy: On Steve Jobs Supposedly Making All Apple Decisions." *The Small Wave*, August 28, 2011.

Scheiber, Noam. "GM's Ex-CEO: Worse Than You Thought." *The New Republic*, October 21, 2009.

"Designed Chaos—An Interview with David Kelley, Founder and CEO of IDEO." Virtual Advisor, Inc., January 1, 2000.

Woolley, Anita Williams, Christopher F. Chabris, Alex Pentland, Nada Hashmi, and Thomas W. Malone. "Evidence for a Collective Intelligence Factor in the Performance of Human Groups." *Science* 330, no. 6004 (2010): 686–688.

"The Man Who Crashed the World." *Vanity Fair*, August 2009.

Lowenstein, Roger. "The Education of Ben Bernanke." *New York Times*, January 20, 2008.

"Top 10 Mistakes Made by U.S. Presidents." *Encyclopedia Britannica Blog*, January 20, 2009.

Stern, Sheldon. "The Cuban Missile Crisis ExComm Meetings: Getting It Right After 50 Years." *History News Network*, October 15, 2012.

Luke, Evan. "The Death Zone: Dangerous Overcrowding on Mount Everest." *News Record*, May 7, 2014.

Bromwich, Kathryn. "Conquering Everest: 60 Facts About the World's Tallest Mountain." *Independent*, May 26, 2013.

Sang-Hun, Choe. "4 Employed by Operator of Doomed South Korean Ferry Are Arrested." *New York Times*, May 6, 2014.

Anicich, Eric M., Roderick I. Swaab, and Adam D. Galinsky. (online) "When Hierarchy Conquers and Kills: Hierarchical Cultural Values Predict Success and Mortality in High-Stakes Teams." *Proceedings of the National Academy of Sciences* 112, no. 5 (2015): 1338–1343.

Schmidle, Nicholas. "Getting Bin Laden." *The New Yorker*, August 8, 2011.

Gawande, Atul. *The Checklist Manifesto: How to Get Things Right.* New York: Metropolitan Books, vol. 200, 2010.

Edmondson, Amy. "Psychological Safety and Learning Behavior in Work Teams." *Administrative Science Quarterly* 44, no. 2 (1999): 350–383.

Cialdini, Robert B. *Influence.* New York: HarperCollins, 1987.

Sutton, Robert I., and Andrew Hargadon. "Brainstorming Groups in Context: Effectiveness in a Product Design Firm." *Administrative Science Quarterly* 41, no. 4 (1996): 685–718.

Chapter 4

"The Big Story: It's Just the Robinson's Family Affair." *Sunday Independent*, August 18, 2014.

Crichton, Torcuil. "Robinson Fights for Political Life Amidst Irisgate Scandal." *Scotland Herald*, January 8, 2010.

Martin, Iain. "The Swish Family Robinson." *Wall Street Journal*, January 12, 2010.

Sachs, Andrea. "A Slap at Sex Stereotypes." *Time*, June 24, 2001.

Price Waterhouse v. Hopkins, 490 U.S. 228, 109 S. Ct. 1775, 104 L. Ed. 2d 268 (1989).

Sandberg, Sheryl, and Nell Scovell. *Lean In: Women, Work, and the Will to Lead*. New York: Alfred A. Knopf, 2013.

Dillon, Sam. "Harvard Chief Defends His Talk on Women." *New York Times*, updated January 20, 2005.

Reis, Harry T., and Bobbi J. Carothers. "Black and White or Shades of Gray: Are Gender Differences Categorical or Dimensional?" *Current Directions in Psychological Science* 23, no. 1 (2014): 19–26.

Rushe, Dominic. "New Census Bureau Survey: Women Earn $11,500 Less Than Men Annually." *The Guardian*, September 17, 2013.

"Statistical Overview of Women in the Workplace." Catalyst.org, March 3, 2014.

Brooks, Alison Wood, Laura Huang, Sarah Wood Kearney, and Fiona E. Murray. "Investors Prefer Entrepreneurial Ventures Pitched by Attractive Men." *Proceedings of the National Academy of Sciences* 111, no. 12 (2014): 4427–4431.

Perry, Mark J. "2013 SAT Test Results Show That a Huge Math Gender Gap Persists with a 32-Point Advantage for High School Boys." American Enterprise Institute, September 26, 2013.

Guiso, Luigi, Ferdinando Monte, Paola Sapienza, and Luigi Zingales. "Culture, Gender, and Math." *Science* 320, no. 5880 (2008): 1164.

Harada, Tokiko, Donna J. Bridge, and Joan Y. Chiao. "Dynamic Social Power Modulates Neural Basis of Math Calculation." *Frontiers in Human Neuroscience* 6 (2012).

Swaab, Roderick I., and Adam D. Galinsky. "Cross-National Variation in Gender Equality Predicts National Soccer Performance." Working paper (2015).

Babcock, Linda, and Sara Laschever. *Women Don't Ask: Negotiation and the Gender Divide*. Princeton, N.J.: Princeton University Press, 2009.

Small, Deborah A., Michele Gelfand, Linda Babcock, and Hilary Gettman. "Who Goes to the Bargaining Table? The Influence of Gender and Framing on the Initiation of Negotiation." *Journal of Personality and Social Psychology* 93, no. 4 (2007): 600.

Magee, Joe C., Adam D. Galinsky, and Deborah H. Gruenfeld. "Power, Propensity to Negotiate, and Moving First in Competitive Interactions." *Personality and Social Psychology Bulletin* 33, no. 2 (2007): 200–212.

Lammers, Joris, Janka I. Stoker, Jennifer Jordan, Monique Pollmann, and Diederik A. Stapel. "Power Increases Infidelity Among Men and Women." *Psychological Science* 22, no. 9 (2011): 1191–1197.

Larson, Selena. "Microsoft CEO Satya Nadella to Women: Don't Ask for a Raise, Trust Karma." *ReadWrite*, October 9, 2014.

Bowles, Hannah Riley, Linda Babcock, and Lei Lai. "Social Incentives for Gender Differences in the Propensity to Initiate Negotiations: Sometimes It Does Hurt to Ask." *Organizational Behavior and Human Decision Processes* 103, no. 1 (2007): 84–103.

Waldman, Katy. "Negotiating While Female: Sometimes It Does Hurt to Ask." *Slate*, March 17, 2014.

Rudman, Laurie A., and Peter Glick. "Prescriptive Gender Stereotypes and Backlash Toward Agentic Women." *Journal of Social Issues* 57, no. 4 (2001): 743–762.

Gregory, Alex. "But When a Woman Has Someone's Head Cut Off She's a Bitch." *New Yorker* cartoon, July 9, 2001, http://www.condenaststore.com/-sp/But-when-a-woman-has-someone-s-head-cut-off-she-s-a-bitch-New-Yorker-Cartoon-Prints_i8543544_.htm, accessed January 2, 2015.

Dickerson, John. "In Ruthlessness We Trust." *Slate*, February 11, 2014.

Duguid, Michelle. "Female Tokens in High-Prestige Work Groups: Catalysts or Inhibitors of Group Diversification?" *Organizational Behavior and Human Decision Processes* 116, no. 1 (2011): 104–115.

Duguid, Michelle M. "Consequences of Value Threat: The Influence of Helping Women on Female Solos' Preference for Female Candidates." Working paper (2015).

Ellemers, Naomi, Henriette Heuvel, Dick Gilder, Anne Maass, and Alessandra Bonvini. "The Underrepresentation of Women in Science: Differential Commitment or the Queen Bee Syndrome?" *British Journal of Social Psychology* 43, no. 3 (2004): 315–338.

Kalev, Alexandra, Frank Dobbin, and Erin Kelly. "Best Practices or Best Guesses? Assessing the Efficacy of Corporate Affirmative Action and Diversity Policies." *American Sociological Review* 71, no. 4 (2006): 589–617.

Gender Diversity and Corporate Performance. Credit Suisse Research Institute, August 2012.

Levine, Sheen S., Evan P. Apfelbaum, Mark Bernard, Valerie L. Bartelt, Edward J. Zajac, and David Stark. "Ethnic Diversity Deflates Price Bubbles." *Proceedings of the National Academy of Sciences* 111, no. 52 (2014): 18524–18529.

"PWC Talks: Leaning In, Together with Facebook COO Sheryl Sandberg." *Bob Moritz Interview* (2013).

Brescoll, Victoria L., Erica Dawson, and Eric Luis Uhlmann. "Hard Won and Easily Lost: The Fragile Status of Leaders in Gender-Stereotype-Incongruent Occupations." *Psychological Science* 21, no. 11 (2010): 1640–1642.

Swaab, Roderick I., and Adam D. Galinsky. "Cross-National Variation in Gender Equality Predicts National Soccer Performance." Working paper (2015).

"Gender Empowerment Measure: Countries Compared." *NationMaster,* http://www.nationmaster.com/country-info/stats/People/Gender-empowerment-measure, accessed January 3, 2015.

McSmith, Andy. "Closing the Gender Gap: Why Women Now Reign in Spain." *The Independent,* April 16, 2008.

Garbett, Paul. "Spain Win World Cup 2010." *The Telegraph,* July 11, 2010.

Keaten, Jamey. "Alberto Contador Wins the 2010 Tour De France." *The Huffington Post,* July 25, 2010.

Sandberg, Sheryl, and Adam Grant. "Speaking While Female." *New York Times,* January 10, 2015.

Goldin, Claudia, and Cecilia Rouse. "Orchestrating Impartiality: The Impact of 'Blind' Auditions on Female Musicians." *National Bureau of Economic Research* no. 5903 (1997).

Van Biema, David. "My Take: The Mother Teresa You Don't Know." CNN, September 10, 2012.

Lord, Charles G., Mark R. Lepper, and Elizabeth Preston. "Considering the Opposite: A Corrective Strategy for Social Judgment." *Journal of Personality and Social Psychology* 47, no. 6 (1984): 1231.

Bowles, Hannah Riley, Linda Babcock, and Kathleen L. McGinn. "Constraints and Triggers: Situational Mechanics of Gender in Negotiation." *Journal of Personality and Social Psychology* 89, no. 6 (2005): 951.

Amanatullah, Emily T., and Michael W. Morris. "Negotiating Gender Roles: Gender Differences in Assertive Negotiating Are Mediated by Women's Fear of Backlash and Attenuated When Negotiating on Behalf of Others." *Journal of Personality and Social Psychology* 98, no. 2 (2010): 256.

Schneider, Andrea Kupfer, Catherine H. Tinsley, Sandra Cheldelin, and Emily T. Amanatullah. "Likeability V. Competence: The Impossible Choice Faced by Female Politicians, Attenuated by Lawyers." *Duke Journal of Gender Law & Policy* 17 (2010): 363.

Amanatullah, Emily T., and Catherine H. Tinsley. "Negotiating for Us: The Unique Advantage of Us-Advocacy for Female Negotiators." Working paper (2015).

Chapter 5

"A Breakdown of All the Nicknames George W. Bush Gave During His Presidency." *Total Frat Move*, 2014. http://totalfratmove.com/a-breakdown-of-all-the-nicknames-george-w-bush-gave-during-his-presidency/, accessed January 6, 2015.

"Bye-Bye Landslide & Fredo." *Parade*, September 30, 2007.

"Deep Inside the Bush White House." *BusinessWeek*, February 18, 2003.

Gavin, Patrick. "Tony Blair: George Bush Was No 'Dumb Idiot.'" *Politico*, updated September 2, 2010.

"Girl, 13, Who Hanged Herself Days After Text Calling Her a 'Slut' Was Forwarded to Girls at Her School 'Sent the Message Herself,'" *The Daily Mail*, updated May 10, 2012.

"Call Sign Generator." *Top Gun Day* RSS. http://www.topgunday.com/call-sign-generator/, accessed November 6, 2014.

"Romantic Nicknames." Lovingyou.com: Romance 101. http://archive
    .lovingyou.com/content/romance/romance101-content.php
    ?ART=nicknames, accessed October 14, 2014.

Gormley, Beatrice. *Laura Bush: America's First Lady*. New York: Simon
    & Schuster, 2010, 89.

Little, Lyneka. "Fired Iowa Civil Rights Investigators Nicknamed Co-
    workers 'Psycho' and 'Rainman.'" ABC News, August 24, 2011.

Haskins, Charles Homer. *The Renaissance of the Twelfth Century*. Vol. 14.
    Cambridge, Massachusetts: Harvard University Press, 1957.

Harmon-Jones, Cindy, Brandon J. Schmeichel, and Eddie Harmon-
    Jones. "Symbolic Self-Completion in Academia: Evidence from De-
    partment Web Pages and Email Signature Files." *European Journal
    of Social Psychology* 39, no. 2 (2009): 311–316.

Berry, Carlotta. "They Call Me Doctor Berry." *New York Times*, Novem-
    ber 1, 2014.

Mullen, Brian, and Joshua M. Smyth. "Immigrant Suicide Rates as a
    Function of Ethnophaulisms: Hate Speech Predicts Death." *Psycho-
    somatic Medicine* 66, no. 3 (2004): 343–348.

Mullen, Brian, and Diana R. Rice. "Ethnophaulisms and Exclusion:
    The Behavioral Consequences of Cognitive Representation of Eth-
    nic Immigrant Groups." *Personality and Social Psychology Bulletin* 29,
    no. 8 (2003): 1056–1067.

Mullen, Brian. "Ethnophaulisms for Ethnic Immigrant Groups." *Jour-
    nal of Social Issues* 57, no. 3 (2001): 457–475.

Peters, William. *A Class Divided: Then and Now* (Expanded ed.). New
    Haven, Connecticut: Yale University Press, 1987.

Zimbardo, Philip. *The Lucifer Effect: Understanding How Good People
    Turn Evil*. New York: Random House, 2007.

McFadden, Cynthia, and Jake Whitman. "Sheryl Sandberg Launches
    'Ban Bossy' Campaign to Empower Girls to Lead." ABC News,
    March 10, 2014.

"Bossy Doesn't Have to Be a Bad Word." *Slate*, March 10, 2014.

"Change It Up: What Girls Say About Redefining Leadership." *Girl
    Scout Research Institute*, 2008, http://www.girlscouts.org/research/
    pdf/change_it_up_ executive_summary_english.pdf.

Plotz, David. "The Washington ********. Why *Slate* Will No Longer Refer to Washington's NFL Team as the Redskins." *Slate,* August 8, 2013.

"The Invention of the Chilean Sea Bass." *Priceonomics,* April 28, 2014.

Schwartz, John. "Philip Morris to Change Name to Altria." *New York Times,* November 16, 2001.

Nelson, Amy K. "Finding Jeff Gillooly: What Happened to Figure Skating's Infamous Villain?" *Deadspin,* December 13, 2013.

Adamu, Zaina. "Matt Sandusky Files Motion to Have Name Changed." CNN, updated July 18, 2013.

Ramos, Zuania. "Bruno Mars Confesses Why He Changed His Hispanic Last Name." *The Huffington Post,* March 20, 2013.

Ball, Molly. "The Agony of Frank Luntz." *The Atlantic,* January 6, 2014.

Galinsky, Adam D., Cynthia S. Wang, Jennifer A. Whitson, Eric M. Anicich, Kurt Hugenberg, and Galen V. Bodenhausen. "The Reappropriation of Stigmatizing Labels: The Reciprocal Relationship Between Power and Self-Labeling." *Psychological Science* 24 (2013): 2020–2029.

Gibson, Megan. "Will SlutWalks Change the Meaning of the Word Slut?" *Time,* August 12, 2011.

Talbot, Margaret. "Don't Ban 'Bossy.'" *The New Yorker,* March 13, 2014.

Jackson, David. "Obama Embraces the Term 'Obamacare.'" *USA Today,* August 9, 2012.

Branstetter, Ziva. "Symbol Has Its Ups and Downs." Philly.com, June 10, 1993.

Whitson, Jennifer A., Eric M. Anicich, Cynthia S. Wang, and Adam D. Galinsky. "Group Identification as a Cause, Consequence, and Moderator of Self-Labeling with a Stigmatizing Label." Working paper (2015).

Hallowell, Billy. "'An Evil Little Thing': Atheists Slam RI State Rep's Comments About Teen Behind Prayer Mural Ban." *The Blaze,* January 17, 2012.

Greenberg, Chris. "Olympic Rings Fail Joke: Sochi Closing Ceremony Includes Nod to Lighting Flub." *The Huffington Post,* February 23, 2014.

Bayless, Skip. "It's Time to Let the N-Word Die." ESPN, November 15, 2013.

Browne, Rembert. "Saying the Word the NFL Doesn't Want to Hear." *Grantland,* February 28, 2014.

"'Chink in the Armor' Fallout: Fired ESPN Employee Writes Long Apology." *Gothamist,* February 22, 2012.

Ferrazzi, Keith. *Who's Got Your Back: The Breakthrough Program to Build Deep, Trusting Relationships That Create Success—and Won't Let You Fail.* New York: Random House, 2009.

Liberman, Varda, Steven M. Samuels, and Lee Ross. "The Name of the Game: Predictive Power of Reputations Versus Situational Labels in Determining Prisoner's Dilemma Game Moves." *Personality and Social Psychology Bulletin* 30, no. 9 (2004): 1175–1185.

Brooks, Alison Wood. "Get Excited: Reappraising Pre-Performance Anxiety as Excitement." *Journal of Experimental Psychology: General* 143, no. 3 (June 2014): 1144–1158.

Lieberman, Matthew D., Naomi I. Eisenberger, Molly J. Crockett, Sabrina M. Tom, Jennifer H. Pfeifer, and Baldwin M. Way. "Putting Feelings into Words: Affect Labeling Disrupts Amygdala Activity in Response to Affective Stimuli." *Psychological Science* 18, no. 5 (2007): 421–428.

Chapter 6

Patterson, Thom. "3 Steps to Make a Murderer Confess." CNN, updated March 28, 2014.

Greenfield, Beth. "Wife of Millionaire Wins 'Unprecedented' Case to Overturn Prenup Agreement." Yahoo! News, March 12, 2013.

Suarez, Joanna. "Long Island Woman Wins 'Groundbreaking' Prenup Battle." ABC News, March 11, 2013.

Fukuyama, Francis. *Trust: The Social Virtues and the Creation of Prosperity.* New York: Free Press, 1995.

Zak, Paul J., and Stephen Knack. "Trust and Growth." *The Economic Journal* 111, no. 470 (2001): 295–321.

Cuddy, Amy, and Nithyasri Sharma. "Congressional Candidate Ron Klein and KNP Communications." *Harvard Business School,* December 11, 2009.

Fiske, Susan T., Amy J. C. Cuddy, and Peter Glick. "Universal Dimensions of Social Cognition: Warmth and Competence." *Trends in Cognitive Sciences* 11, no. 2 (2007): 77–83.

"List of U.S. Presidents and Their Dogs." *Dog Time.* January 11, 2010. http://dogtime.com/list-of-us-presidents-and-their-dogs.html.

Brooks, Alison Wood, Hengchen Dai, and Maurice E. Schweitzer. "I'm Sorry About the Rain! Superfluous Apologies Demonstrate Empathic Concern and Increase Trust." *Social Psychological and Personality Science* 5, no. 4 (2014): 467–474.

Levine, Ross. "Law, Finance, and Economic Growth." *Journal of Financial Intermediation* 8, no. 1 (1999): 8–35.

Horan, Richard D., Erwin Bulte, and Jason F. Shogren. "How Trade Saved Humanity from Biological Exclusion: An Economic Theory of Neanderthal Extinction." *Journal of Economic Behavior & Organization* 58, no. 1 (2005): 1–29.

Miner, Michael. "The Greater of Two Evils." *Chicago Reader,* January 31, 2008.

Schmadeke, Steve. "After 26 Years, a Taste of Freedom." *Chicago Tribune,* April 19, 2008.

Aronson, Elliot, Ben Willerman, and Joanne Floyd. "The Effect of a Pratfall on Increasing Interpersonal Attractiveness." *Psychonomic Science,* no. 4(6) (1966): 227–228.

Galinsky, Adam D., and Maurice E. Schweitzer. "Think Before You Drink: Alcohol and Negotiations." *Negotiation,* no. 10(7), (2007): 4–6.

Chollet, Derek. *The Road to the Dayton Accords: A Study of American Statecraft.* New York: Palgrave Macmillan, 2005, 165–167.

Malhotra, Deepak, and J. Keith Murnighan. "The Effects of Contracts on Interpersonal Trust." *Administrative Science Quarterly* 47, no. 3 (2002): 534–559.

Elliott, Andrea. "The Jihadist Next Door." *New York Times,* January 27, 2010.

Taher, Abdul. "The Middle-Class Terrorists: More Than 60pc of Suspects Are Well Educated and from Comfortable Backgrounds, Says Secret MI5 File." *The Daily Mail,* updated October 15, 2011.

Sageman, Marc. *Understanding Terror Networks.* Philadelphia: University of Pennsylvania Press, 2004.

Tajfel, Henri, Michael G. Billig, Robert P. Bundy, and Claude Fla-
ment. "Social Categorization and Intergroup Behaviour." *European
Journal of Social Psychology* 1, no. 2 (1971): 149–178.

Cohen, Taya R., R. Matthew Montoya, and Chester A. Insko. "Group
Morality and Intergroup Relations: Cross-Cultural and Experimental Evidence." *Personality and Social Psychology Bulletin* 32, no. 11
(2006): 1559–1572.

Lengel, Edward. *General George Washington: A Military Life.* New York:
Random House Trade Paperbacks, 2005.

"Lieutenant Colonel George Washington Begins the Seven Years'
War." History.com, May 28, 2009. http://www.history.com/this
-day-in-history/lieutenant-colonel-george-washington-begins-the
-seven-years-war.

Kollock, Peter. "The Emergence of Exchange Structures: An Experimental Study of Uncertainty, Commitment, and Trust." *American
Journal of Sociology* (1994): 313–345.

Seul, Min Ki. "1950–1959: When Nike Breathed Its First Breath, It
Inhaled the Spirit of Two Men." *Stony Brook University Digication,*
accessed January 6, 2015.

Feinberg, Matthew, Robb Willer, and Michael Schultz. "Gossip and
Ostracism Promote Cooperation in Groups." *Psychological Science*
25, no. 3 (2014): 656–664.

Chapter 7

Bilefsky, Dan. "A Revenge Plot So Intricate, the Prosecutors Were
Pawns." *New York Times,* July 25, 2011.

Bilefsky, Dan. "Man Guilty of Raping Ex-Girlfriend and Then Framing Her." *New York Times,* November 23, 2011.

Stump, Scott. "Woman Framed by Boyfriend: Police 'Didn't Do Their
Job.'" *Today News,* updated April 6, 2012.

Pearce, John M. *Animal Learning and Cognition: An Introduction.* 3rd
edition. London: Taylor & Francis, 2008.

Feldman, Robert S., James A. Forrest, and Benjamin R. Happ. "Self-
Presentation and Verbal Deception: Do Self-Presenters Lie More?"
Basic and Applied Social Psychology 24, no. 2 (2002): 163–170.

Hancock, Jeffrey T., Catalina Toma, and Nicole Ellison. "The Truth About Lying in Online Dating Profiles." *Proceedings of the SIGCHI Conference on Human Factors in Computing Systems*, 449–452. ACM, 2007.

Mazar, Nina, and Dan Ariely. "Dishonesty in Everyday Life and Its Policy Implications." *Journal of Public Policy & Marketing* 25, no. 1 (2006): 117–126.

"Britney Gets a Lighter with Five Finger Discount!" *TMZ*, December 8, 2007.

Finn, Robin. "TENNIS; Shoplifting an Accident, Capriati Says of Charge." *New York Times*, December 11, 1993.

Young, C. "Winona Ryder Busted for Shoplifting." *People*, December 14, 2001.

Abagnale, Frank W., and Stan Redding. *Catch Me If You Can*. New York: Random House, 2002.

Ruedy, Nicole E., Cecilia Moore, Francesca Gino, and Maurice E. Schweitzer. "The Cheater's High: The Unexpected Affective Benefits of Unethical Behavior." *Journal of Personality and Social Psychology* 105, no. 4 (October 2013): 531–548.

Gino, Francesca, Maurice E. Schweitzer, Nicole L. Mead, and Dan Ariely. "Unable to Resist Temptation: How Self-Control Depletion Promotes Unethical Behavior." *Organizational Behavior and Human Decision Processes* 115, no. 2 (2011): 191–203.

Levine, Emma E., and Maurice E. Schweitzer. "Are Liars Ethical? On the Tension Between Benevolence and Honesty." *Journal of Experimental Social Psychology* 53 (2014): 107–117.

Fragale, Alison R., V. Kay, and Francesca Gino. "Lie to Me: Excuse Recipients Prefer Legitimacy over Truthfulness." Working paper (2015).

Iezzoni, Lisa I., Sowmya R. Rao, Catherine M. DesRoches, Christine Vogeli, and Eric G. Campbell. "Survey Shows That at Least Some Physicians Are Not Always Open or Honest with Patients." *Health Affairs* 31, no. 2 (2012): 383–391.

Coenen, Tracy. "Fraud Files: With Madoff, There Were Many Red Flags." *Daily Finance*, updated April 13, 2010.

Zuckoff, Mitchell. "The Perfect Mark: How a Massachusetts Psychotherapist Fell for a Nigerian E-mail Scam." *The New Yorker*, May 15, 2006.

Slepian, Michael L., Steven G. Young, Abraham M. Rutchick, and Nalini Ambady. "Quality of Professional Players' Poker Hands Is Perceived Accurately from Arm Motions." *Psychological Science* 24, no. 11 (2013): 2335–2338.

Minson, Julia A., and Maurice E. Schweitzer. "Ask (the Right Way) and You Shall Receive: The Effect of Question Type on Information Disclosure and Deception." Working paper (2015).

Notebook Entry, January or February 1894, *Mark Twain's Notebook*, ed. Albert Bigelow Paine (1935), 240.

Vrij, Aldert, et al. "Increasing Cognitive Load to Facilitate Lie Detection: The Benefit of Recalling an Event in Reverse Order." *Law and Human Behavior* 32, no. 3 (2008): 253.

"Scott Peterson Sells Missing Wife's Car." ABC News, February 4, 2003.

Nesse, Randolph M. "Fear and Fitness: An Evolutionary Analysis of Anxiety Disorders." *Ethology and Sociobiology* 15, no. 5 (1994): 247–261.

"What Clinton Said." *Washington Post.* http://www.washingtonpost.com/wp-srv/politics/special/clinton/stories/whatclintonsaid.htm, accessed January 4, 2015.

DePaulo, Bella M., and Wendy L. Morris. "Discerning Lies from Truths: Behavioural Cues to Deception and the Indirect Pathway of Intuition." *The Detection of Deception in Forensic Contexts* (2004): 15–40.

Simonsohn, Uri. "Just Post It: The Lesson from Two Cases of Fabricated Data Detected by Statistics Alone." *Psychological Science* 24, no. 10 (2013): 1875–1888.

"Track Star Marion Jones Pleads Guilty to Doping Deception." CNN, updated October 5, 2007.

Benson, Pam, and Jeanne Meserve. "Report: Key Information on CIA Base Bomber Wasn't Relayed." CNN, October 19, 2010.

DeYoung, Karen, and Walter Pincus. "Success Against Al-Qaeda." *Washington Post*, September 30, 2009.

Finn, Peter, and Joby Warrick. "In Afghanistan Attack, CIA Fell Victim to Series of Miscalculations About Informant." *Washington Post*, January 16, 2010.

Chapter 8

Landro, Laura. "Hospitals Own Up to Errors." *Wall Street Journal*, August 25, 2009.

"National Practitioner Data Bank 2006 Annual Report." U.S. Department of Health and Human Services, 2006. http://www.npdb.hrsa.gov/resources/reports/2006NPDBAnnualReport.pdf.

"The Fall of Andersen." *Chicago Tribune*, September 1, 2002.

Barbaro, Michael, and David W. Chen. "Spitzer Rejoins Politics, Asking for Forgiveness." *New York Times*, July 7, 2013.

"Stewart Found Guilty on All Counts in Obstruction Trial." *CNN Money*, March 10, 2004.

Hays, Constance, and Leslie Eaton. "Stewart Found Guilty of Lying in Sale of Stock." *New York Times*, March 5, 2004.

Collins, Scott. "Letterman Blackmail Scandal Boosts Ratings 22%." *Los Angeles Times*, October 2, 2009.

Hylen, Stacey. "Lessons from the Ritz." BusinessOptimizerCoach.com, August 11, 2010.

Denove, Chris, and James D. Power IV. "How a Recall Earned Lexus a Top Reputation." *Automotive News*, March 27, 2006.

Abeler, Johannes, Juljana Calaki, Kai Andree, and Christoph Basek. "The Power of Apology." *Economics Letters* 107, no. 2 (2010): 233–235.

Reed, Dan. "Southwest's 'Goodwill' Should Keep Fliers." *USA Today*, updated December 12, 2005.

Schmeltzer, John. "Southwest Response Called Swift, Caring." *Chicago Tribune*, December 10, 2005.

Rothman, Wilson. "Apple Gives Free Bumpers to All iPhone 4 Owners." NBC News, July 16, 2010.

Warren, Christina. "Apple Sells 3 Million iPhone 4 Units in Three Weeks." *Mashable*, July 16, 2010.

Manjoo, Farhad. "Here's Your Free Case, Jerk." *Slate*, July 16, 2010.

Oliver, Sam. "Apple's $15 Settlement Checks for iPhone 4 'Antennagate' Begin Arriving." *Appleinsider*, April 23, 2013.

Helmore, Edward. "The Writer, the Accident, and a Lonely End." *The Guardian*, September 30, 2000.

Schweitzer, Maurice E., John C. Hershey, and Eric T. Bradlow. "Promises and Lies: Restoring Violated Trust." *Organizational Behavior and Human Decision Processes* 101, no. 1 (2006): 1–19.

De Waal, Frans B. M. *Peacemaking Among Primates*. Cambridge, Massachusetts: Harvard University Press, 1989, 22.

Goffman, E. *The Presentation of Self in Everyday Life*. New York: Anchor, 1959.

Camerer, Colin. Negotiation Lecture at the Wharton School and Conversation with Maurice Schweitzer, Fall 1990.

Okimoto, Tyler G., Michael Wenzel, and Kyli Hedrick. "Refusing to Apologize Can Have Psychological Benefits (and We Issue No Mea Culpa for This Research Finding)." *European Journal of Social Psychology* 43, no. 1 (2013): 22–31.

Chapter 9

Reiss, Diana, and Lori Marino. "Mirror Self-Recognition in the Bottlenose Dolphin: A Case of Cognitive Convergence." *Proceedings of the National Academy of Sciences* 98, no. 10 (2001): 5937–5942.

Piaget, Jean, and Bärbel Inhelder. *The Psychology of the Child*. New York: Basic Books, 1969.

Squires, Jennifer. "Man Claiming to Have a Bomb in Watsonville Bank Gets Talked into Filling Out Loan Paperwork, Then Arrested." *Santa Cruz Sentinel*, September 9, 2010.

Galinsky, Adam D., William W. Maddux, Debra Gilin, and Judith B. White. "Why It Pays to Get Inside the Head of Your Opponent: The Differential Effects of Perspective Taking and Empathy in Negotiations." *Psychological Science* 19, no. 4 (2008): 378–384.

Sebenius, James K. "Six Habits of Merely Effective Negotiators." *Harvard Business Review* 79, no. 4 (2001): 87–97.

Coren, Stanley. "Do People Look Like Their Dogs?" *Anthrozoos: A Multidisciplinary Journal of the Interactions of People & Animals* 12, no. 2 (1999): 111–114.

Zajonc, Robert B., Pamela K. Adelmann, Sheila T. Murphy, and Paula M. Niedenthal. "Convergence in the Physical Appearance of Spouses." *Motivation and Emotion* 11, no. 4 (1987): 335–346.

Neal, David T., and Tanya L. Chartrand. "Embodied Emotion Perception: Amplifying and Dampening Facial Feedback Modulates

Emotion Perception Accuracy." *Social Psychological and Personality Science* 2, no. 6 (2011): 673–678.

Chartrand, Tanya L., and John A. Bargh. "The Chameleon Effect: The Perception–Behavior Link and Social Interaction." *Journal of Personality and Social Psychology* 76, no. 6 (1999): 893.

Sanchez-Burks, Jeffrey, Caroline A. Bartel, and Sally Blount. "Performance in Intercultural Interactions at Work: Cross-Cultural Differences in Response to Behavioral Mirroring." *Journal of Applied Psychology* 94, no. 1 (2009): 216.

Maddux, William W., Elizabeth Mullen, and Adam D. Galinsky. "Chameleons Bake Bigger Pies and Take Bigger Pieces: Strategic Behavioral Mimicry Facilitates Negotiation Outcomes." *Journal of Experimental Social Psychology* 44, no. 2 (2008): 461–468.

Van Baaren, Rick B., Rob W. Holland, Kerry Kawakami, and Ad Van Knippenberg. "Mimicry and Prosocial Behavior." *Psychological Science* 15, no. 1 (2004): 71–74.

Swaab, Roderick I., William W. Maddux, and Marwan Sinaceur. "Early Words That Work: When and How Virtual Linguistic Mimicry Facilitates Negotiation Outcomes." *Journal of Experimental Social Psychology* 47, no. 3 (2011): 616–621.

Romero, Daniel, Brian Uzzi, Roderick I. Swaab, and Adam D. Galinsky. "Mimicry Is Presidential: Linguistic Style Matching and Improved Polling Numbers." *Personality and Social Psychology Bulletin* (In press).

Wagner, Eric T. "Five Reasons 8 out of 10 Businesses Fail." *Forbes*, September 12, 2013.

Moore, Don A., John M. Oesch, and Charlene Zietsma. "What Competition? Myopic Self-Focus in Market-Entry Decisions." *Organization Science* 18, no. 3 (2007): 440–454.

Jeffries, Stuart. "Flying High." *The Guardian*, September 3, 2007.

Santoso, Alex. "5 Dubious Moments in Olympics History." *Neatorama*, August 21, 2008.

Simonsohn, Uri. "eBay's Crowded Evenings: Competition Neglect in Market Entry Decisions." *Management Science* 56, no. 7 (2010): 1060–1073.

Liljenquist, Katie A., and Adam D. Galinsky. "Turn Your Adversary into Your Advocate." *Negotiation Newsletter* 10 (2007): 4–6.

Brooks, Alison Wood, Francesca Gino, and Maurice E. Schweitzer. "Smart People Ask for (My) Advice: Seeking Advice Boosts Perceptions of Competence." *Management Science* (2015).

Baer, Markus, and Graham Brown. "Blind in One Eye: How Psychological Ownership of Ideas Affects the Types of Suggestions People Adopt." *Organizational Behavior and Human Decision Processes* 118, no. 1 (2012): 60–71.

Parker, Ryan. "Five Injured by Turbulence on Flight from Denver to Billings." *Denver Post*, February 17, 2014.

Lublin, Joann S. "Bosses' Small Gestures Send Big Signals." *Wall Street Journal*, December 2, 2010.

Ford, Dana. "Samuel L. Jackson Scolds Reporter: 'I'm Not Laurence Fishburne!'" CNN, updated February 10, 2014.

Ryland, Amber. "Paula Deen Admits Using the N-Word & Making Racial Jokes in Explosive Deposition." *Radar Online*, June 18, 2013.

Norton, Michael I., Samuel R. Sommers, Evan P. Apfelbaum, Natassia Pura, and Dan Ariely. "Color Blindness and Interracial Interaction: Playing the Political Correctness Game." *Psychological Science* 17, no. 11 (2006): 949–953.

Apfelbaum, Evan P., Samuel R. Sommers, and Michael I. Norton. "Seeing Race and Seeming Racist? Evaluating Strategic Colorblindness in Social Interaction." *Journal of Personality and Social Psychology* 95, no. 4 (2008): 918.

Wegner, Daniel M., David J. Schneider, Samuel R. Carter, and Teri L. White. "Paradoxical Effects of Thought Suppression." *Journal of Personality and Social Psychology* 53, no. 1 (1987): 5.

Galinsky, Adam D., and Gordon B. Moskowitz. "Perspective-Taking: Decreasing Stereotype Expression, Stereotype Accessibility, and In-Group Favoritism." *Journal of Personality and Social Psychology* 78, no. 4 (2000): 708.

Todd, Andrew R., Galen V. Bodenhausen, Jennifer A. Richeson, and Adam D. Galinsky. "Perspective Taking Combats Automatic Expressions of Racial Bias." *Journal of Personality and Social Psychology* 100, no. 6 (2011): 1027.

Blatt, Benjamin, Susan F. LeLacheur, Adam D. Galinsky, Samuel J. Simmens, and Larrie Greenberg. "Does Perspective-Taking Increase Patient Satisfaction in Medical Encounters?" *Academic Medicine* 85, no. 9 (2010): 1445–1452.

Long, Edgar, and David W. Andrews. "Perspective Taking as a Predictor of Marital Adjustment." *Journal of Personality and Social Psychology* 59, no. 1 (1990): 126.

Long, Edgar. "Maintaining a Stable Marriage: Perspective Taking as a Predictor of a Propensity to Divorce." *Journal of Divorce & Remarriage* 21, no. 1–2 (1994): 121–138.

Pierce, Jason R., Gavin J. Kilduff, Adam D. Galinsky, and Niro Sivanathan. "From Glue to Gasoline: How Competition Turns Perspective Takers Unethical." *Psychological Science* (2013): 0956797613482144.

Glad, Betty, and Olin D. Johnston. "Carter's Greatest Legacy: The Camp David Negotiations." PBS, updated November 11, 2002.

Swaab, Roderick I., Adam D. Galinsky, Victoria Medvec, and Daniel A. Diermeier. "The Communication Orientation Model: Explaining the Diverse Effects of Sight, Sound, and Synchronicity on Negotiation and Group Decision-Making Outcomes." *Personality and Social Psychology Review* 16, no. 1 (2012): 25–53.

Chapter 10

Seelye, Katharine. "Enigmatic Jobless Man Prepares Senate Campaign." *New York Times*, July 10, 2010.

Krosnick, Jon A., Joanne M. Miller, and Michael P. Tichy. "An Unrecognized Need for Ballot Reform: Effects of Candidate Name Order." *Rethinking the Vote: The Politics and Prospects of American Election Reform*, edited by Ann N. Crigler, Marion R. Just, and Edward J. McCaffery. New York: Oxford University Press, 2004.

"Bush Claims Victory; Gore Fights On." ABC News, November 26, 2000.

Danziger, Shai, Jonathan Levav, and Liora Avnaim-Pesso. "Extraneous Factors in Judicial Decisions." *Proceedings of the National Academy of Sciences* 108, no. 17 (2011): 6889–6892.

Bruine de Bruin, Wändi. "Save the Last Dance for Me: Unwanted Serial Position Effects in Jury Evaluations." *Acta Psychologica* 118, no. 3 (2005): 245–260.

Page, Lionel, and Katie Page. "Last Shall Be First: A Field Study of Biases in Sequential Performance Evaluation on the Idol Series." *Journal of Economic Behavior & Organization* 73, no. 2 (2010): 186–198.

"Lysacek Wins Gold, but Debate Rages." ESPN, February 19, 2010.

Carney, Dana R., and Mahzarin R. Banaji. "First Is Best." *PlOS One* 7, no. 6 (2012): e35088.

Mantonakis, Antonia, Pauline Rodero, Isabelle Lesschaeve, and Reid Hastie. "Order in Choice Effects of Serial Position on Preferences." *Psychological Science* 20, no. 11 (2009): 1309–1312.

Krueger, D. "And the Last Shall Be First: Zero Position Effect in Martial Arts Competition." Working paper (2008).

Tversky, Amos, and Daniel Kahneman. "Judgment Under Uncertainty: Heuristics and Biases." *Science* 185, no. 4157 (1974): 1124–1131.

Loschelder, David D., Roderick I. Swaab, Roman Trötschel, and Adam D. Galinsky. "The First-Mover *Dis*advantage: The Folly of Revealing Compatible Preferences." *Psychological Science* (2014): 0956797613520168.

Strack, Fritz, and Thomas Mussweiler. "Explaining the Enigmatic Anchoring Effect: Mechanisms of Selective Accessibility." *Journal of Personality and Social Psychology* 73, no. 3 (1997): 437.

Galinsky, Adam D., and Thomas Mussweiler. "First Offers as Anchors: The Role of Perspective-Taking and Negotiator Focus." *Journal of Personality and Social Psychology* 81, no. 4 (2001): 657.

Gunia, Brian C., Roderick I. Swaab, Niro Sivanathan, and Adam D. Galinsky. "The Remarkable Robustness of the First-Offer Effect: Across Cultures, Power, and Issues." *Personality and Social Psychology Bulletin* 39 (2013): 1547–1558.

Dell, Donald, and John Boswell. *Never Make the First Offer (Except When You Should): Wisdom from a Master Dealmaker.* New York: Portfolio/Penguin, 2009.

McCannon, Bryan C., and John B. Stevens. "Deal Making in *Pawn Stars*: Testing Theories of Bargaining." *JNABET* 2 (2013): 62.

Wiley, Elizabeth A., Malia F. Mason, and Adam D. Galinsky. "When Going First Leaves You with Less." Working paper (2015).

Loschelder, David D., Roderick I. Swaab, Roman Trötschel, and Adam D. Galinsky. "The First-Mover *Dis*advantage: The Folly of Revealing Compatible Preferences." *Psychological Science* 25, no. 4 (2014): 954–962.

Sinaceur, Marwan, William W. Maddux, Dimitri Vasiljevic, Ricardo Perez Nückel, and Adam D. Galinsky. "Good Things Come to

Those Who Wait: Late First Offers Facilitate Creative Agreements in Negotiation." *Personality and Social Psychology Bulletin* 39, no. 6 (2013): 814–825.

Bowles, Hannah Riley, Linda Babcock, and Lei Lai. "Social Incentives for Gender Differences in the Propensity to Initiate Negotiations: Sometimes It Does Hurt to Ask." *Organizational Behavior and Human Decision Processes* 103, no. 1 (2007): 84–103.

Northcraft, Gregory B., and Margaret A. Neale. "Experts, Amateurs, and Real Estate: An Anchoring-and-Adjustment Perspective on Property Pricing Decisions." *Organizational Behavior and Human Decision Processes* 39, no. 1 (1987): 84–97.

Mussweiler, Thomas, Fritz Strack, and Tim Pfeiffer. "Overcoming the Inevitable Anchoring Effect: Considering the Opposite Compensates for Selective Accessibility." *Personality and Social Psychology Bulletin* 26, no. 9 (2000): 1142–1150.

Galinsky, Adam D. "Should You Make the First Offer?" *Negotiation* 7 (2004): 1–4.

"Debt Ceiling: Timeline of Deal's Development." CNN, August 2, 2011.

Chait, Jonathan. "Obama's Dangerous Credibility Problem." *The New Republic*, July 6, 2011.

Mason, Malia F., Alice J. Lee, Elizabeth A. Wiley, and Daniel R. Ames. "Precise Offers Are Potent Anchors: Conciliatory Counteroffers and Attributions of Knowledge in Negotiations." *Journal of Experimental Social Psychology* 49, no. 4 (2013): 759–63.

Jerez-Fernandez, Alexandra, Ashley N. Angulo, and Daniel M. Oppenheimer. "Show Me the Numbers: Precision as a Cue to Others' Confidence." *Psychological Science* 25, no. 2 (2014): 633–635.

Loschelder, David D., Johannes Stuppi, and Roman Trötschel. " '€14,875?!': Precision Boosts the Anchoring Potency of First Offers." *Social Psychological and Personality Science* 5, no. 4 (2014): 491–499.

Lee, Alice, David D. Loschelder, Malia F. Mason, Martin Schweinsberg, and Adam. D. Galinsky. "Precise First Offers Create Barriers to Entry." Working paper (2015).

Ames, Daniel R., and Malia F. Mason. "Tandem Anchoring: Informational and Politeness Effects of Range Offers in Social Exchange." *Journal of Personality and Social Psychology* 108.2 (2015): 254.

Leonardelli, Geoffrey, Jun Gu, Geordie McRuer, Adam D. Galinsky, Victoria Husted Medvec. "Negotiating with a Velvet Hammer: Multiple Equivalent Simultaneous Offers." Working paper (2015).

Schweinsberg, Martin, Gillian Ku, Cynthia S. Wang, and Madan M. Pillutla. "Starting High and Ending with Nothing: The Role of Anchors and Power in Negotiations." *Journal of Experimental Social Psychology* 48, no. 1 (2012): 226–231.

Chapter 11

Santich, Kate. "Hey, Bob Dole, You Missed a Great VP Candidate." *Orlando Sentinel*, September 8, 1996.

"Discussions with Officer Angel Calzadilla." *Miami Herald*, August 5, 1996.

Kahneman, Daniel, Barbara L. Fredrickson, Charles A. Schreiber, and Donald A. Redelmeier. "When More Pain Is Preferred to Less: Adding a Better End." *Psychological Science* 4, no. 6 (1993): 401–405.

Redelmeier, Donald A., Joel Katz, and Daniel Kahneman. "Memories of Colonoscopy: A Randomized Trial." *Pain* 104, no. 1 (2003): 187–194.

Thompson, Leigh, Kathleen L. Valley, and Roderick M. Kramer. "The Bittersweet Feeling of Success: An Examination of Social Perception in Negotiation." *Journal of Experimental Social Psychology* 31, no. 6 (1995): 467–492.

Walsh, Colleen. "Wise Negotiator." *Harvard Gazette*, April 4, 2012.

Galinsky, Adam D., Vanessa L. Seiden, Peter H. Kim, and Victoria Husted Medvec. "The Dissatisfaction of Having Your First Offer Accepted: The Role of Counterfactual Thinking in Negotiations." *Personality and Social Psychology Bulletin* 28, no. 2 (2002): 271–283.

Index

Note: Abbreviation *C-C dichotomy* stands for *Compete-Cooperate dichotomy*.

Fast, Nathanael, 57
Fédération Internationale de Football
　Association (FIFA), 97
Feinberg, Matt, 159–160
Feinstein, Dianne, 117
Ferrazzi, Keith, 132
FIBA World Championship (2002), 74
"50 Cent" (singer/rapper), 44
"Finding the Right Balance"
　about book sections titled, 11
　concept of "leaning in," 106–112
　exercising psychological safety,
　　87–90
　fairness, creating sense of, 239–248
　first-offer dilemma, 248–250
　making first offer, 258–260
　names matter, 132–135
　perspective-taking, 229–232
　power and social behavior, 58–61
　reputations and relationships,
　　158–161
　saying "I'm sorry," 205–207
　social comparisons, 34–37
　trust but verify, 186–188
Fisher, Jodie, 40
Fiske, Susan, 141
Florida, 139–140, 206, 235, 242
Fragale, Alison, 174
France, 27, 156–157, 245
Franco, Francisco, 110
Franklin, Morton, 250–251
Frank, Marshall, 137–138, 142
Friesen, Justin, 68–69
Fujimori, Alberto, 1–4

Gay/lesbian. See Homosexuality
Gelfand, Michele, 69–70
Gender. See also Sex/sexual activity
　about power and, 98–100, 123
　abuse of power, 91–92
　aggressiveness, penalties, 92–94, 252
　aptitude and performance, 94–97
　assertiveness, 43, 76–78, 103, 114–
　　115, 128–129, 209
　cultural disparities, 97
　diversity training and, 107–108
　hiring and promotion, 109–110
　income disparity, 95, 98
　infidelity, 97, 99
　networking and mentoring, 108–
　　109
　Queen Bee phenomenon, 103–106
　sexual discrimination, 100–103
Gender bias, 114–115

Gender equality, 96–97, 106–114, 124–
　127
General Motors, 81
Genes/genetics, 9, 17, 23–24
George, Francis, 63–66
Germany, 9, 69, 124, 157, 267
"Get Ready for This" (Wild, DeCoster
　and Slijngaard, song), 44
"The Gift of the Magi" (O. Henry), 53
Gillooly, Jeff (aka Jeff Stone), 127
Godart, Frédéric, 72
Goffman, Erving, 203
Goldin, Claudia, 112
Google, 67
Gore, Al, 236
Gossip, 7, 159–161
Grace Hopper Celebration of Women
　in Computing (conference), 100–
　101
Grant, Adam, 111
Gray, John, 94
Greene, Alvin, 233–234
Greenspan, Alan, 82
Groups/group identity, 119–120, 154–
　157
Groysberg, Boris, 75
Gruenfeld, Deb, 44
Guiso, Luigi, 96–97

Haig, Alexander, 55–56
Hammami, Omar, 154–155
Hancock, Jeffrey, 169
Happiness, 20–22, 25–27, 36, 170–171,
　185–186
Happy marriage, 138–139, 229–230
Harding, Tonya, 31–32
Harvard Medical School, 16
Hashimoto, Ryutaro, 2
Hernandez, Peter (aka Bruno Mars),
　127
Hershlag, Natalie (aka Natalie
　Portman), 127
Hewlett-Packard (HP), 39–40
Hierarchy
　benefits and evolution, 66–70
　C-C dichotomy, 70–71
　co-leadership, 71–72
　diversity, 81, 107–110
　function of, 63–66
　leadership and cooperation, 72–78
　Queen Bee phenomenon, 103–106,
　　110
　talent vs. performance, 78–79
　when it doesn't work, 80–87

312   Index

Trust (*cont'd.*)
  warmth and competence builds,
    139–142
Trustworthiness. *See also* Credibility;
    Manipulation
  deception and cheating, 167–173
  deception as good thing and, 173–175
  red flags of deception, 179–186
  role of, 163–166
  scams, successfulness of, 175–179
  when trusting too much blows up,
    186–188
Truth bias, 179
Tupac Amaru Revolutionary
    Movement (MRTA), 1–4
Twain, Mark, 181
"2 Unlimited" (singing group), 44

Uber, 160–161
Uhlmann, Eric, 109
University of Chicago, 237
University of Illinois, 207
University of Michigan, 28–29
University of North Carolina, 20
Unprotected sex, 50
Unstable/dynamic world
  as force for C-C dichotomy, 8–11,
    14–15, 27, 268
  effects of "power," 40–42
  effects of sincere apology, 195–197
  importance of hierarchy, 64–66
"Us advocacy," 115
U.S. Army, 64–65, 68, 88
U.S. Central Intelligence Agency, 83,
    187–188
U.S. Constitution, 55–56
U.S. Federal Reserve, 82
U.S. National Aeronautics and Space
    Administration (NASA), 29–30
U.S. Securities and Exchange
    Commission (SEC), 22, 175–176,
    193
U.S. Supreme Court, 93, 191

The Vagina Monologues (play), 128
Virgin Airlines, 32–33
Vonk, Roos, 60
Vulnerability, benefits of, 148–154

Wade, Dwyane, 73–74
War and military operations. *See also*
    Terrorism/terrorist(s)
  about hierarchy in times of, 69–70
  Abu Ghraib prison scandal, 57

Afghan-Soviet war, 155
American Civil War, 27
American Revolution, 156–157
Bay of Pigs invasion, 83
Bosnian war, 152–153
Cold War era, 266–267
Cuban missile crisis, 83–84
Egyptian revolution, 27
French and Indian war, 157
French revolution, 27
Iraqi War, 57, 155
Russian revolution, 27
World War I, 69
World War II, 9, 29
World War III, 83
Washington, George, 157
Washington Redskins, 126
Watergate scandal, 55
Websites
  Airbnb, 160
  Political Correctness Game, 226
  Top Gun call sign, 119
Weight-gain study, 15–17
Wells, Frank, 71
"We Will Rock You" (May, song), 44
Whitson, Jennifer, 130
Wiley, Elizabeth, 246
Willer, Rob, 68
Williams, Venus and Serena, 18–19,
    35, 44
Willingham, Bob, 25
Wilson, Andrew, 147–148
Wojnilower, Sam, 24
Women. *See* Gender
Women Don't Ask (Babcock), 98
Woolley, Anita, 81
Workplace salary/income
  dealing with disparity, 20–23
  gender and, 98–103
  happiness/satisfaction with, 26–27
  hoarding/sharing, 53
  negotiations, 243, 251, 259, 265–266
  social comparison and, 17, 24
World Aquatics Championships, 239
World Cup soccer, 28
Worley, John, 176–179
Wu-Tang Clan (hip hop group), 44

X-Men: First Class (movie), 129

Yugoslavia, 152–153

Zajonc, Robert, 214
Zapatero, José Luis Rodríguez, 111